≡

Florence Lin's
Complete Book of

Chinese
Noodles,
Dumplings
and Breads

≡

Also by Florence Lin

Florence Lin's Chinese Regional Cookbook (1975)

Florence Lin's Chinese Vegetarian Cookbook (1976)

Florence Lin's Chinese One-Dish Meal Cookbook (1978)

Florence Lin's Cooking with Fire Pot (1979)

Florence Lin's Complete Book of Chinese Noodles, Dumplings ≡ and ≡ Breads

Florence Lin

Illustrations by Peter LaVigna
Calligraphy by Xiong Yang

Quill
William Morrow
New York

It is the policy of William Morrow and Company, Inc., and its imprints and affiliates, recognizing the importance of preserving what has been written, to print the books we publish on acid-free paper, and we exert our best efforts to that end.

Library of Congress Cataloging-in-Publication Data

Lin, Florence.
    Florence Lin's complete book of Chinese noodles,
dumplings, and breads.

    Includes index.
    1. Cookery (Macaroni). 2. Noodles. 3. Dumplings.
4. Bread. 5. Cookery, Chinese I. Title.
TX809.M17L56 1986 64.5951 85-29820
ISBN 0-688-12845-9(pbk.)

Printed in the United States of America

First Quill Edition

1 2 3 4 5 6 7 8 9 10

BOOK DESIGN BY ANN GOLD

Foreword

When I started this book some two years ago, it was to be a brief guide to the pasta of China. But the book quickly evolved to a much broader and extensive collection, which has taken all this time to compile. And that is because the pasta of China really includes a vast range of grain-based foods—starting with the pervasive bowl of rice or bread that is at the center of even the simplest of meals throughout China, and ranging to dumplings and pasta-wrapped foods with elaborate fillings that are important parts of the most formal banquets.

Given the extent of this collection, even I am surprised that there are many more varieties of grain-based dishes that I would like to have shared. For clarity and manageability, however, I have selected those that I think will provide you with a good sample of cooking techniques. From this start, you can easily adapt different ingredients and develop new combinations by interchanging the fillings from one recipe to another.

A great deal of credit for this book goes to my many students who came back to my classes year after year. Because of them, I have searched continuously for new recipes. And because of them, these recipes are time tested and well practiced. My editor Maria's husband, John Guarnaschelli, was one of those students to whom I am especially grateful and who made this book possible. I also want to thank my agent, Barney Karpfinger, who handled the negotiation complexities so expertly, and Suzi Arensberg, who did a wonderful job of editing. Also, thanks to my good friend T. S. Lauh, who helped with many of the historical points. Finally, I thank Maria Guarnaschelli, who has set standards of excellence of which we can all be proud.

For further information on the origin and development of Chinese noodles, dumplings, and breads, the reader is referred to: *Food in Chinese Culture: Anthropological and Historical Perspectives*, edited by K.C. Chang, Yale University Press, 1981.

Contents

≡

**Florence Lin's
Complete Book of**

Chinese
Noodles,
Dumplings
and Breads

≡

The Origin of Chinese Noodles, Dumplings and Breads

Throughout the history of Chinese cooking, vegetables, meat, or seafood (*cai*) have always been considered accompaniments to the basic staples, either a starch made from wheat (*mian shi*) or rice (*fan*). In the north *mian shi* made mainly from wheat was and is predominant. From very early times wheat was milled and used as flour; in the south and central regions, along the Yangtze River, the people ate rice as a grain; it was only occasionally made into flour. A 1930s study postulated that 89 percent of China's food supply came from grains and their products, and even in more prosperous times, such as the southern Sung dynasty (960–1279), something close to that percentage must have prevailed generally for the common people. It follows, as the fourth-century writer Shu Hsi said, that the various kinds of noodles and cakes originated with the common people, although a few of the cooking methods (such as baking) were foreign in origin.

The dominant grains in China through the Han period (206 B.C. –A.D. 219) were millet and wheat; in fact, a poem from 1111 B.C. by Ji Zi describes "wheat . . . maturing, cereal and millet leaves sprouting" in the Shang ruins near the present city of An-yang. There is no archaeological evidence of flour mills before the first century B.C., but another early text gives credence to the proposition that wheat was ground, not eaten as whole grains, long before then. The reason has to do with the scarcity of fuel, a perennial problem in China. In the fifth century B.C., during the Zhou dynasty, Mencius cautioned against the misuse of cutting wood in a poem: "If saws and axes enter mountains and forests at the proper time, there will be more than enough timbers for use." With fuel conservation already an issue so long ago, it seems unlikely that the Chinese would go to the trouble and expense of cooking the whole grain of wheat, which takes up to three hours. Millet, probably the oldest grain used in China, takes only fifteen minutes to cook, and rice takes about twenty. Necessity is the mother of invention, and I believe it possible that in order to save fuel, the grinding of wheat into flour must have been invented sometime during the early Zhou or late Shang dynasty in the fifth century B.C.

Whether or not flour mills were an early, indigenous invention or a late Han borrowing from Persia during the extensive explorations and trade expansion under that dynasty, there is ample evidence that the technology had become widespread by the second half of the first century A.D. The development of food made from flour was a major revolution in the economy. By the end of the Han dynasty, wheat-flour products, such as boiled noodles and steamed sesame breads, were achieving vast popularity; even the emperor ate boiled noodles. From that time on noodle vending became a thriving business—these vendors being among the first of that noisy, colorful array of entrepreneurs who populate the streets of China.

Like other cultures, the Chinese elevated these staples when it came to ceremonial foods and offerings to the gods. The year used to be punctuated by the special cakes made to celebrate festivals; for instance, spring cakes for the first month, green dumplings stuffed with lotus root for the third month, round dumplings for the fifth month dragon boat festival, coiled sugar cakes for the autumn weaver and cowherd festival, glutinous rice dumplings with red bean stuffing for the kitchen god's festival on the eve of the New Year, and pork-and-cabbage-stuffed dumplings for the New Year. In Chinese cuisine there is no such thing as crude, rough food; behind even the simplest bowl of noodles is a deep regard for the ingredients and great attention is paid to the details of cooking and presenting a dish.

During the Tang dynasty (618–906), which is known as China's golden age, Chinese cuisine developed substantially. Many new, foreign foods were borrowed and adapted; the cultivation of rice increased as agricultural techniques were perfected; and fried, baked, and steamed breads, both salty and sweet, began to appear in abundance; these were made with either wheat or rice flour. Two of the most enduring Chinese specialties—*jiao-zi,* or stuffed dumplings (then called *hun-t'un*), and *chun-juan,* or spring rolls—came from Beijing, although it is possible that these little dumplings originated in central Asia. Certainly many cultures there have them also. As wheat flour was used more and more, millet tended to be eaten less. Coarser and less nutritious than wheat, it was commonly prepared as a gruel.

During the Tang dynasty the most popular method of cooking all the new cakes was frying, and some examples have been unearthed from tombs. Many of the cakes were referred to as *hu,* meaning "foreign"—either they were made with foreign ingredients, such as spices, or they were inspired from foreign recipes. A steamed bread with sesame seeds was sold by foreign vendors in the streets of the capital, Chang-an (now called Xian). A rice cake fried in camel fat was thought to cure hemorroids. Dumplings were wrapped in wild rice leaves. Rice cakes were flavored with cherries and other sweet fruits.

These innovations and additions to Chinese cuisine during the Tang dynasty contributed to the extraordinary flowering of cooking during the Sung dynasty (960–1279), as did the flourishing of agriculture, the development of a large civil bureaucracy, and general economic prosperity. It was during this time that restaurants of all kinds came into their own. In Pien Ching, now Kaifeng, the northern Song capital, and particularly in Hangzhow, the southern Song capital, there were lavish multilevel wine restaurants that offered hundreds of dishes. On the shore of West Lake in Hangzhow alone there were more than a hundred of these establishments. But it was the smaller, humbler places, serving no wine and specializing in one kind of food, that sold noodles or pastries. A typical noodle shop would offer noodles with meat or noodles with vegetables; pastries were divided between those shops that served steamed, sugared, or stuffed buns and cakes and those that served only deep-fried pastries in various forms, similar to what is called today *you-tiao.* The two most famous "deep-fry" pastry shops in Kaifeng had fifty stoves each. Still another kind of shop sold only steamed buns with a filling. And then, of course, there were vendors who roamed the streets day and night. Marco Polo called Hangzhow "the greatest city in the world, where so many pleasures may be found that one fancies himself to be in Paradise." Then, after Kaifeng had fallen to the Mongols, the fare there had switched to chunks of mutton.

During the Song period three styles of cooking were recognized—northern, southern, and Sichuan. The characteristics are the same now as then. Northern food was bland, with an emphasis on lamb and preserved foods, and based on wheat and millet, which were turned into buns, dumplings, noodles, and cakes, often with a filling. Southern cooking, from the Yangtze River basin, was more highly spiced and more varied than that of the north; it used pork and seafood to a much greater degree and was based on rice. From the Song period on, the south became the richest source of food and culinary invention. Even in the twelfth century Sichuan cooking was fiery in taste, using peppers and other hot condiments.

From the descriptions of Hangzhow it is obvious that many of the north's less doughy, more dainty wheat products were enjoyed there as well, but what is not so obvious is that in ritual food wheat products predominated—in offerings to the dead, to the gods, and for the enjoyment of the common people on religious holidays. This is because the rituals had become codified very early in the Zhou dynasty (1100 B.C.), when the capital was in the north. Tradition has it that the rituals were compiled by the duke of Zhou, a younger brother of King Wu, the Marshal King, founder of the Zhou dynasty. By the time of the Western Han dynasty, commentaries on Zhou ritual were written by two scholars named Tai. For instance, special cakes were eaten on the ninth day of the ninth month, and during wedding ceremonies the groom's family received steamed cakes called honey-harmonizing-with-oil cakes, symbolizing the union of two differing elements. Even a kind of millet no longer eaten was grown for use in ritual food. Rice also was used in many of these offerings, but not to the extent that wheat products were. A fascinating list of the monthly sacrificial offerings from the first Ming emperor, in Nanjing in the 1370s, reveals that twenty-two of the thirty daily offerings were some kind of bread—clover honey biscuits; open-oven baked breads, sugar-filled steamed breads, marrow cakes, scalded-dough baked breads, pepper-and-salt breads, thousand-layer baked breads, plus buns and cookies. This isn't to say that there were no fresh offerings but to emphasize the particular importance wheat products enjoyed in ritual food.

During the hundred years that the Mongols were in power, from the mid-thirteenth century to the mid-fourteenth, there was little culinary exchange between the conquerors and the Chinese populace. The Mongols ate simply, preferring to carve their mutton (anathema to the Chinese) at the table and to drink mare's milk (*koumiss*) and great quantities of wine. They held lavish feasts, but their importance was much more for the extension of ritual and hospitality than for the display of culinary art. The Mongols remained nomads even when they were in power, and the Chinese viewed them with some disdain.

With the restoration of Chinese power in 1370 under the first Ming emperor, agricultural conditions began to improve, and soon rice was standard fare. With a population that was basically well fed, food once again took on value as something meant to be enjoyed in all its variety. From the sixteenth century on the expansion of commerce and general prosperity began to have an effect on northern cooking, in the sense that more foods were offered. Northern cooking had always been simpler than southern and still is, but the Ming dynasty redistributed many of the riches of the land.

The sixteenth century onward also saw a new culinary pleasure develop—excursion boats that offered prepared foods from restaurants. Among the delicacies delivered were all manner of breads and pastries for the new tourists. It is also revealing of Chinese culinary attitudes that in the mid-sixteenth century a novel called *Chin-p'ing-mei* appeared; it is an unabashed sensual reveling in food and sex, with as much leisurely attention to the delights of the table as to those of the flesh.

Beginning in the Ch'ing dynasty, in the early 1700s, to the mid-1900s, there was a tremendous population explosion in China; the number of Chinese rose from 150,000,000 to 450,000,000. Much of this increase can be attributed to the introduction of foods from the West, such as white potatoes, sweet potatoes, carrots, peanuts, and particularly corn, although these foods never became as pervasive as the indigenous staples. The cultivation of rice in the south intensified, and since it gives the most nutrition for the least amount of land, it is what really permitted this population density.

By the twentieth century, however, the gulf between rich and poor had widened to a very serious degree, and, as mentioned before, almost 90 percent of the food supply came from grains. The very poor existed on a diet of millet, hand-milled wheat flour, and coarse corn flour. This was a far cry even from a noodle recipe extolled by the eighteenth-century writer Li Yü; he liked his noodles done in a light broth with a touch of vinegar or soy sauce, then garnished with a little sesame oil and bamboo shoots, with perhaps a light mushroom or shrimp sauce poured on top. It is to the credit of the People's Republic of China that the rice (*fan*) of the country is now adequately distributed to the entire population, even though it is over a billion in number. The inventiveness and art that the Chinese still lavish on these staples are qualities outside politics, rooted in the culture of the people.

Doughs Made from
Wheat Flour

Since the climate of northern China is more suitable for growing wheat than rice, northerners depend on it for their starch staple in the form of noodles, buns, dumplings, pancakes, and other specialties. For the rest of the country, wheat products are primarily snacks—*dian xin* (Mandarin) or *dim sum* (Cantonese), known as "to dot your heart"—a between-meals refreshment meant only to touch one's appetite. These snacks are light on dough and replete with many varieties of fillings; it is only in the north that you find thick wrappers with just a little filling and plain steamed breadlike buns.

Stir-Fried and Pan-Fried Noodle Dishes with Sauce

Homemade Chinese Egg Noodles

 DAN MIAN

This egg noodle recipe is the master recipe, which may be used for most of the noodle dishes in this book. The dough itself also doubles as the dough for wontons (page 117), spring rolls (page 103), and shao mai (page 124). If you use all-purpose flour, the color of the noodle will be off-white and the texture slightly soft.

Homemade noodles are always better than commercial ones, *and they are not hard to make.* Even 1½ pounds of noodles kneaded and cut by hand take only about 30 minutes to make. Frankly, I prefer hand-rolled and hand-cut noodles. The uneven width and thickness, plus the slightly fluffier texture, make them more interesting to eat than machine-cut noodles. Nevertheless, I've included instructions for processor kneading and pasta-machine kneading, rolling, and cutting; these machines do save time and create an evenly done, handsome product.

(Should you not have the time to make them, there are a number of good commercial noodles available, both fresh and dried. See the notes on commercial noodles at the end of the recipe, page 29.)

Noodle dishes are much loved in my house, and they make wonderful one-dish meals. Since they use little meat, they are also inexpensive. Besides being the base for the sauces and toppings in this book, they can be used very casually indeed. Often I heat up a leftover dish, such as red-cooked meat, chicken with gravy, or a stir-fried combination; add some chicken broth; and make a "noodle-soup" dish with fresh or dried noodles. For these noodle-soup dishes I prefer a noodle about ⅛ inch wide. It's substantial and holds its texture better in the broth than very thin ones do. Once you try several noodle-soup dishes from the book (see pages 78–92), I guarantee you'll become a devotee of this enormously popular way of eating noodles in China.

This recipe produces 1½ pounds of fresh noodles, enough for five or six people for a light meal. While you have to divide the dough at points to work with it easily, and while many of the stir-fried dishes call for only ¾ pound of noodles, making this amount is worth your time. After all, it's a special and delicious treat for guests or family.

Yield: 1½ pounds

3 cups all-purpose flour
2 extra large eggs (½ cup)
2 teaspoons coarse salt
2 teaspoons corn oil or peanut oil
½ cup water, approximately (pasta flour takes 2 to 3 tablespoons more water than all-purpose flour)
About ½ cup flour for dusting

About ½ cup cornstarch for sprinkling on finished noodle sheets so noodles won't stick together when refrigerated or frozen (I use a large tin salt shaker to shake out the cornstarch—it is easier and more effective than your hands)

MIXING THE DOUGH BY HAND

Put the flour in a large mixing bowl or on a work surface. Make a well in the center and add the eggs, salt, and oil. Slowly add the water while you stir with your fingers or a wooden spoon, out from the center, to incorporate the flour. As you form the dough, add more water or flour if needed. For instance, if some dry flour remains, stir in 1 or 2 teaspoons of water at a time; stir in about 1 or 2 tablespoons of flour at a time if the dough is too soft. Pat and knead the dough in the bowl until a fairly smooth dough is formed. A dough scraper is useful if you're mixing the dough on a work surface; you can easily scrape up any flour that scatters.

KNEADING THE DOUGH BY HAND

(If you have a pasta machine, you can skip the following 5 minutes of kneading by hand; instead, do the kneading by machine—see page 26.)

Put the ball of dough on a lightly floured surface; then knead it with the heel of one hand as you give the dough a quarter-turn with the other after each kneading. The dough should be firm but manageable. Wet your hands from time to time if the dough is too firm to knead, or add 1 to 2 tablespoons of flour at a time if the dough is too soft to knead. Sprinkling some flour on the surface from time to time, knead for about 5 minutes or until the dough is smooth and elastic. If your kneading is slow, you may need a little more time.

Cover the dough with plastic wrap and let it rest at room temperature for 30 minutes, so that it won't fight back when you roll it. You can let it rest in the refrigerator, but bring it to room temperature before you roll and cut it.

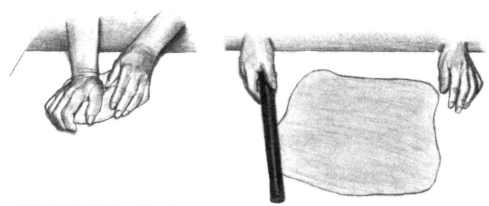

ROLLING THE DOUGH BY HAND

After the dough has been formed and kneaded and it has rested, divide it into four pieces. Put aside three of them, covered with plastic wrap, while you work on one.

On a lightly floured surface, push and flatten the dough with your fingers, then, with a long rolling pin or a large heavy one, roll the dough out from the center to the far edge and lift the pin, then roll it back from the center toward you; turn the dough sheet halfway at regular intervals to maintain an even thickness. You should be creating a squarish shape; you may stretch the dough a little if you need to. To prevent the dough from becoming sticky, periodically dust it with a little flour and smooth the flour with your hand. Dust the work surface, too, but not so much that the sheet slides. Always roll back and forth from the center of the dough sheet as you work. When the sheet of dough is an approximately 14-inch-roundish square and a little less than ⅛ inch thick, it is done (this takes less than 5 minutes); spread it out on a cloth towel to dry, hanging about one-third of it over the edge of the table, while you work the other three sheets. By the time you finish the fourth sheet, the first will be ready to cut.

CUTTING THE NOODLES BY HAND

Liberally dust the first sheet of dough with cornstarch on both sides, smoothing it in with your hand; from one side and then the opposite, fold the dough over toward the center until the edges meet; the width at that point should be about 3 inches. Lightly press the folded sheet. With a sharp knife cut across the folds to make even strips about ⅛ inch wide (or any width you desire).

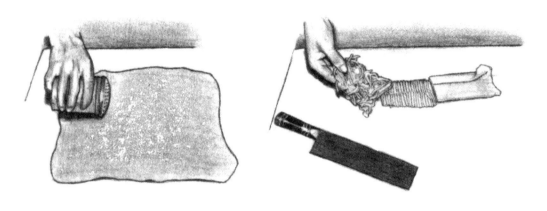

Unroll the noodles by tossing them loosely with your fingers. Spread them all out on two 10- by 15-inch baking sheets or trays and let them dry uncovered for 10 to 20 minutes to firm up. At this point you may cook them or put them in a plastic bag and refrigerate or freeze them.

If you want to dry and store them, mound them in loose piles about 3 to 4 inches in diameter and less than ½ inch thick; it will take at least 24 hours for them to dry completely if they are drying near a window or drying outdoors. In a heated room they will dry faster. Humid weather makes the drying process much slower.

Cut the other three sheets of dough in the same fashion.

MIXING AND KNEADING THE DOUGH
IN A FOOD PROCESSOR

Machine-kneaded dough takes less water—about 1 to 2 tablespoons less—and it needs a longer rest than hand-kneaded dough, because in the rapid spin there is not enough time for the liquid to be fully absorbed. The finished noodles, therefore, are slightly tougher than hand-kneaded ones, but a processor does save time and energy, and the small sacrifice may be worth it for some cooks. The 60 seconds of spinning is equivalent to the 5 minutes of hand-kneading.

Insert the steel blade in the food processor. Pour the flour and salt into the work bowl (if you have the small food processor, make half the recipe at a time). Slowly pour the eggs, oil, and water (1 to 2 tablespoons less than the amount in the ingredients) through the food tube, making twenty to thirty pulse actions so that the flour can absorb the liquid

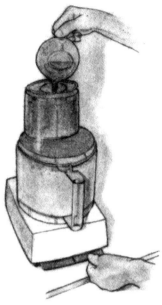

gradually. Then press "on." Within 10 seconds the mixture should start to form a ball that cleans the sides of the work bowl as it spins. If a ball doesn't form, add more water 1 or 2 teaspoons at a time. The dough must be firm-soft, but not so soft that it sticks to the bowl, so don't add any water unless it's absolutely necessary. Flours vary from season to season and from one part of the country to another. Some may absorb less water than I call for in this recipe, so if your dough is too soft and sticks to the bowl, add 1 or 2 tablespoons more flour at a time and continue the spin. (You can uncover the food processor and check the dough with your fingers.) After the dough forms a ball, let it spin for 60 seconds—this is the equivalent of kneading. Then turn off the machine and remove the dough, including any small pieces that remain in the bowl. Knead very briefly—only a few turns; then cover the dough with plastic wrap and let it rest at room temperature for 1 hour (or longer in the refrigerator—bring to room temperature before proceeding).

KNEADING THE DOUGH WITH A PASTA MACHINE

After you have formed the dough by hand (before the kneading and resting periods), you could knead it immediately in a pasta machine. (If you have formed and kneaded the dough in a food processor, skip this rolling step.) Divide the hand-formed dough into four pieces. Work with one piece at a time at first (two or more pieces in quick succession after you are familiar with the machine) and cover the other three with plastic wrap.

Push the piece of dough with your fingers into a squarish shape and lightly dust both sides with flour; smooth it in with your hand. Set the rollers of the pasta machine wide open. Pass the dough square through the rollers and quickly pull the rolled sheet out onto the work surface. Lightly flour and smooth each side. Fold the sheet crosswise in half or in thirds. Press it a little to flatten it, and then flour and smooth both sides. Pass the layered sheet, folded edge first, through the rollers again. Repeat the flouring, folding, flouring, and rolling at least five more times, until the dough is totally smooth. The sheet should be ½ inch less than the width of the rollers on each side.

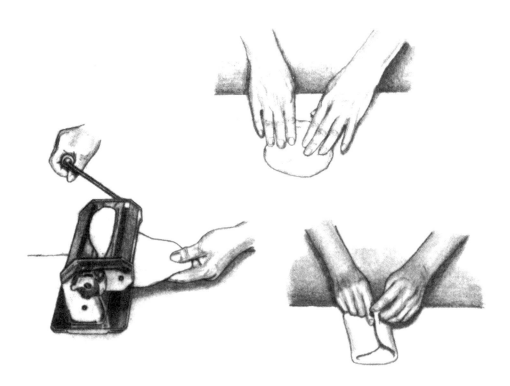

ROLLING WITH THE PASTA MACHINE

This rolling step makes the dough thin enough to cut noodles from. Each time you pass the dough sheet through the rollers, you will be decreasing the gap between the rollers one notch at a time (you may work two sheets of dough, one after the other, before changing the notch). (If you want to roll out hand-kneaded or processor-kneaded dough with a pasta machine, first pat, flour, and smooth the ball of dough into an oblong shape and pass it through the fully open rollers

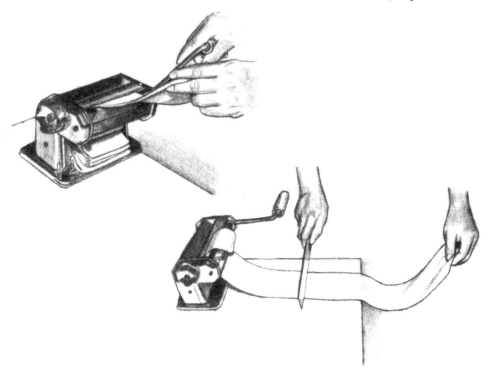

once before starting this procedure.) Each time flour the sheet on both sides, smoothing it in, and then pass it through the rollers, quickly pulling it out as it comes through the other side. The sheet will get longer in the process; when it is more than 20 inches long, cut it in half and work with one, then the other. At the next to last setting, you will make the last roll, which creates a thickness appropriate for most egg noodle dishes—a little less than ⅛ inch thick.

After the final rolling of all the sheets, do not dust with flour, since you'll be dusting them with cornstarch later; simply spread each sheet on dry towels, and hang them halfway over the edge of a table. The drying takes about 20 to 30 minutes, depending on whether it is dry or humid. Sheets that are to be cut by machine need to be drier than those you do by hand. You want to be sure not to have the sheet get caught on the cutting teeth. Repeat this entire rolling and drying process with the other three pieces of dough.

CUTTING THE NOODLES WITH A PASTA MACHINE
When the first noodle sheets are slightly dry at the edges but still pliable, dust and smooth them on both sides lightly with cornstarch—approximately 2 teaspoons for each sheet. (The salt shaker approach makes this dusting very even.) Pass each through the cutter you need; most machines come with two widths—¼ inch and ¹⁄₁₆ inch. You can

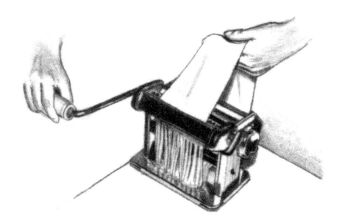

buy other sizes of cutters to suit your needs. Gather the ends of the noodles as the sheet is being cut. Spread them on a baking sheet, tray, or towel and let them dry for 10 minutes to firm up. Cut the other sheets of dough.

After the 10-minute rest period, you can cook the noodles or put them in a plastic bag and refrigerate them. If you want to keep them dried, pile them in loose mounds about 3 to 4 inches wide and less than ½ inch thick. They will take at least 24 hours to dry completely; they will be thin and brittle and feel light to the touch.

STORING FRESH NOODLES
If you aren't cooking the noodles right away but will within 4 hours, simply cover the tray with a dry towel. If you are waiting longer than that, put the noodles in a plastic bag and refrigerate them; they will stay fresh for as long as 3 days, and you can freeze them for up to 2 months. If you want to keep them dried, let them dry uncovered for at least 24

hours or longer and then store them in a tightly closed container, where they will keep for up to 3 months.

A GUIDE TO BUYING FRESH AND DRIED NOODLES

The simple fact is that the Chinese use essentially only two or three widths of noodles, the thinnest being about 1/16 inch wide and the others either 1/8 or 1/4 inch wide or somewhere in between. Therefore, if you are buying fresh or dried noodles from an Italian pasta shop or specialty store, get the linguine or spaghetti shape for the thin noodle, the fettucini shape for the wider noodle.

Many Chinese stores carry fresh noodles, sold by the pound in plastic bags and available in different widths (approximately those just mentioned). For instance, the West Lake Noodle Company in New York City's Chinatown carries two widths of egg noodles—one less than 1/16 inch wide and the other about 1/8 inch wide. The flour used is equivalent to all-purpose flour. The egg noodles are made with 2½ ounces of eggs to 1 pound of flour (less than I use), and a vegetable coloring is added to give them a pale yellow look. The eggless noodles made at West Lake are a little less than 1/4 inch wide. Both egg and eggless noodles are also sold dried, in 2½- and 5-pound boxes. Always be sure to refrigerate fresh noodles after you buy them.

COOKING FRESH NOODLES

The key to cooking any pasta is using a large amount of water (4 quarts per pound of pasta). The rapidly boiling water and an occasional stir will keep the pasta from sticking, especially when it's frozen.

For homemade Chinese egg noodles, bring 4 quarts of water to a rolling boil over high heat. Since fresh noodles cook so rapidly, have the sauce or topping ready if possible so you can serve them immediately; or, if you're stir-frying them briefly later, you can decrease the cooking time and let them rest in the pot, drained and covered, for a few minutes.

Loosen the noodle strands, drop them gradually into the boiling water, and stir them once or twice with chopsticks to separate them. When the water returns to a boil, lower the heat a little so the water doesn't boil over but still maintains a rolling boil. Stir occasionally and cook the noodles until done—from 1 to 3 minutes, depending on the width of the noodle and your preference. Commercial fresh noodles will take about 1 to 2 minutes longer to cook. With both homemade and store-bought noodles, start tasting after the noodles have been boiling for 1 minute, since the only true test is taste: Chinese noodles should be tender but firm to the bite (a little softer than *al dente*). For very thin noodles taste them *before* the water returns to a boil, since they take such a short time to cook. Again, if you are going to stir-fry or simmer them after this first cooking, decrease the time just a little.

To Serve Hot: When the noodles are done, pour them into a large colander and shake to drain off the water; then immediately return them to the cooking pot and toss with a little oil to keep them warm and to keep them from sticking while you finish making any sauce or topping. If the noodles get cold, simply dip them in boiling water to heat them.

To Serve Cold: Rinse the cooked noodles well with cold water in a colander and drain them thoroughly. Put them in a serving bowl, toss with a little oil, and refrigerate, covered. Before serving them, toss to loosen the noodle strands.

COOKING FROZEN OR DRIED NOODLES
When you are cooking fresh noodles that you've frozen, you can defrost the noodles in the refrigerator (this takes about 2 to 3 hours), or at room temperature (this takes about 30 minutes to an hour); then gently loosen the strands and drop them into rapidly boiling water. If you don't have the time to defrost them, you may drop the noodles, still frozen, into the boiling water but be careful to stir gently to separate them. In that case cook them a minute or two longer than you would fresh noodles—3 to 4 minutes in all. Noodles that you've dried should be cooked as long as completely frozen ones. Store-bought dried noodles will need even longer to cook—approximately 5 minutes or according to the directions on the package.

Homemade
Chinese Eggless Noodles

白
面　BAI MIAN

These are a staple of the Chinese home because they are used so often in soups, such as Shredded Pork and Red-in-Snow Noodle Soup (page 87). They are also especially tasty with a rich sauce, such as Sichuan Spicy Beef Sauce and Noodle Soup (page 80) or Brown Bean and Meat Sauce on

Noodles (page 59), since their soft texture and bland taste take readily to seasonings. Good accompaniments are Shanghai Spring Rolls (page 105), Cantonese Spring Rolls with Shrimp and Pork (page 110), or Boiled Dumplings, Beijing-Style (page 135), when you want a substantial meal.

The trick here is to produce a firm dough that is well kneaded, so the noodles will have enough texture to hold their shape, either in a broth or against a strong sauce. The wider-size noodle is best for both soups and rich sauces. If you don't have the time to make them, they are readily available fresh from Chinese markets and they keep well in the freezer.

Yield: 1 1/4 pounds

3 cups all-purpose flour	2 teaspoons corn oil or peanut oil
2 teaspoons coarse salt	1 cup water, approximately

Mix and knead the dough by hand (page 22) or in a food processor (page 24). Let it rest, covered with plastic wrap, for 30 minutes if done by hand and for 1 hour if done in a food processor.

Roll and cut the dough by hand (pages 23–24) or with a pasta machine (pages 26–27).

Steamed Noodles

蒸
蛋   ZHENG MIAN
面

The process of first steaming fresh noodles and then boiling or pan frying them is often used by the Chinese. As a result, the noodles not only retain their fresh flavor but become crispier when fried. They also become separate and bouncier and fluffier than fresh noodles that are merely boiled. They won't turn sticky or mushy even if you overcook them. In fact, this process is a trade secret most Chinese noodle shops and restaurants have used for years. Nowadays restaurateurs often ask the noodle factories to do the initial steaming.

I am very fond of cooking with noodles that have been already steamed. I prefer refrigerating or freezing already-steamed noodles to drying them, because it is easier and takes less time. But I remember with pleasure that when I was very young, my mother used to steam fresh egg noodles in nests and then dry them in the sunlight. There is no question that the steaming process prolongs the fresh flavor of noodles; they also keep fresh longer without refrigeration.

Dried, pre-steamed noodles are on sale in almost all Oriental grocery stores. You need to select them by their appearance (the packages are not marked). They are a little shinier, darker in color, and more neatly stacked than regular dried noodles.

STEAMING THE NOODLES

If you want to savor the unusual texture of noodles try this recipe with 1 pound homemade or store-bought medium-thin soft fresh noodles (not frozen or dried, since they can't be arranged in the steamer). Divide them into two piles, and if possible use two 10-inch bamboo steamers, stacked one on top of the other. In each steamer rack spread the noodles into an 8-inch-round patty, keeping it loose and evenly distributed, or arrange them in eight nests, four in each steamer, with some space between them. The individual noodle patties and nests shouldn't be piled more than 1 inch high. The steamers should sit in a 12-inch wok, with the boiling water 1½ inches lower than the rack. If you don't have a steamer, place the patties or nests on two large plates and elevate them in a large pot, such as a roasting pan, with tuna-fish cans, both ends removed, or heatproof cups with a little water in them to anchor them. The boiling water should be about 1½ inches beneath the plates so it will just steam, not bathe, the noodles. Cover tightly, and when the water is back at a rolling boil, start to time the steaming process. The noodles should steam over high heat 10 minutes for homemade and 15 minutes for store-bought, until they are a little shiny, slightly darker in color, and a little heavier because they are dense.

Remove the racks or plates from the steamer and loosen the noodles with your fingers so they won't stick together when they cool, which occurs in a few minutes. At that point you may put them in a plastic bag and refrigerate them (for up to 2 weeks) or freeze them (for up to 2 months), or let the unloosened mounds dry completely in cool air or sunlight. Once dried, steamed noodles can be kept in a tightly closed container for 3 or 4 months.

For Soup Noodles (such as Yangzhou Noodle Soup in Casserole, page 82): To cook the steamed noodles, drop them into boiling water and stir briefly to loosen the strands. When the water returns to a boil, cook the noodles for about 3 to 4 minutes, or to taste—they take longer to cook than fresh noodles.

For Cold Noodles (such as Cold Noodle Salad with Sesame–Peanut Butter–Chili Sauce or Soy-Vinegar Sauce, page 72): After cooking, drain the noodles well in a colander, and rinse in cold water and drain thoroughly. Use chopsticks to fluff them up and dry until all moisture is gone. For storing, simply put them in a plastic bag and refrigerate them; they will stay fresh for up to 3 days.

For Browned Noodle Patty with Sauce (page 66): For fresh pre-steamed noodles (the soft kind; not dried) that are very fine, you don't need to boil them. Just put them directly in the pan with the heated oil (for ½ pound of noodles, use 2 tablespoons of oil for each side) and fry, but while you cook the first side, sprinkle about ¼ cup of water on the noodles, then cover the pan, and fry for 5 minutes, or until it is browned. Flip the patty over, add more oil and fry, uncovered, for another 5 minutes, or until browned.

If you are using pre-steamed noodles that are thick, you will need to boil them first (2 minutes for homemade; about 5 minutes for store-bought), before frying the patty.

Yi Fu Noodles

 YI FU MIAN

The Chinese, especially those from Canton, take the texture of food so seriously that they sometimes go to extreme lengths to achieve a special effect. *Yi fu* noodles are a superb example of this passion. *Yi fu* means "house of Yi," referring to a famous nobleman in the imperial court during the eighteenth century. These equally famous noodles were probably made at his instigation.

Fresh soft noodles (egg or eggless) are first boiled, then deep-fried, then boiled again, and finally, as part of a dish, they are stir-fried or used as noodle soup. They have a rich flavor and a magically smooth, soft and fluffy texture. The noodle strands are separate.

Dried *yi fu* noodles are available in Chinese markets, packed in boxes. They have been boiled and deep-fried. All you have to do is boil them and then prepare them in a dish.

Yi fu noodles can be substituted for fresh noodles in any stir-fried dish. See the suggestions at the end of this recipe.

Yield: 1 pound

**1 pound soft egg noodles, about ⅛   4 cups oil for deep-frying
inch wide (page 21)**

Bring 4 quarts of water to a boil in a large pot. Loosen the noodle strands, drop them gradually into the boiling water, and stir briefly. Bring the water to a second boil as quickly as possible. When the boil returns, lower the heat a little so the water doesn't boil over. Cook the noodles for 1 to 2 minutes from the time the water boils. You want them to be slightly unerdone. Pour them into a large colander, rinse well with cold water, and drain thoroughly. Spread them out on a plate and let them dry for about 15 minutes, lifting them occasionally so they dry evenly.

Heat the oil to 365 degrees in a wok or deep casserole. Mound one-quarter of the noodles in a loose pile on a 10-inch plate to make an 8-inch noodle pie. Slide this "pie" into the oil and let it fry for about 2 minutes, or until the noodles turn very light brown and become hardened on the bottom. Turn the "pie" over and fry the other side until the noodles are crisp and light brown all over. Remove with a large slotted spoon, and drain on paper towels. Repeat with the other nest. This frying can be done hours or days ahead of time; in that case store the "pies" in a plastic bag in a cool place.

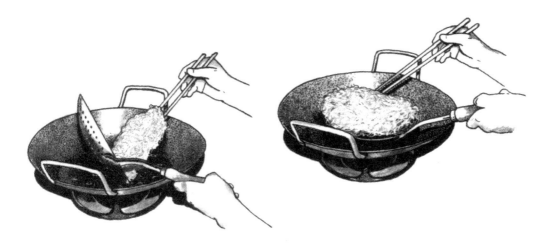

THE FINAL COOKING

Bring 2 to 3 cups of water to a boil in a large pot (just enough water to submerge the noodles so that the oil will hold its own during the cooking and give the noodles a rich flavor), drop in the noodle "pies," and stir gently to separate the noodle strands in each of the "pies"; cook the noodles for about 3 to 4 minutes, or until they become soft again. Drain in a colander and toss to cool. The noodles are now ready for stir-frying or boiling (see, for example, *Yi Fu* Noodles with Hearts of Chinese Broccoli, below; Roast Pork with Tossed Noodles, page 63; or Yangzhou Noodle Soup in Casserole on page 82).

Yi Fu Noodles with Hearts of Chinese Broccoli

干烧伊府面 KAN SHA YI FU MIAN

This is a delicious noodle dish made with vegetables only. It would go beautifully with traditional American dishes such as roast beef or chicken, or Chinese dishes such as meat or fowl cooked in a "master marinade sauce," roast pork (page 208), or spicy crisp sea bass or carp. *Guo tie,* or Fried Dumplings, Beijing-Style (page 141), would also be an excellent match if you wanted a lighter meal.

Chinese broccoli has a thinner stalk and not as pronounced a head as American broccoli. Use the tender inner stalks and heads. Homemade or store-bought Steamed Noodles (page 31) or Homemade Chinese Egg Noodles (page 21) may be used instead of the *yi fu* noodles if you prefer.

Yield: 4–6 servings as part of a larger meal or 2 servings as a light meal

2 tablespoons corn oil or peanut oil
2 cups hearts of Chinese broccoli cut into pencil strips 2 inches long × ¼ inch wide (if Chinese yellow chives are available, use 1 cup chives cut into 2-inch lengths and 1 cup broccoli; if neither is available, use 2 cups regular leeks cut into 2-inch lengths and ¼-inch wide)

1 cup Best Chicken Broth (page 77)
1 recipe *Yi Fu* Noodles (page 33)
2 tablespoons oyster-flavored sauce
Salt and black pepper to taste

STIR-FRYING THE DISH

Heat a wok over moderate heat for 30 seconds. Add the oil and swirl; then add the broccoli and stir-fry for 30 seconds. Add the chicken broth and bring to a boil. Put in the noodles and lift and stir them with chopsticks to distribute them evenly in the broth; then cover and cook for 2 to 3 minutes, or until they absorb the broth. Uncover and toss the noodles a few times with a spatula. Dribble the oyster-flavored sauce all over and continue to scoop and toss for a few seconds. Taste for seasoning, adding salt and pepper if needed. Dish out onto a heated platter and serve hot.

Green Jade Noodles
(Fresh Spinach Noodles)

  FEICUI MIAN

Years ago, on a visit to Taiwan, I met a famous Hunan chef, Mr. Peng, who later came to New York City and opened a Hunan restaurant. He taught me to make several Hunan dishes, both in Taiwan and New York, among them these lovely bright-green noodles, which he prepared by hand-chopping fresh spinach leaves and combining them with noodle dough. He served them cold, with meat, vegetables, and sauce, just as in the cold noodle salad recipe on page 72.

I have simplified Chef Peng's work by using a food processor, so that in a half hour you can make 1½ pounds of lovely green jade noodles. If you need to use frozen spinach in a pinch, the noodles will be flecked with dark-green spots, but they will be just as tasty.

If you don't have time to make fresh noodles, dried, pre-steamed spinach noodles are available in most Chinese grocery stores. The Long Life brand from China is very good, sold in 250 G. (8.8 oz.) packages.

Yield: 1½ pounds

1 cup fresh spinach leaves with stems removed (about 1 pound), parboiled for 1 minute and squeezed very dry, or use a 10-ounce package frozen chopped spinach, thawed and squeezed very dry

3 cups all-purpose flour
2 teaspoons coarse salt
2 extra large eggs
2 teaspoons corn oil or peanut oil
2 tablespoons or more cold water

MIXING THE DOUGH IN A FOOD PROCESSOR
Insert the steel blade in the food processor. Put the spinach, flour, and salt into the work bowl (for a small food processor, make half the recipe at a time). Chop the spinach with the flour until the spinach is very fine—about 60 seconds. Then turn the machine off.

Break the eggs into a measuring cup and add the oil and 1 tablespoon of the cold water. Gradually pour the egg-oil-and-water mixture through the processor feed tube, pressing the pulse action about twenty or thirty times. Then press "on." Within 10 seconds the mixture should start to form a ball that cleans the sides of the work bowl as it spins. If the ball doesn't form, add more water 1 or 2 teaspoons at a time. The dough should be firm but smooth, so don't add too much water, which would make it sticky. After the dough forms a ball, continue to let it spin for 1 minute. Then turn off the machine, remove the dough ball along with any small pieces, and knead by hand a few turns. Cover the dough with plastic wrap and let it rest at room temperature for 1 hour.

MIXING THE DOUGH BY HAND
Chop the parboiled fresh or thawed frozen spinach very fine, until it is almost a paste. Put it in a large mixing bowl or on a work surface, pour

the flour around the spinach, add the eggs, salt, and oil in the center, and start working it together with your hands. Add water when needed as you follow the directions on pages 22 and 23 for mixing and kneading. Cover the dough with plastic wrap and let it rest for 1 hour. Then either roll and cut the dough by hand (pages 23 and 24) or roll and cut the dough with a pasta machine (pages 26 and 27).

Shrimp Roe Noodles

虾 XIA ZI MIAN
子
面 Most Italian pasta is made from wheat, with or without eggs, and then formed into an endless array of imaginative shapes—angel's hair, spaghetti, twists, bow-ties, and butterflies are only a few. Chinese noodles are almost always cut into two basic forms—wide like fettucini or thin like spaghetti—but its great variety derives from the many food products it is made from, such as wheat, rice, beans, tapioca, and other grains. Particularly with wheat noodles, other ingredients besides eggs are often added, such as chicken extract or tiny shrimp roe. In this way the noodles are flavored from the start, and all you have to do is boil them and toss them with oil, salt, and pepper to produce a very tasty dish. The Chinese very often put flavored noodles in chicken broth to serve as a noodle soup.

Wheat noodles that contain special ingredients can be completely dried, needing no refrigeration. That is why most Oriental markets can stock a full line of dried velvet chicken noodles (chicken broth and monosodium glutamate), shrimp roe noodles, and egg noodles. They come boxed or in cellophane, containing small round or oval nests of dried noodles. Some have a shiny appearance, which means they were steamed before being dried (see page 31). They can be stored for up to three months if kept in a tightly closed container in a cool, dry place.

The recipe for these delicious shrimp roe noodles is almost the same as the one for egg noodles (page 21), except that the shrimp roe is an additional ingredient. Homemade shrimp roe noodles are really so much tastier than the commercial ones that it is well worth your effort to make them.

Yield: 1½ pounds; enough for 6 people

1 tablespoon shrimp roe (sold in Chinese supermarkets by the ounce), about ⅓ ounce
2 tablespoons water
3 cups all-purpose flour

2 extra large eggs
1 tablespoon coarse salt
2 teaspoons corn oil or peanut oil
½ cup Best Chicken Broth (page 77)

MAKING THE SHRIMP PASTE
AND THE NOODLE DOUGH

In a small bowl combine the shrimp roe with water and steam over high heat for 10 minutes; it will become a paste. Set aside to cool. You will be adding it with the eggs, salt, oil, and broth, when you make the noodle dough.

Mix and knead the dough by hand (pages 22 and 23) or in a food processor (page 24), adding the shrimp roe paste with the other ingredients as you make the noodle dough. Roll and cut the dough by hand (pages 23 and 24) or in a pasta machine (pages 26 and 27).

COOKING AND SERVING THE NOODLES

Cook the noodles in 4 quarts of boiling water for 1 to 2 minutes, or until tender but firm to the bite, a little softer than *al dente*. Drain them in a colander and shake off the water. Put the noodles in a serving bowl, add 3 tablespoons of sesame or corn oil, depending on your preference, and salt and pepper to taste.

Serve the noodles hot as a plain pasta dish. Or use the noodles in a noodle soup dish, such as Best Chicken Broth (page 77) and add vegetables—in that case don't add the oil, salt, or pepper, but simply boil the noodles and add them to your soup.

Silver Needle Noodles

YIN ZHEN MIAN

These shiny transparent noodles from Canton look very much like cellophane noodles, although their size is that of a very thick needle. The texture is very smooth, bouncy, and slightly chewy; the flavor is pleasingly bland—a perfect foil for a rich sauce, such as Sichuan Spicy Beef Sauce and Noodle Soup (page 80), Noodles with Spicy Fish Sauce (page 57), or Baby Squid and Hearts of Celery on Noodles (page 60). They would be an excellent substitute for Drop Noodles in Two Soups (page 90) or for the rice sticks in Spicy Beef with Fried Rice Noodles (page 229). The main ingredient—wheat starch—is flour that has no gluten in it—thus the very smooth texture.

The recipe can easily be doubled or more.

Yield: 2 cups

1 cup wheat starch	**¾ cup boiling water,**
¼ teaspoon coarse salt	**approximately**
	1 tablespoon corn or peanut oil

FORMING THE DOUGH

Put the wheat starch and salt in a mixing bowl. Add the boiling water all at once, stirring with chopsticks or a fork until the starch is damp. Add the oil, then knead the dough, while it is hot, with your hands, until it forms a soft, smooth ball—about 2 minutes. Cover the dough with plastic wrap and let it rest for 10 minutes.

ROLLING THE NOODLES

Divide the dough into six portions. With your fingers, roll each portion into ropelike strips about ¼ inch wide. Break these into peanut-size bits. Roll each bit on your palms into the shape of a thick knitting needle, ¼ inch thick and 1½ inches long.

Yield: about 150 pieces

STEAMING THE NOODLES

Grease a plate that will be approximately ½ inch smaller in diameter than the steamer you will be using. Place the shaped noodles on the plate and steam them for 5 minutes. They will be slightly shiny and off-white in color.

These noodles can be made ahead of time and refrigerated for a few days wrapped in plastic.

Dragon's Beard Noodles or Pull Noodles

 LONG XU MIAN OR LA MIAN

These noodles are hard to believe unless you've seen someone make them. The dough, made from 3½ cups of flour, creates noodles 5 feet long in 2,048 hairlike strands. They are deep-fried, and they are so fine they will melt in your mouth. This noodle making, however, is very difficult. You need strength and a good deal of practice to accomplish it.

The dough can make two types of noodles. The first, after six or seven pulls, becomes a regular thick kind of noodle, ready to be boiled. The second, after ten pulls, becomes 2,048 strands, ready to be deep-fried. A skilled master can go even further—I have seen up to twelve pulls. Kun Jing Mark, our senior instructor at China Institute's Bilingual Vocational Chef Training Program, did this many times in classes and on television. I want to describe the whole process so that you can make this famous noodle if you want to. The nest of fine deep-fried noodles is usually served inside Mandarin pancakes.

Yield: 10 servings for a first course

1 cup unsifted unbleached flour
2½ cups unsifted bread flour
1½ cups cold water,
   approximately
   Peanut oil or corn oil for
   deep-frying, about 6 cups
3 teaspoons baking powder
1 teaspoon salt

1 piece velvet or velvetlike
   cloth, double-layered,
   measuring approximately
   5 × 3 feet
1 large electric wok
1 recipe warm Mandarin
   Pancakes (page 157)

MIXING THE DOUGH

Put the flours in a large mixing bowl and make a well in the center.
Gradually pour the water into the center and mix with your hands until
a soft dough forms. Because the dough is too soft to knead with the heel
of your hand, pick it up and throw it to the table until it is smooth—
about 3 minutes.

Keep the dough in a covered bowl at room temperature for at least
4 hours or up to overnight.

PULLING THE NOODLES

Place the cloth on a large table and put plenty of flour in the center of
the cloth. Set up the electric wok nearby, pour oil up to 1 inch below the
wok's rim, and heat the oil to 350 degrees. Place a large bowl of cold
water next to the cloth.

Sprinkle 3 teaspoons baking soda, 1 teaspoon salt, and 2 teaspoons
water on top of the dough and mix them into the dough with your
fingers. Pull the elastic dough out from the bowl by letting it stretch
straight down with one hand. Then grasp the end of the dough with
your other hand and shake the dough up and down to create as long a
strand as possible. Join the ends into one hand with a whirling motion
to make one twisted strand. If the dough starts to stick to your fingers,
dip your fingers in the cold water. Continue shaking and twisting the
dough. When it begins to feel tight, pass the whole loop through the
water from one end to the other, still holding on with two hands. This
gives the dough a softer texture. Do this two or three times in the process of shaking down and twisting.

When the dough is pliable, shiny, and absolutely smooth, stretch it
out as long as your arm can reach to make a long "rope" and quickly lay
the rope on the floured cloth. Push the flour over on top of the dough.
Fold the dough back over itself, so you have the two ends in your left
hand and the first and second fingers of your right hand in the folded
end. Keeping your left hand stationary, stretch the folded end out and

up with your right hand's two fingers to arm's length. Fold the dough over itself again. Now you have four ends in your left hand. Quickly cut off a few inches of the left-hand end of the dough to reduce the amount you have to hold. Liberally flour the stretched-out dough by moving it around on the floured cloth and repeat the folding, stretching, cutting, and flouring ten times. This will create 2,048 strands of very fine noodles when you do the final cutting.

CUTTING AND DEEP-FRYING THE NOODLES
Lay the dough on the cloth. With a sharp knife, cut off a few inches of dough from the two ends and discard, then cut the rest of the length into three sections. Using a pair of long chopsticks, lift up from bottom of the fine noodles and transfer the three sections, one at a time, to the hot oil and fry them until lightly browned on both sides, about 1 to 2 minutes. Remove the noodles from the oil with a sieve and lay them on paper towels to drain. When they are cool, sprinkle a little salt on top. Serve the noodles wrapped in Mandarin Pancakes.

Fried dragon's beard noodles can be stored in an airtight container in the refrigerator for weeks or in the freezer for months. Reheat them for 2 to 3 minutes in a preheated 350 degree oven.

Pull Noodles (Simple Version)

拉 LA MIAN

面 During my recent trip to China (spring, 1985), I had an unusual lesson from one of my nieces, Er-mei. During China's cultural revolution, Er-mei was sent to Gansu Province in northwest China for more than ten years. Her daily meal was made from wheat. She had to make noodles without equipment, not even a rolling pin or board. So her skills in hand-pulling noodles are excellent. The kneading the dough and letting it rest are important. The pulling part is not hard. She just pulls and drops the noodles in boiling water, then drains the noodles and mixes them with sauce or in a soup for the meal. Oddly enough, the noodle has a nutty and sweet taste, although a few grains of salt are all that is added to the flour.

Since we have modern equipment, making the dough becomes very easy. You can use a food processor to mix and knead the dough. First I use the pulse action to absorb the liquid slowly, then spin to knead a soft, smooth, elastic texture into the dough. After pulling, place the noodles on a floured board or surface. You can cook the noodles later or store them in the refrigerator or freezer.

1 cup all-purpose flour
¼ teaspoon coarse salt

½ cup cold water (leave out 2
tablespoons, adding when
needed)

MIXING THE DOUGH BY HAND
Put the flour in a large mixing bowl, make a well in the center, and add the salt; then gradually add water in the well, mixing it into the flour with your fingers to form a dough. The dough must be firm in the beginning so that the gluten will develop; then add a little water, about 1 teaspoon at a time, or wet your fingers with the remaining water to knead the dough until you have a ball that is soft, smooth, elastic, and shiny, about 5 minutes.

Make a hole in the center of the dough with your fingers, smooth the hole as you make it larger, then break the circle to form a rope. Break the rope into six pieces, smooth each piece, and then lightly coat them with corn oil and set them in the mixing bowl without letting them touch each other. Cover the bowl with plastic wrap and let it sit from 2 to 3 hours up to 8 hours at room temperature.

MIXING THE DOUGH IN A FOOD PROCESSOR
Put the flour and salt in a food processor with the steel blade on. Use pulse action to mix the flour while you add the water, about twenty to thirty pulses—first 6 tablespoons of water, then more as needed, total about 7 tablespoons. The dough should be soft but not sticky. Then let it spin for 1 minute or until the dough is soft, smooth, and does not stick to your fingers. Remove the dough from the bowl. Shape a ball, make a hole, break the pieces, coat them with oil, and let them rest as with mixing dough by hand.

PULLING NOODLES
Sprinkle some flour on a working surface. Working with one piece at a time, gently pull the dough by pressing it flat with the fingers and thumbs of both hands. Press the dough evenly to about 1-inch width. As you press, the dough will grow longer, about two feet. Hold both ends of the dough and shake up and down to make it even longer, about three feet. Then, from the center of the flat long rope, use your fingernails to split the rope lengthwise and pull it apart into two long ropes. Put one half on the working surface and split the other from the center once more to make it thinner, like a ¼-inch-wide noodle. Work the other half rope in the same fashion. If the rope breaks, leave it on the work surface and split again. Ideally, you should end up with each piece

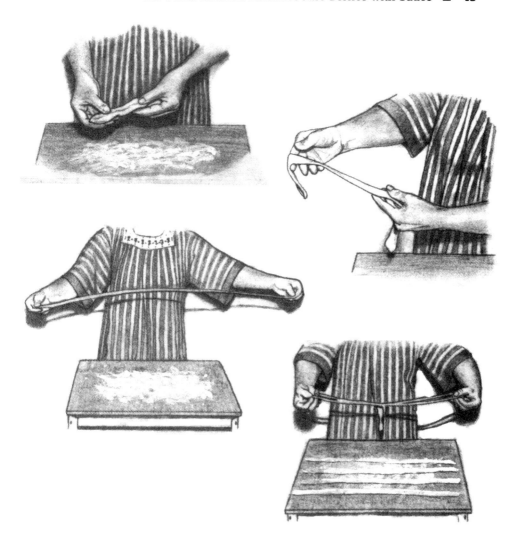

of dough (total six pieces) split into four ropes less than ¼ inch wide and three feet long.

You can cook the noodles right away or you can leave the finished noodles on a floured surface and let them dry for 15 to 20 minutes. Sprinkle on cornstarch to coat them, then put them in a plastic bag and keep in the refrigerator for three days or freezer for one month.

Beef with Onions on Noodles

洋 葱 牛 肉 面 YANG CONG NIU ROU MIAN

Stir-frying is a technique the Chinese developed many centuries ago to conserve fuel; it is the quick cooking of small pieces of food in a little oil over high heat. The amount of food cooked must be small so that the heat will seal in the juices, and all the ingredients must be cut approximately in the same size and shape (such as thin slices 1 by 1½ inches, matchstick shreds 2 inches long, or large or small cubes) so they will be done at the same time and also have visual integrity. This sliced steak and onion dish is a perfect example of simple stir-frying. The two following recipes illustrate further variations on stir-frying: The meats are parboiled in water or oil (sometimes called *velveting*) before being stir-fried.

In this classic, uncomplicated dish you can substitute other ingredients with equally superb results. You could fry pork, veal, lamb, or even chicken (use light soy sauce, not dark, with the chicken) instead of steak; you could replace the onions with fresh asparagus, snow peas, or broccoli—whatever you prefer and is in season.

Yield: 4 servings for a light meal

¾ **pound flank steak or round steak, semi-frozen for easier slicing**
3 **medium yellow onions**
¼ **teaspoon coarse salt**
1 **teaspoon minced fresh ginger**
1 **small clove garlic, minced, about ½ teaspoon**

¾ **pound Homemade Chinese Egg Noodles (page 21) or Homemade Chinese Eggless Noodles (page 30)**
5 **tablespoons corn oil or peanut oil**

THE MARINADE

¼ **teaspoon coarse salt**
1 **tablespoon dark soy sauce**
2 **teaspoons cornstarch**

1 **tablespoon cold water**
1 **tablespoon peanut oil or corn oil**

THE SAUCE

2 **tablespoons dark soy sauce**
1 **teaspoon sugar**
2 **teaspoons sesame oil**

1 **tablespoon cornstarch**
1 **cup Best Chicken Broth (page 77)**

THE SEASONINGS FOR THE NOODLES

2 tablespoons corn oil or peanut oil	**1 tablespoon light soy sauce** **Dash white pepper**

PREPARING THE MEAT AND VEGETABLES

If you are using flank steak, cut it lengthwise (with the grain) into strips about 2 inches wide; then cut the strips against the grain into ⅛-inch-thick slices. If you use round steak, slice it against the grain into pieces ⅛ inch thick, 1 inch wide, and 1½ inches long. Put the meat in a large bowl and add the marinade ingredients in the order listed, but don't pour in the oil until you've used your fingers to mix the first ingredients well with the meat. Let the meat marinate at room temperature while you combine the sauce ingredients in a bowl and slice the onions. You can marinate the beef for up to 8 hours if you cover the bowl and refrigerate it. Remove it from the refrigerator 10 minutes before the cooking.

Combine the sauce ingredients in a bowl and set aside. Cut the onions vertically in half, then vertically again into slices a little less than ½ inch thick. Separate the slices—you should have about 2 cups. Put the minced ginger and garlic in a small dish.

COOKING THE NOODLES

Cook the noodles in 3 quarts of boiling water for about 2 minutes, testing for doneness after 1 minute. When they are tender but firm to the bite, a little softer than *al dente,* drain them in a colander, shake off the water, and return them to the pot. Sprinkle on the seasonings, toss well, and cover to keep the noodles hot while you cook the topping.

STIR-FRYING THE TOPPING

Heat a wok over medium-high heat for 30 seconds, add 2 tablespoons of the oil and swirl, then add the onions. Stir-fry for about 2 minutes, or until the onions are translucent and still crunch but not soft or burned. Add the salt and toss; then scoop the onions out onto a plate. Give the marinated beef a good stir. Reheat the wok over medium-high heat, add the remaining 3 tablespoons of oil and swirl, then add the ginger and garlic and stir for 5 seconds; then add the beef with marinade and stir and toss to separate the slices. Cook, stirring, until most of the beef changes color—about 1 minute. Then add the onions and toss well to heat through. Stir the sauce well, turn up the heat fairly high, and gradually pour the sauce into the wok; stir and toss until the sauce thickens slightly and glazes the ingredients. Remove the wok from the heat.

Dish out the noodles on a large heated platter. Pour the beef, onions, and sauce on top. Serve immediately.

Doubling the Recipe. If you want to make more than 1 recipe, stir-fry the meat in two batches and the onions or vegetables in one large batch. Dish out the meat and vegetables on a large plate, but keep them separate. Now pour the sauce into the wok and bring to a boil while stirring. Turn the heat high. Add first the vegetables and then the meat to the sauce and bring just to a boil again, to avoid overcooking the meat. Serve over noodles.

Variation: *Curry-flavored beef with onions.* After stir-frying the onions for 2 minutes, add 2 to 3 teaspoons of Madras curry powder and stir together for 30 seconds; then add the salt and also 1 teaspoon of sugar and mix well. Scoop out onto a plate, wash the wok, and then stir-fry the meat.

Variation: *For matchstick shreds of meat with onions,* cut the meat to match the noodles, cut shreds *with* the grain. This will prevent them from breaking into bits while cooking. Cut the onions into shreds too to match the meat and noodles.

Noodles with Velveted Chicken and Smithfield Ham

 HUI TUI JI PIAN MIAN

Velveting chicken, seafood, or meat in cornstarch and egg white and then parboiling it before stir-frying is a favorite Cantonese cooking method. It makes the meat soft on the outside while sealing in all the flavor and tenderness. In this dish the salty Smithfield ham balances the subtle flavor of the chicken and vegetables. The dish would go well with Shanghai Spring Rolls (page 105), which are crisp, and Sichuan Pickled Cabbage (page 308), which is spicy.

Yield: 4 servings as a light meal

1 **large whole chicken breast or 2
small whole chicken breasts,
skinned and boned, about 10
ounces, semi-frozen for easier
slicing**
1 **bunch broccoli**
2 **tablespoons corn oil or peanut
oil**
¾ **pound Homemade Chinese Egg
Noodles (page 21) or
Homemade Chinese Eggless
Noodles (page 30)**
4 **tablespoons corn oil or peanut
oil**

1 **teaspoon minced fresh ginger**
1 **clove garlic, minced**
¼ **teaspoon coarse salt**
1 **tablespoon light soy sauce**
½ **cup thinly sliced cooked
Smithfield ham or any other
salty ham, each slice about
⅛ × 1 × 1½ inches**
1 **cup Best Chicken Broth
(page 77)**
1 **tablespoon cornstarch
combined with 2 tablespoons
water**

THE SEASONINGS FOR THE NOODLES

2 **tablespoons corn oil or peanut
oil**

1 **tablespoon light soy sauce**
⅛ **teaspoon white pepper**

THE MARINADE FOR THE CHICKEN

1 **small egg white**
½ **teaspoon coarse salt**

¼ **teaspoon sugar**
3 **tablespoons cornstarch**

PREPARING THE CHICKEN AND BROCCOLI

Cut each chicken breast in half crosswise and then slant-cut, with the grain, into slices each approximately ⅛ inch thick by 1 inch wide by 2 inches long. Put them in a shallow bowl and mix gently with all the marinade ingredients except the cornstarch; then sprinkle on the cornstarch and mix well with your fingers for 30 seconds, until the chicken is well coated. Cover and refrigerate the chicken.

Peel and cut the broccoli stalks into slices about 2 inches long and ¼ inch thick and set aside with the florets, which should have just a little stem still attached. You should have about 4 cups. Mince the ginger and the garlic and place them in a small dish.

Heat 4 cups of water and 1 tablespoon of oil in the saucepan over high heat until boiling; then plunge in the broccoli florets and sliced stalks and parboil for 2 minutes total. Scoop them out with a slotted spoon and reserve on a plate.

Keeping the same water in the pan, turn the heat down to medium so that it continues at a slow boil. Add the slices of chicken breast and gently stir them to separate the slices. "Velvet," or parboil, them for 30 seconds, or until the slices whiten and just turn firm (about 90 percent cooked). Remove them with a slotted spoon to a plate. Up to this point the broccoli florets and stems and the chicken may be prepared ahead of time—up to 2 hours at room temperature or up to 8 hours if covered and refrigerated.

BOILING THE NOODLES

Heat 3 quarts of water in a large pot over high heat until it boils. Add the noodles gradually and cook them for about 2 minutes (test for doneness after 1 minute), until tender but firm to the bite, a little softer than *al dente*. Drain thoroughly in a colander and then return them to the pot. Sprinkle on the seasonings, toss well, and cover to keep the noodles hot while you finish the topping.

COOKING THE TOPPING

Heat a wok over medium-high heat for 30 seconds. Add 3 tablespoons of the oil, swirl, then add the ginger, garlic, chicken, and broccoli. Stir and toss for 30 seconds. Add the salt and light soy sauce and toss to mix; then add the ham and chicken broth. Raise the heat to high and bring the liquid to a boil. With a spatula or large spoon, push all the food to the sides of your wok to leave the liquid in the center exposed.

Stir the cornstarch-and-water mixture well and gradually add it to the center of the wok, stirring until the liquid thickens slightly. Now toss and mix so the sauce thoroughly coats the meats and vegetables. Splash in the remaining 1 tablespoon of oil and stir once, then remove from the heat. Dish out the noodles on a large heated platter. Pour the topping over them and serve hot.

Variation: One-half pound veal cutlets may be used instead of chicken breast. Substitute ½ pound snow peas or 4 cups cut-up cauliflower for the broccoli.

Stir-Fried Chicken Breast and Green Peppers on Noodles

青
茭
鸡
面

QING JIAO JI MIAN

In his best-selling cookbook, *Jim Lee's Chinese Cookbook,* my friend Jim Lee described "velveting" chicken in water long before other writers gave due credit to this popular Cantonese cooking technique. In the Beijing region and Sichuan province, another technique is preferred—velveting in oil, which makes the meat richer and more lustrous. This oil velveting has been used extensively by restaurants in the West. To do it properly, the wok must be very hot before the oil is poured in, so the meat won't stick to the pan, but the temperature of the oil should be only about 300 degrees, so the meat doesn't fry but is cooked quickly.

This simple but colorful dish is a real home favorite, perfect for an impromptu meal. The broth must be rich, however, so that the bland flavor of the chicken will be enhanced.

Yield: Serves 4 as a light meal

2 whole chicken breasts skinned and boned, about 12 ounces
2 medium green peppers or ½ pound snow peas
2 teaspoons minced fresh ginger
1 cup corn oil or peanut oil, for velveting the chicken and cooking
¾ pound Homemade Chinese Egg Noodles (page 21)

½ teaspoon coarse salt or to taste
¼ teaspoon sugar
1 cup Best Chicken Broth (page 77)
1 tablespoon dry sherry
2 tablespoons light soy sauce
1 tablespoon cornstarch combined with 2 tablespoons cold water

THE MARINADE FOR THE CHICKEN

½ teaspoon coarse salt
1 egg white
1 tablespoon cornstarch

1 tablespoon corn oil or peanut oil

THE SEASONINGS FOR THE NOODLES

2 tablespoons corn oil or peanut oil
½ teaspoon coarse salt or to taste

⅛ teaspoon white pepper or to taste

VELVETING THE CHICKEN IN OIL AND PREPARING THE PEPPERS

Cut the chicken into strips with the grain, approximately ¼ inch wide and 1½ inches long. Place in a shallow bowl. With your fingers or chopsticks, mix them first with the salt and egg white of the marinade mixture; then stir in the cornstarch and oil. Cover and refrigerate the coated chicken for 30 minutes or as long as overnight.

Remove the seeds from the peppers and cut them into strips ¼ inch wide by 1½ inches long. Set aside on a plate. Mince the ginger and also set aside.

Heat a wok for 30 seconds or until very hot. Add 1 cup oil and heat to 300 degrees. (If a piece of scallion sizzles slowly in it, the oil is ready.) Slide the chicken strips into the oil and stir to separate them. Velvet until they whiten—this takes less than 1 minute. Pour the chicken and oil into a strainer over a bowl (save the oil for other uses; you will need 3 tablespoons of it for this recipe).

As soon as the oil has drained, transfer the chicken to a plate. There is no need to wash the wok, which will be used again. This velveting can be done up to an hour ahead of time. Keep the chicken at room temperature.

COOKING THE NOODLES

Bring 4 quarts of water to a boil in a large pot over high heat. Cook the noodles in the boiling water for 2 minutes (taste for doneness after 1 minute), until *al dente*. Drain in a colander and shake off the water. Return the noodles to the pot, add the seasonings for them, toss well, and cover to keep them hot.

STIR-FRYING THE TOPPING

Heat the wok over high heat for 30 seconds. Add 3 tablespoons of the drained oil, swirl, then stir-fry the ginger and peppers for 1 minute. Add ½ teaspoon salt, ¼ teaspoon of sugar, and stir in. Add the chicken broth, cover, and cook for 1 minute. Place the velveted chicken strips on top of the peppers or snow peas without mixing them in. Sprinkle on the sherry and soy sauce, then stir to mix. Push the chicken and vegetable to the sides of the wok. Stir the cornstarch-and-water mixture very well and pour it into the center of the wok. Stir and then toss and mix so the ingredients are glazed by the sauce. Remove from the heat.

SERVING THE DISH

Scoop the hot noodles into a serving bowl, add the topping, and toss lightly. Serve immediately.

Stir-Fried Shrimp with Egg Sauce on Noodles

BOLI XIA MIAN

I grew up in Ningbo, a seaport in the eastern central part of China, where every meal included rice. Noodles and buns, breads, and pastries were served as snacks and, for company, with tea. This noodle dish is one my family very often served to guests. It is bright with color, and crunchy from the shrimp, snow peas, and straw mushrooms, and the velvety egg sauce coats the noodles beautifully, giving the dish a soft, smooth texture and sheen. The topping is also very good with Browned Noodle Patty with Sauce (page 66).

Yield: 4 servings as a light meal

¾ pound medium raw shrimp (about 20–25)
1 teaspoon coarse salt
20 snow peas, strings removed, cut in half crosswise, washed and drained
15-ounce can straw mushrooms, drained
1 teaspoon minced fresh ginger
1 clove garlic, minced
¾ pound Homemade Chinese Egg Noodles (page 21)

5 tablespoons corn oil or peanut oil
½ teaspoon coarse salt
¾ cup Best Chicken Broth (page 77)
1 tablespoon cornstarch combined with 2 tablespoons water
2 large egg whites, beaten till frothy

THE MARINADE FOR THE SHRIMP

½ teaspoon coarse salt
2 teaspoons dry sherry

2 teaspoons cornstarch

THE SEASONINGS FOR THE NOODLES

1 tablespoon corn oil or peanut oil

1 tablespoon light soy sauce
⅛ teaspoon white pepper

PREPARING THE SHRIMP AND VEGETABLES
Shell and devein the shrimp, put them in a bowl, sprinkle the salt and 4 tablespoons water on top. Stir around with your fingers for about 10

seconds. Let sit for 20 minutes. (This process removes the sticky substance from the shrimp, making them crisper after they are cooked.) Rinse the shrimp, drain them in a colander, and pat dry with paper towels; then put them in a mixing bowl.

To coat the shrimp with the marinade, first mix in the salt and sherry with your fingers; then add the cornstarch and mix again. Set aside.

Put the snow peas, mushrooms, ginger, and garlic on a plate. The shrimp and vegetables can be prepared ahead of time; cover them with plastic wrap and refrigerate them, but bring them out 15 minutes before cooking.

COOKING THE NOODLES

Put 3 quarts of water in a large pot and bring to a boil. Loosen the noodles and add them to the pot, stirring them with chopsticks a few times. Cook the noodles for about 2 minutes or longer, tasting for doneness after 1 minute of boiling; the noodles should be just soft but not chewy. Drain them in a colander, then return them to the pot and toss with the seasonings. Cover the noodles so they stay hot while you finish the dish.

**STIR-FRYING THE SHRIMP AND VEGETABLES
AND MAKING THE SAUCE**

Heat a wok over medium-high heat until very hot. Add 3 tablespoons of the oil and swirl; then add the shrimp and stir-fry with a spatula for less than 1 minute, or until the shrimp is about 80 percent cooked. Scoop out the shrimp to a plate. Clean the wok and heat it again; add the remaining 2 tablespoons of oil and swirl; then add the ginger and garlic and stir-fry till they are fragrant but not brown—a few seconds. Add the snow peas and mushrooms and stir-fry for 1 minute. Return the shrimp to the wok and toss with the vegetables. Sprinkle in ½ teaspoon salt and then pour in the chicken broth, turn heat to high, and bring to a boil. Stir the cornstarch-and-water mixture again and pour it into the wok. Stir until the sauce thickens, which happens within 10 seconds. Pour in the beaten egg white and let it begin to set without stirring for a few seconds; then with a spatula gently lift the mixture from the bottom of the wok a few times. Splash in 1 tablespoon of oil to give the dish a shine, if desired.

Scoop the hot noodles onto a large heated platter, pour the shrimp, vegetables, and egg sauce on top and serve immediately.

Variation: Fresh scallops may be used instead of shrimp; leave bay scallops whole and slice sea scallops in half. Stir-fried sliced zucchini (1 small zucchini) and fresh mushrooms (½ pound) may be used instead of snow peas and straw mushrooms.

Shrimp Paste Noodles

虾 XIA MIAN
面

Shrimp paste noodles are small noodles, or really sections of mashed shrimp and other ingredients—a stunningly unusual food idea created by the Chinese.

Making the shrimp paste for these noodles in a food processor is much easier than doing it the old-fashioned way with knives. A small pastry tube also makes the job easy and fun. If you have a large pastry tube, cut the resulting noodles into 1½- to 2-inch lengths.

In addition to being served alone, these shrimp paste noodles could be the topping for 1 pound of egg noodles, making more servings. Simply boil 1 pound of egg noodles and lightly season them with salt, pepper and a little oil. Scoop the shrimp noodles on top and toss to serve.

Yield: 4 servings if eaten alone; 8 servings with egg noodles

2 ounces fresh pork fat or blanched fatty bacon, about ½ cup diced
3 egg whites
1½ pounds raw shrimp, shelled and deveined
3 tablespoons cornstarch
2 teaspoons coarse salt
½ teaspoon sugar

⅛ teaspoon white pepper
2 tablespoons dry sherry
2 teaspoons chili pepper flakes
2 tablespoons minced fresh ginger
2 teaspoons minced garlic, about 2 cloves
½ cup plus 2 tablespoons minced whole scallions
5 tablespoons corn oil

THE SAUCE

½ cup wine rice (page 264) or rice wine mixed with ½ teaspoon sugar
½ cup chicken broth
2 tablespoons Hot Chili Bean Paste, Sichuan- or Hunan-Style (page 302)

2 tablespoons tomato catsup
2 tablespoons dark soy sauce
½ tablespoon sugar
1 tablespoon white vinegar
1 tablespoon cornstarch

PREPARING THE SHRIMP NOODLES

Put the pork fat and egg whites in a food processor fitted with the steel blade and grind until foamy. Add the shrimp, cornstarch, salt, pepper, sugar and sherry. Spin for 30 seconds, or until the mixture is smooth (you may have to stop the machine and use a rubber spatula to scrape down the sides of the bowl once or twice). The shrimp paste is now ready to be made into shrimp noodles; it can be made ahead of time, covered, and refrigerated for up to 8 hours.

If you are making the paste by hand, simply chop the shrimp and pork fat with a cleaver or large heavy knife until the mixture is a paste, and then add the other ingredients in stages as given.

Spoon half the shrimp paste at a time into a pastry bag that has been fitted with a number 8 or 9 pastry tube if you are making shrimp noodles to be served in their own right, or to make shrimp paste sections as a topping for egg noodles.

BOILING THE SHRIMP NOODLES

Put 2 quarts of water in a large saucepan. Set it on the stove without heat. Squeeze the tube over the pot of water in a circular motion, and as the paste drops, cut it into 2-inch sections for topping or 10-inch sections for noodles. After squeezing out all the shrimp paste, turn on the heat and cook until the water is about to boil, or taste a piece when firm; do not overcook. Drain and run under cold water. The noodles can be used right away or stored, covered with cold water, for up to two days in the refrigerator. You will have 1½ pounds shrimp noodles or shrimp paste sections.

MAKING THE SAUCE AND
FINISHING THE DISH

Set out the chili pepper flakes, ginger, garlic, and scallions on a plate. Combine the sauce ingredients in a bowl. Drain and pat the shrimp noodles dry with paper towels, and set them on another plate.

Heat a wok over medium heat for 30 seconds, add 4 tablespoons of the oil and heat, then add the pepper flakes and fry for 5 seconds. Add the ginger, garlic, and ½ cup of the scallions, and stir for 30 seconds. Add the drained shrimp noodles or shrimp paste sections and stir together for another 30 seconds. Give the sauce ingredients a good stir and pour them into the wok, stirring until the sauce thickens slightly. Add the remaining 1 tablespoon of oil and mix into the sauce.

Dish out the noodles on a large heated platter with some sauce on top and garnish with 2 tablespoons chopped scallions. For a topping, pour shrimp paste sections and sauce on top of cooked egg noodles. Garnish with the 2 tablespoons scallions. Toss and serve hot.

Noodles with Spicy Fish Sauce

 YU SI XIANG MIAN

Two years ago four chefs from Shanghai came to New York to demonstrate their skills at Fortune Garden Restaurant. This noodle dish is one of their specialties. The slivered fish complements the thin noodles, and the sauce is spicy and hearty. The taste and texture are fabulous. It is truly worth the effort and time involved in making it. Shrimp or scallops may be used instead of fish; they can also be sliced instead of shredded.

Yield: 6 servings as a light meal

1½ pounds fillet of sea bass, yellow pike, or gray sole
2 teaspoons chili pepper flakes
2 tablespoons minced fresh ginger
2 cloves minced garlic
½ cup plus 2 tablespoons chopped whole scallions

3 cups oil for velveting the fish, approximately
1 pound fresh thin Homemade Chinese Egg Noodles (page 21) or Homemade Chinese Eggless Noodles (page 30)
1 tablespoon cornstarch mixed with 3 tablespoons water

THE MARINADE

1 teaspoon coarse salt
1 egg white

2 teaspoons cornstarch

THE SAUCE

½ cup wine rice (page 264) or
rice wine mixed with ½
teaspoon sugar
½ cup chicken broth
2 tablespoons Hot Chili Bean
Paste, Sichuan- or Hunan-
Style (page 302)

2 tablespoons tomato catsup
2 tablespoons light soy sauce
½ teaspoon coarse salt or to taste
½ tablespoon sugar
1 tablespoon white vinegar

PREPARATIONS

With a sharp knife shred the fish with the grain into matchstick strips
about 2 inches long. Put them in a mixing bowl and add the marinade
ingredients. Mix with your fingers and refrigerate for at least 30 minutes or up to 8 hours; in that case remove from the refrigerator 30
minutes before cooking.

Mix the sauce ingredients in a bowl, and set the chili pepper, ginger, garlic, and scallions on a large plate.

Heat a well-seasoned wok for 30 seconds, add 3 cups oil, and heat
to 300 degrees. Gently stir in the fish and blanch for less than 1 minute,
or until the fish shreds turn firm and white. Then pour the fish and oil
into a strainer over a bowl. (You will need 5 tablespoons later in this
recipe.) As soon as the oil drains off, set the fish aside on a plate. The
fish can be prepared up to 2 hours ahead of time; cover with plastic
wrap. You can reuse the oil; when it is cool, bottle and refrigerate it.

COOKING THE SAUCE AND THE NOODLES

In a large pot bring 4 quarts of water to a boil, then reduce the heat to
low—you will need this for boiling the noodles later. Heat the wok
again over medium heat for 30 seconds. Add 4 tablespoons of the
drained oil and swirl. When the oil is hot, add the chili pepper flakes
and fry, stirring, for about 5 seconds. Add the ginger, garlic, and ½ cup
of the scallions and toss lightly. Stir the sauce ingredients thoroughly
and pour into the pan. Stir until the sauce boils, then keep it hot over
very low heat.

Bring the pot of water to a rolling boil and add the noodles; cook
them for about 2 minutes, or until tender but firm to the bite, a little
softer than *al dente*. Drain thoroughly in a colander and then put them
on a large warm platter. Ladle one-third of the hot sauce over the noodles and toss to mix well. Working quickly so the noodles don't cool,
heat the remaining sauce over medium-high heat, add the fish, and let it
heat through, stirring it gently.

Mix the cornstarch and water well and slowly add to the sauce, stirring gently, until the sauce thickens. Dribble 1 tablespoon of the oil on top, then pour the sauce and fish over the noodles. Garnish with the 2 tablespoons chopped scallions.

Brown Bean and Meat Sauce on Noodles

  ZHA JIANG MIAN

This is a typical one-dish northern noodle meal. The sauce has the richness and tastiness of an Italian meat sauce, but instead of tomatoes, the Chinese use a soybean sauce made from fermented soybeans and wheat flour mixed with salt and water. In Chinese cooking the bean sauce is generally used as a seasoning agent when a thick sauce is needed.

This meat sauce can be made ahead of time and kept in a tightly covered jar for a week in the refrigerator.

Yield: 6 servings as a light meal

¼ cup brown bean sauce
¼ cup sweet bean sauce or hoisin sauce
¼ cup water
¼ cup corn oil
¼ cup chopped scallions, white part
1 pound ground pork with some fat

¼ cup chopped scallions, green part
1 pound Homemade Chinese Eggless Noodles (page 30)
1 cup finely shredded cucumber or lettuce or blanched bean sprouts for garnish

Combine the brown bean sauce and sweet bean sauce in a small bowl, add the water, and mix well.

Heat a wok for 30 seconds, add the oil and swirl, then toss in the white part of the scallions and stir while they sizzle for a few seconds; then add the pork. Stir-fry over medium heat until the pork pieces are separated. Add the water-sauce mixture and stir and toss gently over medium-low heat for about 5 minutes, or until the liquid begins to smell fragrant and the water has cooked away (when this happens, the oil will start floating up along the sides). Then add the green part of the scal-

lions. Stir only once to mix. Remove from the heat and dish out immediately into a bowl.

Boil the noodles in 4 quarts of boiling water for about 2 minutes.
Drain and shake off the water.

To serve, scoop about 1 cup of cooked noodles into each of six
large soup bowls and spoon 2 heaping tablespoons of sauce on top.
Sprinkle the shredded garnish over the sauce and serve at once.

Baby Squid and Hearts of Celery on Noodles

 XIAN YOU YU MIAN

For this wonderful example of Chinese home cooking, try to buy small
squid if you can, since they are more tender than the larger ones. The
flavors of squid and oyster sauce blend marvelously, giving the sauce a
rich, robust dimension.

To create a complete meal, serve this with Flaky Pastry Filled with
White Turnips and Ham (page 185) and Flaky Pastry Egg Custard Tarts
(page 190) for dessert. The recipe can be doubled easily.

Yield: 4 servings for a light meal

1 pound fresh squid, preferably
the small ones
½ cup carrots cut on the
diagonal into very thin slices
½ inch wide × 1½ inches
long
1½ cups tender celery or
unpeeled cucumber, seeds
removed, cut in very thin
slices ½ inch wide × 1½
inches long

2 teaspoons minced fresh
ginger
1 teaspoon minced garlic
2 tablespoons chopped scallions
¾ pound Homemade Chinese
Egg Noodles (page 21) or
Homemade Chinese Eggless
Noodles (page 30)
6 tablespoons corn oil or peanut
oil

THE SAUCE

2 tablespoons light soy sauce
1 tablespoon oyster sauce
2 tablespoons dry sherry

⅛ teaspoon white pepper
2 teaspoons cornstarch

THE SEASONINGS FOR THE NOODLES

**2 tablespoons corn oil or peanut
  oil**

**1 tablespoon light soy sauce
Dash white pepper**

PREPARING THE SQUID

Clean the squid body and the firm part of the tentacles. Drain and dry. Cut the body into rings if the squid are small, into 1- by 2-inch pieces if large. Place in a bowl; cover, and refrigerate.

**PREPARING THE SAUCE, VEGETABLES,
AND NOODLES**

Prepare the vegetables and ginger, garlic, and scallions, and put them all on a large plate. Combine the sauce ingredients in a mixing bowl.

Just before cooking the squid and sauce, boil the noodles in 3 quarts of water for 2 minutes, or until tender but firm to the bite, a little softer than *al dente*. Drain and return to the pot, add the noodle seasonings, cover, and keep the noodles warm.

Mix the sauce with the squid (do not mix ahead of time). Then heat a wok for 30 seconds, add 2 tablespoons of the oil and swirl, then stir-fry the carrots over moderate heat for 1 minute; then add the celery or cucumbers and stir-fry for 2 minutes. Transfer to a bowl with a slotted spoon. Heat the wok again, add the remaining 4 tablespoons oil, and swirl. When the oil is hot, scatter in the ginger, garlic, and scallions and stir while they sizzle for about 10 seconds. Then add the squid and stir-fry for 2 minutes, or until the squid are firm and white. Return the vegetables to the pan and stir just long enough to heat through.

Scoop out the noodles onto a large heated platter. Pour the squid and vegetables on top and serve hot.

Variation: Using the same sauce, you can create a totally different dish with these substitutions: For the squid, use instead 1 pound bay or sea scallops, leaving the bay scallops whole and slicing the sea scallops in half. Instead of celery and carrots, use 6 dried black Chinese mushrooms, soaked in warm water for 30 minutes, then remove stems and slice; ½ cup sliced bamboo shoots; and 1 cup snow peas. Stir-fry the vegetables for 2 minutes over high heat and transfer to a dish with a slotted spoon. Heat the wok again, add the 4 tablespoons of oil and swirl, then stir-fry the ginger, garlic, and scallions for 10 seconds. Add the scallops and stir-fry for 1 minute over high heat. Return the vegetables to the wok and toss. Add the sauce and stir until it thickens and coats the scallops and vegetables.

Noodles with Scallion and Dried Shrimp Sauce

蔥
油
开
洋
面

CONG YOU KAI YANG MIAN

This Shanghai specialty features an unusual pungent sauce made of deeply browned scallions and dried shrimp that have been steamed with sherry. Because of the long cooking time, it has a rather dry base of the chopped ingredients, with plenty of fragrant oil on top, so you don't need much to put on the noodles.

Because of its rich taste, plain eggless noodles go well with this dish—or try it with boiled wontons. A chilled cucumber salad makes a tasty accompaniment to this light and strongly flavored dish.

Yield: 8 small servings for a snack or side dish; 4 servings as a main course

⅓ cup dried shrimp, about 2 ounces
Dry sherry or white wine, to cover the shrimp
¾ cup corn oil
2 bunches whole scallions, cut into ¼-inch sections (about 3 cups)

1½ tablespoons dark soy sauce
1 pound Homemade Chinese Eggless Noodles (page 30)
½ teaspoon salt
Black pepper
Chopped fresh coriander, watercress, or Italian parsley for garnish

MAKING THE SAUCE

Put the shrimp in a heatproof bowl, add sherry or white wine to cover, and steam for 30 minutes. Remove the shrimp, reserving the liquid. Finely chop the shrimp and set aside.

Heat a wok over medium-high heat, add the corn oil, and when the oil is hot add the scallions. Stir-fry, tossing frequently, for about 5 minutes, or until most of the scallions are lightly browned. Add the shrimp and cook, stirring, for 1 minute. Turn the heat low and add the soy sauce and reserved shrimp-steaming liquid.

This sauce can be made ahead of time and kept in the refrigerator for up to a month, because the oil covering the scallions and shrimp acts as a preservative. Reheat briefly to serve hot.

COOKING THE NOODLES AND ADDING THE SAUCE

Bring 4 quarts of water to a boil in a large pot. Add the noodles and cook until slightly soft—homemade noodles take 1 to 2 minutes. Pour the noodles into a colander and shake to drain off all the water. Return the noodles to the pot, add 2 to 3 tablespoons of oil from the top of the sauce, ½ teaspoon salt, and several grindings of black pepper. Toss briefly; then scoop about 1 cup of the noodles into individual bowls. Put 2 to 3 tablespoons of the sauce on top of each serving and garnish with the chopped coriander.

Roast Pork with Tossed Noodles (Roast Pork Lo Mian)

叉 CHA SHAO LO MIAN
烧
捞 *Lo* in the Cantonese dialect means "tossing and scooping"; *mian* means
面 "noodle." A roast pork *lo mian* means "a tossed noodle" dish with shredded roast pork and vegetables. This dish has been an established one in
foreign countries for a long time. The fact that many Americans think the
noodles are the *lo mian* rather than the dish itself probably stems from an
early misunderstanding of American buyers in Chinese markets; the true
term for egg noodles is *dan mian*.

Fresh egg noodles (homemade or store-bought) are best for this dish,
because they are smooth and flavorful. It is also a good idea to use a wok,
which makes the tossing and scooping very easy. Roast Pork Lo Mian goes
well with Cantonese Fried Glutinous Rice Dumplings (page 260) or Fried
Taro Fritters with Pork Filling (page 286) and a soup for a more complete
meal.

For more servings cook one recipe at a time so the ingredients are easy
to handle; keep the cooked portion in a warm oven while you prepare
more.

Yield: 4 servings as a light meal; to double the recipe, make the dish twice

¼ **pound Chinese Roast Pork (page 208)**
2 **small whole scallions**
½ **pound Homemade Chinese Egg Noodles (page 21)**
3 **tablespoons corn oil or peanut oil**

½ **pound fresh bean sprouts, about 3 cups**
1 **tablespoon light soy sauce**
½ **teaspoon coarse salt**
1½ **tablespoons oyster sauce**

Cut the roast pork into ⅛-inch-thick slices, then cut again into 2-inch-long julienne strips to make about 1 cup. Shred the scallions into 2-inch-long slivers and set aside with the roast pork, both covered with plastic wrap.

Boil the noodles in 2 to 3 quarts of water for 2 to 3 minutes, or until *al dente*. Drain in a colander and rinse with cold water; shake to remove all excess water. Put the noodles in a bowl, add 1 tablespoon of the oil, toss well, and set aside.

Heat a wok for 30 seconds, then add 2 tablespoons of the oil and swirl. Stir-fry the scallions and roast pork over high heat for 1 minute. Add the bean sprouts, stir and toss for a few seconds, then add the soy sauce, salt, and oyster sauce. Spread the noodles on top of this mixture and immediately start tossing over high heat; continue for 2 to 3 minutes. Dish out onto a warm platter and serve hot. If you are making more portions, cover this and keep it in a low oven for up to 30 minutes.

Vegetables with Tossed Noodles (Vegetarian Lo Mian)

 SU LO MIAN

Here is a wonderful light vegetarian *lo mian* dish with two Chinese ingredients that may be unfamiliar to most Americans—*mu er* and *zha cai*.

Mu er, or dried wood ears, are a very large tree fungus, black on top and white underneath. After being soaked, some of them expand to 6 inches in diameter (at least four times their size) and they all become dark brown on both sides. Wood ears don't have a pronounced flavor or fragrance, but their texture, prized by the Chinese, is wonderful though hard to describe—it is, say, a resilient crispness. Wood ears are particularly good combined with fresh or dried mushrooms.

Zha cai is a preserved vegetable, a specialty of the province of Sichuan. It consists of a special variety of mustard greens that has stems with many knobs. These knobs are preserved in salt and chili pepper. They are greenish brown in color, hot and salty in taste, and I love them.

When I sailed from Shanghai to come to the United States in 1947 as a student, my family provided me with a trunkful of clothing and a jar of *zha cai* in case I didn't like the food on board.

The ship I was on was the *General Mac,* a liner that had been turned into a U.S. Army transport during the war. More than three hundred students slept way below deck, in three tiers of bunk beds. I slept on a bunk in the middle tier, and after only one American cafeteria–style meal in the dining room, I barely left my bunk bed because of seasickness for the next fifteen days. A Chinese cook who worked in the kitchen, bless his heart, made a huge pot of congee (rice gruel, page 296) at each meal for all the sick students. It was the congee and the preserved vegetable that saved my life. I lost only ten pounds.

This recipe can easily be doubled or tripled.

Yield: 4 servings for a light meal

1 ounce *mu er* (wood ears), the thick kind, black on one side and grayish white on the other when dry (optional)

8 dried black Chinese mushrooms

2 tablespoons shredded Sichuan *zha cai* (preserved vegetable)

¼ cup shredded carrots

4 cups shredded green cabbage

1 teaspoon minced fresh ginger

½ pound dried eggless noodles (available in 5-pound boxes in Chinese markets) or Homemade Chinese Egg Noodles (page 21)

4 tablespoons corn oil

1 tablespoon light soy sauce

1 teaspoon coarse salt

THE SEASONINGS FOR THE NOODLES

1 tablespoon light soy sauce

1 tablespoon corn oil or peanut oil

Dash white pepper

PREPARING THE VEGETABLES AND THE NOODLES

Soak the wood ears in about 4 cups of hot water until they have fully expanded—about 1 hour or longer. Rinse well, remove the hard point in the center, and shred them finely; you should have about ½ cup.

Rinse the dried mushrooms and cover with 1 cup of warm water in a bowl to soak until soft—about 30 minutes. Squeeze out the mushrooms' water in the bowl, remove the stems, and finely shred the caps; you should have about ½ cup. Pour ½ cup of the mushroom liquid into a measuring cup, making sure you don't pour any of the residue into it.

Rinse one whole piece of *zha cai* in cold water and finely shred it; you need about 2 tablespoons. Set the shreds on a large plate; then shred the carrots, cabbage, and ginger, and put them on the same plate.

Boil the noodles in 3 quarts of water until they are tender but firm to the bite, a little softer than *al dente*—about 5 to 6 minutes for the Chinese dried noodles and 2 minutes for fresh egg noodles. Drain and return to the pot. Add the seasonings, toss well, and cover the pot to keep the noodles warm.

STIR-FRYING THE VEGETABLES AND NOODLES

Heat a wok over medium heat for 30 seconds, then add 2 tablespoons of the oil and swirl. Add the ginger, mushrooms, wood ears, and soy sauce and stir lightly. Add the *zha cai* and ¼ cup of the mushroom soaking water. Cook for 1 minute, stirring, then pour contents into a bowl and set aside.

Heat the wok again, add the remaining 2 tablespoons of oil, and swirl. Stir-fry the carrots and cabbage over high heat for 2 minutes. Add the salt and mix well, then pour in the remaining ¼ cup of mushroom soaking liquid. Return the mushroom–wood ear–*zha cai* mixture to the wok and stir together with the fresh vegetables for 2 minutes.

Scoop the contents of the wok onto the warm noodles and mix well to serve. The dish can rest in a warm oven, covered, for up to 30 minutes.

Browned Noodle Patty with Sauce

LIANG MIAN HUANG

In this sumptuous dish, a bed of noodles is pan-fried in a skillet or a wok. What results is a thin noodle patty with a brown, crunchy crust on both sides and a soft, plush interior. A chicken, shrimp, and vegetable sauce is then poured on top of the noodles, and the dish is garnished with shredded egg crepes and scallions. You may use any other meat or sauce for noodles from the book to vary the taste of the patty.

Yield: 6 one-dish servings

1 **whole boneless chicken breast, about 6 ounces, semi-frozen and then cut into matchstick strips**	½ **pound raw shrimp, shelled, deveined, and coarsely chopped**

6 dried black Chinese
mushrooms
2 Egg Crepes (page 74), shredded
for garnish
3 cups finely shredded celery
cabbage or fresh bean sprouts
2 scallions, white part only,
finely shredded

¾ pound thin Homemade
Chinese Egg Noodles (page 21)
or Steamed Noodles (page 31)
1 tablespoon light soy sauce
8 tablespoons peanut oil or corn
oil for browning the noodles
7 tablespoons peanut oil or corn
oil for cooking the sauce

THE MARINADE FOR THE CHICKEN

½ teaspoon coarse salt
1 teaspoon cornstarch

1 tablespoon chicken broth
2 teaspoons corn oil or peanut oil

THE MARINADE FOR THE SHRIMP

¼ teaspoon coarse salt

1 teaspoon cornstarch

THE SAUCE

¾ cup chicken broth
1 tablespoon light soy sauce

1 tablespoon oyster sauce
½ tablespoon cornstarch

PREPARATIONS

Put the chicken strips and chopped shrimp in separate bowls and add
the respective coating ingredients. Mix well and set in the refrigerator
for a few minutes so the chicken and shrimp firm up. You could refrigerate them for hours if you wish, but leave them out at room temperature for 30 minutes before cooking.

Rinse the mushrooms, then soak them in warm water for 30 minutes. Drain, remove the stems, and shred the caps. Put them on a large
plate with the shredded egg crepes, cabbage, and scallions. Cover with
plastic wrap if you are doing this hours in advance.

Cook the fresh or steamed egg noodles in 3 quarts of boiling water
for 1 to 2 minutes until tender but firm to the bite, a little softer than *al
dente*. For very fine steamed noodles, omit the boiling step; see page 31.
Briefly rinse with cold water, drain well, and transfer to a bowl. Mix 1
tablespoon each of soy sauce and oil with the noodles and toss to fluff
them. The dish may be made ahead to this point. Cover the noodles and
refrigerate if you are going to cook the dish later.

Mix the sauce ingredients in a small bowl and set aside.

FRYING THE NOODLES

Heat a wok over medium heat until very hot. Add 2 tablespoons of the oil to coat the pan. Curl the cooked noodles in a circular pattern in the pan and cook without stirring for about 5 minutes; the noodles will start to brown and even burn a little. Flip the noodle patty over or, if you aren't experienced in flipping, slide the patty onto a large plate and then invert it into the skillet. Dribble 2 tablespoons of oil down the side of the pan and brown the other side of the patty—about 5 minutes. Transfer the patty to a large platter and keep it warm in a low oven, about 200 degrees.

In the same pan, over moderate heat, stir-fry first the chicken, then the shrimp with 2 tablespoons each of the oil, which you heat first. The chicken will take about 1 minute; the shrimp, 30 seconds. Set them on the same plate.

Add the remaining 2 tablespoons of oil to the pan, swirl, then add the mushrooms and cabbage and stir-fry for 2 minutes. Return the cooked chicken and shrimp to the pan and toss lightly with the vegetables to heat them through. Pour the mixed sauce into the pan with the meat and vegetables, stirring and tossing. Cook until a light glaze coats the ingredients—about 1 minute.

Pour the entire contents of the pan on top of the hot noodle patty and garnish with the shredded egg crepes and scallions. Serve hot as a one-dish meal with hot tea.

≡

Cold
Noodle
Dishes

≡

Shredded Chicken with Sichuan Peppercorn Sauce on Cold Noodles

 JIAO MA YOU BAN MIAN

 Sichuan peppercorns have a pleasant fragrance and a slightly numbing taste. Here they are roasted, crushed, and mixed with hot oil to provide the base for this pungent, scrumptious sauce.

This recipe can easily be doubled or tripled.

Yield: 4 servings for a light meal

½ **pound medium or thin Homemade Chinese Egg Noodles (page 21)**
1 **tablespoon sesame oil**
2 **tablespoons dark soy sauce**
2 **tablespoons Zhejiang vinegar or red wine vinegar**
1 **teaspoon sugar**
2 **tablespoons minced whole scallions**

1 **tablespoon Sichuan peppercorn oil (recipe follows)**
1 **small whole chicken breast with bone, about 6 ounces, steamed and boned, and finely shredded, using your fingers, with the grain**
½ **teaspoon coarse salt**

COOKING AND CHILLING THE NOODLES

Bring 2 quarts of water to a rolling boil over high heat. Add the noodles and stir immediately to separate the strands. When the water returns to a boil, cook for 1 minute if noodles are thin, 2 minutes if thick. Taste to make sure—the noodles should be tender but firm to the bite, a little softer than *al dente.*

Drain and run cold water over the noodles immediately to cool them quickly and thoroughly. Shake off the excess water. With chopsticks, fluff them up for a few minutes to dry them completely. Then put the noodles in a serving bowl and add the sesame oil, tossing to coat them evenly.

MAKING THE SAUCE AND FINISHING THE DISH

Combine the soy sauce, vinegar, sugar, scallions, and peppercorn oil in a small bowl. Prepare the chicken. Sprinkle on the salt. Add the sauce and the chicken to the noodles, toss again, and serve. If you like the dish cold, refrigerate it, but not for more than two hours.

Sichuan Peppercorn Oil

Yield: a generous ¼ cup

**2 tablespoons Sichuan
peppercorns**

**1 teaspoon white peppercorns
¼ cup corn oil or peanut oil**

Roast the Sichuan and white peppercorns in a small dry skillet over low heat until they release their fragrance—about 3 minutes. Using the butt of a cleaver handle or a mortar and pestle, crush them to a fine powder. Put the peppercorn powder in a heatproof jar. Heat the oil until it starts to smoke; then remove it from the heat and wait 30 seconds. Pour the oil over the peppercorns in the jar and cover. Leftover oil will keep for a month, tightly covered, at room temperature.

Cold Noodle Salad with Sesame–Peanut Butter–Chili Sauce or Soy-Vinegar Sauce

LIANG BAN MIAN

This colorful dish would be perfect for a cold buffet or picnic as well as lunch at home. It consists of cold egg noodles, finely shredded meat, and an assortment of crunchy fresh vegetables, and it is served with two sauces—the well-known sesame–peanut butter–chili sauce and a simple tart soy-vinegar sauce. Use either sauce or both in the same meal.

Thin steamed egg noodles (pages 21 and 31) have the best texture for this cold dish, but you could also use fresh or dried noodles or spaghettini.

The sesame–peanut butter–chili sauce is marvelous by itself served with either hot or cold egg noodles. It makes a simple but tasty quick dish for lunch or dinner.

Yield: 6 servings

**1 pound medium or thin
Homemade Chinese Egg
Noodles (page 21)
2 tablespoons sesame or corn oil**

**2 teaspoons finely chopped garlic
and 2 tablespoons finely
chopped scallions for garnish,
optional**

THE SESAME–PEANUT BUTTER–CHILI SAUCE

¼ cup smooth peanut butter
2 tablespoons corn oil or peanut oil
2 tablespoons sesame oil
½ teaspoon coarse salt or to taste
4 teaspoons sugar

2 tablespoons dark soy sauce
2 tablespoons red wine vinegar
4 tablespoons cold water, add more for thin sauce
2 teaspoons Hot Chili Bean Paste, Sichuan- or Hunan-Style (page 302)

THE SOY-VINEGAR SAUCE

¼ cup dark soy sauce
¼ cup Zhejiang or red wine vinegar

2 tablespoons sesame oil
2 teaspoons sugar

THE SUGGESTED MEATS AND VEGETABLES FOR THE SALAD

2 cups shredded roast pork, chicken, turkey, duck, or ham
1 recipe shredded Egg Crepes (recipe follows)

2 cups shredded cucumber, radish, lettuce, blanched fresh bean sprouts

COOKING THE NOODLES

Bring 4 quarts of water to a rolling boil in a large pot over high heat. Add the egg noodles and bring to a boil again. Stir with chopsticks or a fork and turn heat slightly lower. Cook for about 1 to 2 minutes. Drain and rinse the noodles immediately under cold water to stop the cooking. With chopsticks, fluff them up for a few minutes to dry them completely. Then put them in a large bowl, dribble the 2 tablespoons of oil on top, and toss to coat them completely. Serve right away. Or cover and chill in the refrigerator for not more than 2 hours.

PREPARING THE SESAME–PEANUT BUTTER–CHILI SAUCE

Put the peanut butter in a mixing bowl; add the corn oil and sesame oil. Stir together until very smooth; then add the remaining ingredients, except the garlic and scallion, and mix well. The sauce can be made ahead of time and kept, tightly covered, in the refrigerator for several weeks. Before serving it, stir well—and bring to the table in a sauce boat with a ladle. Garnish with garlic and scallion if you wish.

PREPARING THE SOY-VINEGAR SAUCE

Mix all the ingredients together and serve at room temperature in a sauce boat with a ladle. This sauce also can be made ahead of time and kept, tightly covered, in the refrigerator for several weeks.

SERVING THE SALAD

For serving, arrange the meats and vegetables on a platter and place the noodles in a large bowl. Give each person a soup bowl with a ladling of noodles. Then everyone can help himself to the meats and vegetables and the desired sauce.

Egg Crepes

Yield: 4 crepes

2 eggs	**½ teaspoon cornstarch**
Pinch salt	

Combine the eggs with the salt and cornstarch and beat till frothy with a wire whisk. Pour the beaten eggs through a fine strainer.

Lightly grease and heat a nonstick 8-inch skillet or crepe pan. Pour in one-quarter of the beaten egg, tipping the pan so it spreads thinly and evenly, and cook over low heat until the egg sets—about 30 seconds. Flip it over and cook the other side 30 seconds more. Lay the finished crepe on a plate.

Repeat the process to make three more crepes. Let them cool, then cut them in half, stack them, and shred into fine strips about 2 inches long.

One-Dish Meals:
Noodles in Soup

Best Chicken Broth

火 HUO TUI JI TANG
腿
鸡　The best chicken broth I've ever had was at my friend Jane Ho's house.
汤　This broth is appreciated by her entire family, from grandmother to
grandchildren. The broth is so clear and tasty that all you have to do is
put in some cooked noodles, rice cakes, or wontons, and it becomes a
whole meal.

The Smithfield ham gives the broth extra flavor, and saves you from
adding salt. If you prefer plain chicken broth, omit the ham and add 2
teaspoons of coarse salt during the cooking.

If you want to use the chicken for other dishes, use a roasting chicken
and take it out when you remove the ham. The broth will not be as rich.

Yield: 2½ quarts best chicken broth; 4 cups broth for soup

1　1½-inch-thick slice center-part 　　　　5-pound stewing fowl, or
　　Smithfield ham, with skin, fat, 　　　　roasting chicken, cut in half
　　and bone attached 　　　　　　　　1　stalk scallion
　　　　　　　　　　　　　　　　　　　½-inch slice fresh ginger

Wash and scrape the ham under hot water; then remove the discolored
parts and any bone marrow. Blanch the ham in boiling water for 2 minutes and set aside.

Wash the chicken. Pour 3 quarts of water into a large, heavy pot,
add the ham and the chicken, including the neck and gizzard (save the
liver for another use), and bring to a boil. Remove the foam that floats
to the top. Add the scallion and ginger. Turn heat to very low, cover,
and cook at a very gentle simmer for about 2 hours.

Transfer the ham to a bowl, ladle enough broth over it to cover,
and refrigerate to chill. Continue to cook the broth for another 2 hours.

Skim off the oil floating on top of the broth. Pour the broth
through a strainer. Keeping the chicken in the pot, add water to cover
and cook at a simmer 2 hours to make a less flavorful but nevertheless
good chicken broth, useful for making soups. Pour this through the
strainer; then discard the chicken. The first broth will be very clear and
tasty. Store both broths in the refrigerator for up to five days, or in the
freezer for about two months.

Now, remove the ham bone, thinly slice the ham with or without
the skin and fat, and serve one very thin slice at the bottom of each soup
bowl if desired, or serve the ham separately.

Beijing Egg Sauce Noodle Soup

大 DA LU MIAN
卤
面 This rich, creamy noodle soup dish is a favorite Beijing specialty, as popular with the Chinese as the Brown Bean and Meat Sauce on Noodles
(page 59). Brimming with pork, mushrooms, tree ears, and bamboo
shoots, the broth thickened with eggs, this is a one-dish meal I frequently
serve to my family, and everyone usually has a second helping.

Yield: 4 servings for a light meal

¾ pound lean fresh bacon or
pork belly or pork butt in 1
piece
¼ cup dried tree ears
4 dried black Chinese
mushrooms
½ cup bamboo shoots cut in
matchstick strips 1½ inches
× ½ inch, or 1 cup celery or
cabbage stems in strips
1 teaspoon minced fresh ginger
2 tablespoons chopped scallions
½ cup Smithfield or boiled ham
cut in matchstick strips 1½
inches × ½ inch

1 cup Best Chicken Broth
(page 77)
2 tablespoons corn oil or peanut
oil
1½ teaspoons coarse salt or to
taste
1 tablespoon light soy sauce
1 pound Homemade Chinese
Eggless Noodles (page 30)
3 tablespoons cornstarch
combined with 3 tablespoons
water
2 extra large eggs, beaten
2 teaspoons sesame oil
⅛ teaspoon pepper or to taste

PREPARING THE MEAT AND VEGETABLES

Put the bacon or pork in a saucepan, add water to cover, and bring to a
boil. Skim off the foam, cover, and lower the heat so the water is at a
gentle simmer; cook for 30 minutes. Turn off the heat and let the meat
cool down in the liquid.

Soak the tree ears and mushrooms in separate bowls in warm water
to cover for 30 minutes. Then rinse the tree ears several times, remove
and discard the hard ends if any, and cut the tree ears into small
pieces—you should have about 1 cup. Squeeze the mushrooms gently
over the bowl and reserve the water without the residue. Remove and
discard the mushroom stems and slice the caps into thin strips. Set aside
on a plate with the tree ears, bamboo shoots, ginger, and scallion.

Remove the bacon or pork, reserving the liquid. Remove and discard the pork skin. Cut the pork into very thin slices, then cut again into ½- by 1½-inch strips. Set aside with the ham; you should have about 1½ cups.

Skim off the fat from the pork cooking liquid; then pour the liquid into a 4-cup measuring cup and add the reserved mushroom water and chicken broth to make 4 cups.

MAKING THE SOUP AND THE NOODLES
Heat a large saucepan or casserole. Add the oil and swirl to coat the bottom of the pan. Add the ginger and scallions and stir for a minute till they become fragrant. Add the mushrooms, bamboo shoots and tree ears (and shrimp if you are using them). Now, pour in the 4 cups of broth and bring to a boil; then add the salt and soy sauce, lower the heat, and let the broth simmer for 5 minutes.

Meanwhile, bring 4 quarts of water to a boil in a large pot. Add the fresh noodles and cook for 2 minutes, or until just soft. Drain in a colander and then transfer to a large bowl and keep warm. Add the bacon or pork and ham to the soup, turn heat to high, and bring to a boil. Stir the cornstarch mixture well, then gradually stir it into the soup. Continue to stir until it thickens. Lower the heat. Beat the eggs again and slowly pour them into the soup, then gently stir once, so that the eggs will be floating like smooth petals. It will resemble egg-drop soup. Add the sesame oil and pepper.

Take the soup and noodles to the dinner table. Divide the noodles into individual soup bowls, ladle the soup on top, and serve hot. Eat the noodle soup with chopsticks and a spoon.

Variation: For extra bite, I often add 20 medium-size dried shrimp. Soak them in 2 tablespoons of dry sherry for about 15 minutes, and then chop them coarsely. Add them with the mushrooms and bamboo shoots to stir-fry together.

Sichuan Spicy Beef Sauce and Noodle Soup

☷ SICHUAN NIU ROU MIAN

川
牛
肉
面

In 1943 I went to Chengdu in Sichuan province and entered Nanking University. Chengdu is referred to by most Chinese as Little Beijing. There are many famous restaurants in the city, but as a student, I could afford to go only to the small noodle shops. These eateries, however, also had a great reputation. One of them—always packed with people— served this Sichuan spicy beef noodle dish. The sauce was really a thick soup, and it was delicious! I went there often, and finally the chef-owner revealed his secret: he saved some of the "soup" sauce to add to the next day's cooking. When you make this recipe, do the same—put away at least 1 cup in the refrigerator for as long as two weeks or in the freezer for two months, and add it to your new sauce the next time you make it.

Another secret to the succulent richness of the sauce is the addition of beef sinew. At Chinese markets when you buy shin beef, there is always some sinew attached. Ask the butcher to cut it out and save it for you (uncooked sinew is very hard to cut), and buy an extra half-pound of it. Uncooked sinew comes in long pieces, sometimes a foot long, and it is very hard and tough; after long cooking, however, it becomes soft and absorbs all the good flavor from the beef. The texture is slightly chewy but very smooth and easy to eat.

Yield: 6 servings as a light meal

2 **pounds shin beef plus ½ pound beef sinew**
4 **quarter-size slices fresh ginger**
4 **cloves garlic, peeled and crushed**
1 **teaspoon dried chili pepper flakes**
1 **teaspoon Sichuan peppercorns (optional)**
2 **star anise (optional)**

2 **tablespoons peanut oil or corn oil**
¼ **cup Sichuan brown bean sauce**
2 **tablespoons dry sherry**
2 **tablespoons dark soy sauce**
1 **teaspoon sugar**
6 **cups water**
1 **pound Homemade Chinese Eggless Noodles (page 30)**

THE GARNISHES

2 **whole scallions, finely chopped**
1 **teaspoon white pepper**

2 **teaspoons sesame oil**

**PREPARING THE SINEW AND
SIMMERING THE SOUP**

Put the sinew pieces in a saucepan and pour in enough cold water to cover by 2 inches. Bring to a boil, cover, and let the sinew simmer for 2 hours. Drain and discard the water. With a knife, remove and discard any fat attached to the sinew, then cut it into 1-inch chunks. Set aside.

Cut the shin beef into 1-inch cubes and set aside with the sinew, ginger, garlic, chili pepper flakes, and peppercorns and star anise if you are using them.

Heat a wok over moderate heat for 10 seconds, then add the oil and swirl. Add the ginger and garlic first and let them sizzle for 2 seconds; then add the chili pepper flakes and stir-fry till fragrant—about 2 more seconds. Add the beef pieces and continue stir-frying until all the pieces change color—about 2 minutes. Add the sinew, bean sauce, sherry, soy sauce, sugar, and water. Add the peppercorns and star anise if desired, stir to mix, and bring to a boil. Cover, lower the heat, and let the soup simmer gently for 1½ hours or until the beef and sinew are very tender. Taste for seasoning—the broth should taste strong-flavored and spicy, and be slightly thick. Remove the anise, peppercorns, and ginger. Keep the spicy beef warm over very low heat.

The sinew and soup may be prepared ahead of time and reheated over moderate heat until very hot.

**COOKING THE NOODLES AND
ASSEMBLING THE DISH**

When ready to serve, heat the spicy beef over low heat. Cook the fresh noodles in 4 quarts of boiling water for 1 to 2 minutes, until they are tender but firm to the bite, a little softer than *al dente*. (Dried noodles will take a few minutes longer.) Drain the noodles thoroughly, then return them to the pot. Ladle some sauce from the beef on top and heat briefly so the noodles soak up the sauce a little; then ladle the noodles into individual bowls. Scoop some spicy beef and sauce on top of each serving of noodles and garnish with a little of the scallion –pepper–sesame oil mixture. The Chinese usually eat the noodles and beef with chopsticks and the brothy sauce with a porcelain spoon.

Yangzhou Noodle Soup in Casserole

杨
州
窝
面

YANGZHOU WO MIAN

Yangzhou is a city near Shanghai renowned for its snacks and light meals. Whenever the city's name is used with a dish, it means it is full of sumptuous ingredients, particularly meat and seafood. Some famous dishes are Yangzhou fried rice, looking like bright jewels; Yangzhou meatballs, as light as clouds; Yangzhou Steamed Juicy Buns with Two Fillings (page 212), succulently delectable; and this delicious one-dish meal—noodle soup served in chicken broth with an array of colorful meats, seafood, and vegetables on top. The chicken broth you use in this dish must be homemade and of the highest quality (see page 77), and the noodles are best if they are steamed (page 31) or *Yi Fu* Noodles (page 33). In a pinch, you could use plain egg noodles or eggless noodles, but the dish won't be quite so special.

All preparations for this casserole can be done hours in advance, leaving only a few minutes of cooking at the end. It doubles easily.

Yield: Serves 4 as a light meal

1 chicken breast half, skinned and boned, about 4 ounces, cut with the grain into slices ⅛ inch thick × 1 inch wide × 1½ inches long

4 ounces lean loin of pork, cut into slices ⅛ inch thick × 1 inch wide × 1½ inches long

8 raw medium shrimp, shelled and deveined, about ¼ pound

2 tablespoons corn oil or peanut oil

2 quarter-size pieces fresh ginger, crushed with the side of a knife

1 small clove garlic, crushed with the side of a knife

½ cup snow peas, strings removed and cut in half crosswise

6 dried black Chinese mushrooms, soaked in warm water for 30 minutes, stems removed and caps cut in half; or 6 large fresh mushrooms, thickly sliced

½ cup thinly sliced bamboo shoots, approximately ⅛ × 1 × 1½ inches

½ cup thinly sliced cooked Smithfield ham, in pieces ⅛ × 1 × 1½ inches

4 cups Best Chicken Broth (page 77)

¾ pound Steamed Noodles (page 31) or *Yi Fu* Noodles (page 33)

1 tablespoon finely chopped whole scallion, for garnish

THE MARINADE FOR THE CHICKEN AND PORK

1 small egg white	**⅛ teaspoon white pepper**
½ teaspoon coarse salt	**3 tablespoons cornstarch**

THE SEASONINGS FOR THE BROTH AND NOODLES

1 tablespoon light soy sauce	**Dash white pepper**
2 teaspoons sesame oil	

PREPARING THE MEATS AND VEGETABLES

Place the chicken and pork in a shallow bowl. Add all the marinade ingredients but the cornstarch, and mix thoroughly with your fingers for 30 seconds. Then sprinkle on the cornstarch and mix again until all the slices are evenly coated. Cover and refrigerate. Prepare the shrimp, ginger, garlic, bamboo shoots, snow peas, mushrooms, and ham.

Bring 4 cups of water to a boil in a large saucepan. Turn the heat down to medium, so the water remains at a slow boil. Slip in the coated meat, gently stirring the slices to separate them. Parboil for about 1 minute in slowly boiling water, or until firm but tender. Scoop them out onto a plate with a slotted spoon.

Parboil the shrimp in the same slowly boiling water for 30 seconds, or just until they are firm. Scoop them out with a slotted spoon onto the same plate with the chicken and pork.

Heat a wok for 30 seconds over moderate heat. Add 2 tablespoons oil, swirl, then stir and press the ginger and garlic in the oil until they brown lightly. Remove with a slotted spoon and discard. Add the snow peas, mushrooms, bamboo shoots, and ham, and stir-fry for 5 seconds. Add 2 tablespoons of the chicken broth and stir and toss for 1 minute. Scoop contents of the wok into a bowl and set aside.

PREPARING THE NOODLES

Prepare according to the directions on page 31 or 32. Place them in a plastic bag. Up to this point, the dish may be made ahead of time. You can cover all the ingredients and refrigerate them for up to 8 hours.

FINISHING AND SERVING THE DISH

Bring 2 cups of the Best Chicken Broth to a boil over high heat, then add the seasonings for the broth and noodles. Add the noodles, loosening the strands, and bring the broth to a boil; cook the noodles for 1 minute, just to heat them through. Pour the broth and noodles into a soup tureen.

Bring the remaining 2 cups of chicken broth to a boil. Add the chicken, meat, shrimp, and vegetables, and bring the broth to a boil again just to heat the ingredients through. Pour into the soup tureen. Garnish with the scallions.

At the table, using chopsticks or a pasta fork, put the noodles in the individual soup bowls. Then, with a soup ladle, scoop the meat, vegetables, and broth on top. Each person should have a porcelain spoon and a pair of chopsticks to eat this dish.

Red-Cooked Chicken, Ginger, and Noodle Soup

红 HONG JI MIAN
鸡
面

When I was growing up in China, our family cook usually prepared several appetizers for my father to have alone at the table with his rice wine (the famous Shao-xing rice wine from Zhejiang province). This simmered chicken dish, in which the meat and bones are cut into small pieces, is wonderful to chew on while sipping wine slowly. I first had it—and the wine—when I was seven years old and my father asked me to join him at the table. I really didn't appreciate the wine that day, but I have loved this dish ever since. And because I appreciated food so much, even at that early age I became my father's constant companion, even when he traveled for his business selling silk. It is because of him that I learned to love good food.

In addition to being excellent served alone, this very simple and economical braised chicken, served in a little pungent ginger-flavored broth, makes a very tasty topping for noodles. The soup noodle dish would go well with Flaky Pastry Filled with White Turnips and Ham (page 185) or with steamed buns filled with Chopped Pork, Mushroom, and Leafy Green Filling (page 210).

Yield: 6 servings for a light meal

2½- to 3-pound whole chicken	**2 tablespoons corn oil or peanut**
2-inch piece fresh ginger	**oil**

½ cup dry sherry
2 tablespoons light soy sauce
3 tablespoons dark soy sauce
¼ teaspoon coarse salt
1 teaspoon sugar

1 pound Homemade Chinese
Egg Noodles (page 21) or
Homemade Chinese Eggless
Noodles (page 30) or store-
bought

THE SAUCE AND BROTH

3 cups chicken broth
4 tablespoons light soy sauce or
to taste

1½ teaspoons sesame oil
⅛ teaspoon coarse salt
⅛ teaspoon white pepper

PREPARING THE CHICKEN

With a cleaver or kitchen shears, cut the chicken into 1½-inch chunks, with skin and bone, discarding the fat and any very thick skin. Rinse the pieces. Peel the ginger and cut it into ¼-inch dice; you should have about ¼ cup. Set aside with the chicken.

Heat a wok over medium-high heat for 30 seconds. Add the oil, swirl, add ½ of the ginger, let brown a little (about 1 minute), then put in half the chicken pieces in one layer. Fry on one side for about 2 minutes, until lightly browned; then turn the pieces and fry on the other side for 2 more minutes. With a slotted spoon, remove the chicken and ginger, but leave the oil in the wok. Fry the second batch of chicken pieces, adding the rest of the ginger after you turn the pieces. Return the first batch of chicken to the pan and toss the pieces. Sprinkle the sherry, both soy sauces, salt, and sugar over the chicken. Bring the liquid to a boil and toss to coat the chicken with the soy sauces. Cover, reduce heat to medium-low, and cook for 30 minutes. Stir twice during this time. There will be very little sauce left when the chicken is done.

The chicken can be cooked ahead of time and reheated, covered, for 30 minutes in a 325-degree oven or for about 10 minutes on top of the stove over very low heat.

HEATING THE BROTH, COOKING THE NOODLES,
AND SERVING THE DISH

Heat the chicken broth in a small saucepan over low heat. Set up six large soup bowls; into each put 1 to 2 teaspoons light soy sauce, ¼ tea-spoon sesame oil, a dash each of salt and white pepper.

Cook the noodles in a large pot with 4 quarts boiling water for 2 minutes if fresh (test for doneness after 1 minute of boiling), longer if dried. Drain and shake off the water.

Divide the noodles into the six soup bowls. Toss with chopsticks to coat them with the sauce. Put equal amounts of chicken on top of the noodles. Pour ½ cup hot chicken broth on top of each serving. Serve with chopsticks and soup spoons, using the chopsticks to pick up the noodles and chicken, the spoon to drink the broth.

Red-Cooked Fresh Bacon, Squid, and Noodle Soup

乌
贼
大
烤
面
WU ZEI DA KAO TANG MIAN

In the Shanghai area (including Zhejiang and Jiangsu provinces), the method of cooking called *hong shao* ("red-cooking") developed; it involves simmering meats over a slow fire in a rich sauce based on sherry, dark soy sauce, ginger, and other seasonings.

Fresh bacon (pork belly) is a favorite red-cooked meat, combined with bamboo shoots and dried Chinese black mushrooms. It is almost as common in China as pot roast is in the United States. In this recipe I've added large squid to the bacon, giving the dish an exotic flavor. If you don't like seafood with meat, you can make the dish without the squid.

The concentrated sauce resulting from the long stewing is very good added to a clear chicken broth containing noodles. Divide ¾ pound hot boiled eggless noodles among four large bowls, add 1 cup hot chicken broth to each, and ladle a quarter of this pork dish on top of each serving. Serve hot as a light meal. The recipe can easily be doubled.

Yield: 4 servings for a light meal

2 tablespoons corn oil or peanut oil
1 pound fresh bacon (pork belly) including the skin or 1 pound boneless fresh pork butt, cut into 1-inch pieces
2 quarter-size slices fresh ginger
1 clove garlic, crushed
2 whole scallions, cut into 2-inch sections

¼ cup dry sherry
3 tablespoons dark soy sauce
¼ teaspoon coarse salt or to taste
2 teaspoons sugar
½ cup water
1 large squid, cleaned, scored, and cut into 1- by 2-inch sections, about 10 ounces

Heat a well-seasoned wok or heavy-duty saucepan that has a tight-fitting lid. Add the oil, swirl, add the ginger, garlic, and scallions and stir until fragrant. Then add the bacon and let the pieces brown lightly. Add the sherry, soy sauce, salt, sugar, and water. Bring to a boil, cover, and cook at a slow simmer for 30 minutes.

Put the cleaned squid pieces in a mixing bowl. Add very hot water to cover, stir, and then drain. (This keeps the squid from releasing too much water.) Lay the drained squid on top of the meat and continue cooking, covered, for one more hour at a slow simmer. During that time, stir once.

Shredded Pork and Red-in-Snow Noodle Soup

咸
菜
肉
丝
面

XIAN CAI ROU SI MIAN

The people of Zhejiang and Jiangsu provinces pickle a delicious vegetable called red-in-snow. It is a leafy green much like the top of a turnip, but it tastes like mustard greens, and the Chinese preserve both its leaves and its stems. It appears in late winter, and because it is so hardy, even snow doesn't prevent it from growing. The name should, of course, be green-in-snow, but since the Chinese love red, they put that color in the name. This plant is also grown in the United States, and you can buy it fresh in Chinese markets in late winter or early spring.

To pickle it, prepare it a week before it's to be eaten: Rinse and thoroughly dry 1 pound of fresh red-in-snow. Chop it coarsely and put it in a bowl. Sprinkle 2 tablespoons of coarse salt on top and toss well. Pack in a tightly closed jar and refrigerate. You can use the salted red-in-snow after a week. The canned red-in-snow, labeled pickled cabbage, is also quite good. I particularly like the Ma Ling brand.

The red-in-snow in this soup not only gives it a lovely flavor but also preserves it. When my daughters were in college, they missed home cooking. This is one of the dishes I sent to them often. Food editor Cecily Brownstone of the Associated Press wrote about the dishes my daughter Kay received from me under the headline "Chinese Food Goes to College."

Cantonese Spring Rolls with Shrimp and Pork (page 110) or Scallion Pancakes (page 162) would go well with this soup.

Yield: 6 servings as a light meal

8 dried black Chinese
  mushrooms
2 cups winter bamboo shoots
1 pound pork tenderloin or
  center-cut pork chop or
  boneless pork butt, semi-
  frozen for easier slicing
1 small can (7 ounces)
  preserved red-in-snow
6 tablespoons corn oil or
  peanut oil

1 tablespoon dry sherry
1 tablespoon light soy sauce
1 teaspoon sugar
¾ pound Homemade Chinese
  Egg Noodles (page 21) or
  Steamed Noodles (page 31)
6–8 cups Best Chicken Broth
  (page 77)
  Light soy sauce or salt to taste

PREPARING THE VEGETABLES AND PORK

Rinse and then soak the dried mushrooms in warm water to cover for 30 minutes. Squeeze them over the bowl and reserve the liquid. Remove and discard the stems; shred the caps and set them on a large plate. Shred the bamboo shoots in Matchstick strips and set them on the same plate with the mushrooms.

Slice the pork thin with the grain; then cut again into matchstick strips 1½ inches long; you should have about 2 cups. Set aside.

Scoop out the red-in-snow, discarding the liquid. Coarsely chop the vegetable and set aside with the mushrooms and bamboo shoots.

STIR-FRYING THE TOPPING

Heat a wok for 30 seconds, pour in 3 tablespoons of the oil, swirl, and then add the pork; stir-fry for 2 minutes or until the meat whitens a little and separates into shreds; then add the sherry and soy sauce and stir once or twice. Scoop the pork and liquid onto a plate.

Add the remaining 3 tablespoons of oil to the wok, swirl, and then stir-fry the mushrooms for 30 seconds. Add the red-in-snow and stir together for 1 minute, then add the sugar and stir to mix. Add the bamboo shoots, stir-fry for 2 minutes, then return the pork to the wok, add ¼ cup of the mushroom liquid, cover, and cook for 2 minutes. Scoop the contents of the wok out into a bowl.

You can do this stir-frying in advance; simply cover the bowl and refrigerate; it will keep for 1 week. You can also boil the noodles in advance. Put them in 3 quarts of boiling water and cook for 1 to 2 minutes, until they are tender but firm to the bite, a little softer than *al dente*. Drain and rinse with cold water, then put them in the refrigerator in a covered bowl and, before using them, rinse with cold water again to separate.

MAKING THE SOUP

Bring the chicken broth to a boil in a large pot. Add the cooked noodles and the pork-vegetable topping. When the broth boils again, turn the heat to low and simmer for 2 minutes. Add light soy sauce or salt to taste. Serve the soup from this pot or a tureen: Scoop out the noodles with a spaghetti fork or chopsticks into six individual soup bowls, then ladle the pork, vegetables, and broth on top.

Variation: Instead of wheat noodles, use fresh or dried rice sticks.

Clam, Pickled Vegetable, and Noodle Soup

XIAN CAI GELI TANG MIAN

This delicious noodle dish, created by my friend Elsie Hsu, is truly an innovation. The rich chicken soup and salty pickled vegetable are perfect complements to the clams. This soup makes a very satisfying meal.

Yield: 6 servings as a light meal

2 dozen fresh littleneck clams, shucked, meat removed and juices reserved
4 tablespoons corn oil or peanut oil
1 large clove of garlic, minced
1 cup chopped red-in-snow (page 87)

4 cups Best Chicken Broth (page 77)
¾ pound cooked Homemade Chinese Egg Noodles (page 21) or Steamed Noodles (page 31)
Salt and white pepper to taste

Rinse the clams in the juice and put them on a chopping board. Chop all the clams coarsely and set aside. Strain the clam juice in a sieve lined with cheesecloth and reserve.

Heat 2 tablespoons of the oil in a large saucepan over moderate heat. Add the garlic and stir-fry for 5 seconds. Add the clams and stir together for 1 minute. Transfer to a bowl. Heat the remaining 2 tablespoons of oil in the saucepan over moderate heat and stir-fry the red-in-snow for 2 minutes. Return the clams to the pan, add the chicken broth, and bring to a boil. Add the cooked noodles and boil for 2 minutes. Add salt and pepper to taste.

Either pour the soup into a tureen or serve directly from the pan: Dish out the noodles into individual soup bowls with a spaghetti fork or chopsticks, then ladle out servings of the clams, red-in-snow, and broth.

Drop Noodles in Two Soups

 MIAN GEDA

 In China drop noodles are a specialty of little noodle shops and roadside stands; when done professionally, they are made of a well-kneaded firm dough containing flour, water, and salt. The cook cuts off the dough in pieces with a thin curved knife directly into a pot of boiling water. After the noodles have boiled for 2 minutes, the cook strains them and adds them to a prepared soup. This skillful act of cutting is great fun to watch.

When drop noodles are made at home, they are made from a softer dough consisting of flour, egg, salt, and water, and you need only a spreader or knife to cut the batterlike dough.

These drop noodles in broth make a quick meal, an excellent base for leftover meat and vegetables. Homemade chicken broth or canned chicken broth diluted with water may be used. Following the noodle recipe are two soup recipes, one using leftovers, the other, fresh vegetables. If you don't want to make the drop noodles, substitute ½ pound cooked noodles of your choice.

This recipe can easily be doubled.

Yield: 3–4 servings for a light meal

1 cup unbleached flour	**1 beaten egg plus enough water**
¼ teaspoon coarse salt	**to equal ⅔ cup**

MAKING THE DROP NOODLES

Put the flour and salt in a thin-lipped mixing bowl and make a well in the center. Beat the egg in a measuring cup and add enough water to bring the liquid to almost ⅔ cup. Gradually stir the liquid into the center of the flour with a pair of chopsticks or a spoon, and keep stirring until the mixture is a smooth, very thick batter. (You can also use a wire whisk to do this job.) Tilt the bowl; the mixture should slowly slide over the edge.

Bring 5 to 6 cups of water to a boil and turn the heat to medium-high so the water is boiling rapidly. Have an icing spreader or a thin-bladed knife ready. Tilt the bowl of batter slightly over the pot of water, and as the batter begins to slide over the edge, press the blade of the icing spreader or knife against the rim of the bowl and cut the batter into thin strips, letting them drop into the water. Dip the blade in the

water from time to time to wet it. Stir the drop noodles gently with a spoon. They will cook in 2 minutes. Drain them in a colander and run them under cold water.

Drop noodles may be made in advance and put in the refrigerator covered with plastic wrap. Rinse them under cold water to separate before you slip them into the soup. You can also cut the drop noodles directly into a prepared soup and let them cook there for 2 minutes.

Leftover Meat and Vegetable Soup with Drop Noodles

4 cups chicken broth or beef
  broth
2 cups cut-up vegetables

1 cup cut-up cooked meat
1 recipe Drop Noodles (page 90)
Salt and pepper to taste

Bring chicken or beef broth to a boil. Add cut-up leafy vegetable, such as spinach, watercress, or Romaine or leafy lettuce, and any left-over cut-up cooked meat, such as chicken, turkey, duck, pork, ham, or beef or any leftover dish that isn't a sweet-and-sour one. Add already cooked drop noodles and simmer for 1 minute (2 minutes if you are putting uncooked drop noodles into the broth). Add salt and pepper to taste and serve hot in a large bowl.

Fresh Meat and Vegetable Soup with Drop Noodles

2 tablespoons corn oil or peanut
  oil
1 medium-size tomato, diced
1 medium-size carrot, sliced thin
4 cups green cabbage cut in 1-
  inch squares

4 cups chicken broth or water (or
  simmer 2 pounds beef neck
  bones in 8 cups water for 2
  hours; then cut up the meat,
  discarding the bones and fat,
  and measure out broth)
Salt and pepper to taste
1 recipe Drop Noodles (page 90)

Heat the oil in a large saucepan for 30 seconds; then stir-fry the diced tomato for 2 minutes. Add the sliced carrot and stir for 1 minute. Add the cabbage squares and stir and toss for a few seconds until glossy. Add the chicken broth or water and bring to a boil. Cover, lower the heat, and simmer for 20 minutes. Add the already cooked drop noodles and simmer for 1 minute (2 minutes if uncooked). Add salt and pepper to taste and serve hot.

Wrappers

Spring Roll Wrappers

The light brown fried wrappers filled with meat and vegetables, called egg rolls in Chinese restaurants here, are, in China, the Cantonese version of spring rolls. Like the brittle, pale white filled wrappers from Shanghai, they are one of the most important celebratory foods of the Chinese New Year. According to the Chinese lunar calendar, New Year's Day is also the first day of spring, hence the name.

Cantonese spring rolls are made of noodle dough that has egg in it; Shanghai spring rolls (not as common in the United States) are made of a thin eggless dough that is briefly cooked on a griddle. Cantonese spring rolls are rather thick and crunchy after deep-frying; Shanghai spring rolls are thin and brittle. When Shanghai spring rolls are steamed, they are known as Amoy *Popia,* which are like soft and tender pancakes. Both the following recipes detail the making of spring rolls at home as well as give notes about the commercial ones that are available. Recipes follow for the classic fillings.

Cantonese Spring Roll Wrappers

广 卷 GUANGDONG CHUN JUAN PI
东 皮
春

Wonton Wrappers

馄 HUNTUN PI
饨
皮

Shao Mai (Open-Faced Steamed Dumpling) Wrappers

烧 SHAO MAI PI
卖
皮

The traditional dough for Cantonese spring roll wrappers is also suitable for wontons and shao mai; I have included instructions for all three shapes in the recipe here. You will find that they are not very difficult to make, and the irresistible fresh taste and texture of the wrappers is well worth the effort. Should you not have the time, however, you can easily buy commercially made ones; they are very good (see page 97).

Yield: 24 thick or 40 very thin 6-inch-square Cantonese spring roll wrappers
96 thick or 180 very thin 3-inch-square wonton wrappers
112 thick or 200 very thin 2½-inch shao mai wrappers

3 cups all-purpose flour	**¾ cup water, approximately**
1 extra large egg	**Flour and cornstarch for**
3 teaspoons coarse salt	**dusting**

MIXING AND KNEADING THE DOUGH
Following the instructions in the recipe for egg noodles, either mix and knead the dough by hand (pages 22–23) or mix and knead in a food processor (pages 24–26).

ROLLING THE DOUGH BY HAND
After the dough has rested for 30 minutes (if hand-kneaded) or 60 minutes (if processor-kneaded), divide it into four portions. Work with one portion at a time, covering the others with plastic wrap.

With a rolling pin, roll out the dough on a lightly floured surface, turning the dough sheet halfway at regular intervals to maintain an even thickness. Dust with flour when needed and smooth in the flour with your fingers. When the sheet is almost translucent, about 1/16 inch thick and 12 by 18 inches, lay it on a dry towel. Let it dry for 10 minutes. Work the other three portions of dough.

Working with one sheet at a time, sprinkle cornstarch on both sides and smooth it in with your fingers. (The cornstarch prevents the wrappers from sticking together when stacked or when stored in the refrigerator or freezer.)

CUTTING THE WRAPPERS
For Cantonese spring roll wrappers, cut each sheet into 6-inch squares.

For wonton wrappers, cut each sheet into 3-inch squares to make about 24 per sheet.

For shao mai wrappers, use 2½-inch cookie cutter to make about 28 small circles.

ROLLING THE DOUGH WITH A PASTA MACHINE

After the dough has rested for 30 minutes, divide it into four portions. Work with two portions at a time, covering the other two with plastic. Flatten the two portions a little with your fingers, and set the rollers of the machine fully open. Taking one portion at a time, lightly flour both sides and smooth the flour in with your fingers. Pass the dough through the rollers, fold the sheet crosswise in half or thirds, sprinkle with flour and smooth it in, and pass through the rollers again. Repeat the process at least five times, or until the dough is very smooth and elastic.

After the last roll fold the sheet in thirds, almost to the width of the rollers. With the smooth edges at the sides, pass the sheet through the rollers. Pull the sheet out quickly. Decrease the gap between the rollers one notch at a time. Each time flour the sheet on both sides and smooth the flour with your fingers. Then pass the sheet through the rollers. When the sheet is more than 20 inches long, cut in half for easy handling. At the next-to-last setting you will have a thicker wrapper; the finest setting will produce a very thin wrapper. If the sheet is less than 6 inches wide, use a rolling pin to widen it.

To dry the sheet, lay it on a dry towel for 10 minutes. Repeat the final rolling steps with the other two portions of dough and let them dry for 10 minutes before you cut the sheets into wrappers. If you aren't going to use the dough immediately, dust the sheets with cornstarch and smooth it in with your fingers.

CUTTING THE WRAPPERS

Follow the directions on page 96 for cutting out spring roll, wonton, or shao mai wrappers.

STORING FRESH WRAPPERS

Stack the wrappers, each dusted with cornstarch, and wrap them with aluminum foil. They will keep in the refrigerator for up to three days or in the freezer for up to a month.

COMMERCIAL WRAPPERS

Cantonese spring roll wrappers are sold in 7-inch squares, by the pound; each pound contains fourteen to twenty-five wrappers, depending on the thickness. They will keep for about a week in the refrigerator or a month in the freezer. If you freeze them, you must defrost them thoroughly before using them.

Commercial wonton and shao mai wrappers, which are excellent, are sold in 1-pound packages and in two thicknesses. Thick ones, usually made from eggless noodle dough, number about 80 per package; thin ones, numbering about 120 per package, are made from egg noodle dough, and sometimes pasta flour or cornstarch is used. Like spring roll wrappers, wonton and shao mai wrappers stay fresh for about one week in the refrigerator and one month in the freezer. Thoroughly defrost them, then wrap with a damp towel before using.

With any kind of wrapper, always rewrap in aluminum foil before storing.

Shanghai Spring Roll Wrappers

 SHANGHAI CHUN JUAN PI

More than twenty years ago, when I was trying to master the art of making these wrappers, I made many mistakes—and a mess of the kitchen's stove, counter, sink, floor, sometimes even the wall. This recipe, the result of years of trial and error, should eliminate all the trouble and mess; but it does take time. It is a challenge, and it's fun.

On the other hand, commercial frozen Shanghai spring roll wrappers are very handy to have. They are square, and can be frozen for as long as two months (handmade wrappers are round and can be kept in the freezer no more than one month; the one packed for Summit Co. is particularly good). Lately, I buy the Oriental Mascot brand from Hong Kong, which offers twenty-three wrappers in one package. Before I use them I let the sealed package sit at room temperature for 3 to 4 hours or overnight. By that time they will be completely defrosted and very soft. First, gently pull off two or three wrappers together; then peel them apart one by one. While you are making the rolls, restack the wrappers in one pile and wrap them in a damp dish towel.

If the wrappers aren't pliable and they crack when you are filling and rolling them, whether machine-made or handmade, wrap them in a damp dish towel and steam them in a covered steamer over low heat for 10 to 30 minutes. After 10 minutes, check them; rearrange them if necessary to make them all pliable.

Yield: Thirty 7-inch wrappers

3 cups all-purpose flour　　　　**1½ cups water, approximately**
2 teaspoons coarse salt

MAKING THE DOUGH

Combine the flour and salt in a large mixing bowl. Gradually add all but two tablespoons of the water while you mix the dough with your hands.

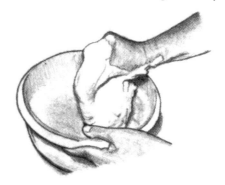

If the dough is too dry, add only as much of the remaining water as you need to make a very soft dough. When all the water has been added, knead the dough in the bowl for approximately 5 minutes, until it is smooth and elastic though very soft—this process means using your fingers or fist to knead the dough against the bottom of the bowl and turning the bowl frequently or hit onto a work surface; the dough is too soft to turn. If you have an electric mixer with a dough hook, this kneading will take approximately 2 minutes.

When you've finished kneading the dough, cover the bowl tightly with plastic wrap and refrigerate for at least 2 to 3 hours or up to overnight. Before you work it, let the dough stand for a while to loosen a little of its chill; it shouldn't be at room temperature, however.

MAKING THE WRAPPERS

Heat a large ungreased electric griddle or skillet to 300 degrees. The temperature is important, for if the pan is too cold, a thick layer of dough will stick to it, and if the pan is too hot, the dough will not stick at all. For that reason a temperature-controlled surface is preferable. Put a large plate and several folds of paper towel next to the pan.

Take up all the dough in one hand. The dough will be very soft,

and it will drip slowly. To work it a little, rotate your wrist slowly, palm down, and let the dough fall away a little; gather it back with your fingers. Do this for about 3 minutes; while the dough is still slightly cool, press it in a circular motion onto the skillet or griddle—you want to make about a 7-inch circle. Quickly pull the dough back; a very thin film of dough will remain on the hot surface. If some small dots of soft

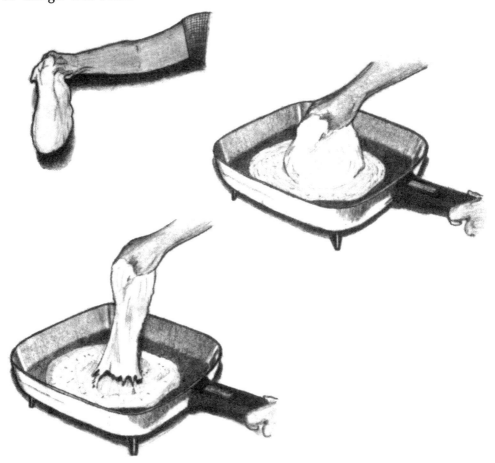

dough are on the surface, use the tips of your finger to flatten them. The circle of dough will start to dry at the edges in a few seconds. With your free hand, peel the whole wrapper off the pan and put it, bottom side up, on the plate. If some dry dough remains in the pan, push to the side with a paper towel, but don't worry if the dough sticks on the sides. Make another wrapper and put it on top of the first; this stacking warms the bottom wrapper and softens the edges.

Continue making wrappers until all the dough is used up. Re-

member that the dough will drip, so keep rotating your wrist slowly to control the dough.

Cover the wrappers with a pot cover or a slightly damp towel until ready to use. You may steam them in a damp towel to produce a hot, soft pancake. If served the same day, they needn't be refrigerated.

STORING AND REHEATING FRESH WRAPPERS
A stack of fresh wrappers in aluminum foil can be stored in the refrigerator for up to one week or in the freezer for up to two months. Once the wrappers are chilled, however, the texture does change, and the only way to make them pliable again is to steam them, wrapped in a damp towel. Over low heat ten wrappers would take about 10 minutes to heat up and become soft again, but you could keep them in a steamer over very low heat for up to 30 minutes without them becoming soggy. After steaming them, you must wrap or cover them while you fill them.

Spring Rolls

Shanghai Spring Rolls

上
海
春
卷

SHANGHAI CHUN JUAN

Here is the treasured Shanghai spring roll filling of shredded pork, vegetables, and seafood for these delicate wrappers. This filling should be made ahead of time and chilled so that it's firm when you roll it in the wrappers. If you can manage to serve the spring rolls freshly fried, they will be at their best, but you can fry them ahead of time.

For years my oldest son-in-law, Jimmy, used to say, "I could have your Shanghai spring rolls anytime." Recently my brand-new son-in-law, Eddy, made the same remark. I'm very flattered by their love for this recipe, and no matter how busy I am, I try to make these spring rolls when my sons-in-law are in the house.

Yield: Twenty 5-inch-long spring rolls

20 **Shanghai Spring Roll
    Wrappers, round or square,
    about 7 inches in diameter
    (page 98)
    Oil for deep-frying**
½ **pound pork tenderloin,
    semifrozen for easy slicing**
¼ **pound raw shrimp, shelled,
    deveined, and coarsely
    chopped**
6 **dried Chinese mushrooms**

4 **cups shredded celery cabbage
    or ½ pound bean sprouts**
½ **cup shredded winter bamboo
    shoots**
3 **tablespoons peanut or corn oil**
1½ **teaspoons coarse salt**
1½ **tablespoons cornstarch
    combined with 3 tablespoons
    mushroom liquid**
1 **egg**

THE MARINADE FOR THE PORK

1 **tablespoon light soy sauce**
½ **teaspoon sugar**

½ **tablespoon cornstarch**

MAKING THE FILLING

Cut the pork with the grain into very thin slices. Cut again into 2-inch-long matchstick strips; you should have about 1 cup. Put them in a mixing bowl, add the marinade ingredients, and mix well. Refrigerate the pork as well as the shrimp.

Rinse the mushrooms, then soak them in 1 cup of warm water for 30 minutes. Drain, reserving 3 tablespoons of the liquid for the cornstarch mixture. Cut off and discard the stems, then cut the caps into very thin strips. Put the shredded mushrooms on a large plate with the shredded celery, cabbage, and bamboo shoots.

Heat a wok for 30 seconds, or until very hot. Add 1½ tablespoons of oil, swirl, then add the pork. Stir-fry the pork until it separates into shreds—about 1 minute. Add the shrimp and stir-fry together for 30 seconds. Dish out onto a plate.

Heat the wok again, add 1½ tablespoons oil and swirl, then toss in the mushrooms, celery, cabbage, and bamboo shoots. Stir-fry until the cabbage becomes soft—about 3 minutes. Add the salt and toss well. Return the meat mixture to the pan and toss with the vegetables to heat through. Transfer to a plate with a slotted spoon (you may push the food to the side).

There should be about 3 tablespoons of liquid in the wok; remove any excess. Stir the cornstarch mixture, add it to the wok, and stir into the liquid; then return the meat and vegetables to the wok and stir to coat them. Dish out the filling onto a plate, cover with plastic wrap, and refrigerate to chill it.

WRAPPING THE SPRING ROLLS

Beat the egg till frothy in a small bowl and set aside with a pastry brush. As you fill the wrappers, keep the ones still to be filled in a stack covered with a damp cloth. (If the wrappers are too stiff because of refrigeration, wrap them in a damp cloth and steam them over low heat for 10 to 20 minutes, or until they are soft and pliable. After 10 minutes, check them; rearrange if necessary to make them evenly soft.)

Take one spring roll wrapper at a time and place on a work surface. Scoop about 2 tablespoons of filling onto the lower corner of the wrapper and, with your fingers, spread it into a 4-inch line. Then fold the edge over the filling and roll the wrapper to the center. Bring the two end flaps over the top of the enclosed filling and gently press down. Brush all exposed edges of the wrapper with beaten egg. Now finish rolling the cylinder into a neat 5-inch-long spring roll. The beaten egg will seal the edge and keep the wrapper intact. Fill the other wrappers, lay them on a plate, and cover with plastic wrap until ready to cook. The filled spring rolls may be kept in the freezer, but you don't have to defrost them before frying them.

FRYING THE SPRING ROLLS

Pour enough oil into a wok or skillet so that it will come at least halfway up the spring rolls during the frying. Heat the oil to about 350 degrees. Place a few rolls in the oil at a time and fry both sides until crisp and

golden brown—about 5 minutes in all. Drain on paper towels and put them in a 200-degree oven with the door ajar. Continue deep-frying the remaining rolls.

If you want to make the spring rolls in advance, it is best to freeze them after frying them. Reheat them on a rack set in a pan, in a preheated 450-degree oven, for about 10 minutes. You can also fry them to a light brown, cover them with a dry towel, and then fry them to a golden brown at the last minute. An electric fryer with a basket is very handy for this.

When ready to serve, cut each hot spring roll in half and set out small bowls of vinegar and chili pepper oil to use as dips.

Variation: Make smaller spring rolls by cutting the wrappers in half before filling them—make two triangular pieces. Spread 1 tablespoon of filling in a line along the cut edge. Bring the two end flaps over the top of the enclosed filling; then fold the edge over and gently press down. Brush the exposed edges of the wrapper with beaten egg. Then finish rolling the cylinder into a spring roll.

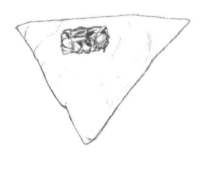
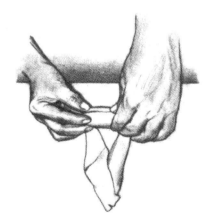

Variation: After you have finished wrapping the Shanghai Spring Rolls, put a little oil in a frying pan over medium-low heat and pan-fry the spring rolls on all sides for about 3 to 4 minutes or until they are lightly brown and crispy. Or steam the wrapped spring rolls briefly and serve them like Amoy spring rolls, page 114.

Spring Rolls with Beef Sausage

 ROU CHANG CHUN JUAN

 Here is an old family recipe for a steamed sausage filling. There's no shredding of meat and vegetables; all you have to do is make the sausages ahead of time.

Yield: Ten 5-inch-long spring rolls

10 **Shanghai Spring Roll Wrappers (page 98)**	1 **beaten egg** **Oil for deep-frying**

FOR THE FILLING

½ **pound ground round beef**
2 **tablespoons finely chopped bamboo shoots**
3 **large dried black Chinese mushrooms, rinsed, soaked in warm water till soft, stems removed and caps finely chopped**
1 **teaspoon finely chopped fresh ginger**

1 **tablespoon finely chopped scallion**
1 **tablespoon light soy sauce**
½ **teaspoon coarse salt**
Dash ground black pepper
1 **tablespoon peanut oil or corn oil**
2 **tablespoons chicken broth or water**
1 **tablespoon cornstarch**

MAKING THE SAUSAGE FILLING
Combine the filling ingredients in a mixing bowl and stir well in one direction until the meat holds together. Divide the filling into ten portions and shape each portion into a sausage shape about 4 inches long. Set these on a plate and steam them for 5 minutes. Let them cool com-

pletely. This can be done ahead of time and kept in the refrigerator for up to two days.

WRAPPING THE SPRING ROLLS

Stack the wrappers and wrap them in a damp cloth. Steam them over low heat for 10 to 20 minutes, or until they are soft and pliable (after 10 minutes of steaming, check and rearrange the wrappers if necessary so the inside ones are outside; that way all of them will be evenly soft).

Take one spring roll wrapper at a time (leaving the rest covered) and set it on a work surface. Put a sausage filling at one edge; then lift the edge over the sausage and roll the wrapper toward the center. Turn the two end flaps over the top of the enclosed sausage and gently press down. Brush the exposed edge with beaten egg. Then finish rolling the cylinder; the beaten egg will keep the wrapper intact. Repeat with the other wrappers, set them on plate, and cover with plastic wrap until ready to cook. The filled spring rolls may be kept in the freezer, but you don't need to defrost them thoroughly before frying them.

FRYING AND SERVING THE SPRING ROLLS

Pour about ½ inch of oil into a 12-inch skillet (the oil should come at least halfway up the sides of the spring rolls during the frying). Heat the oil to about 350 degrees. Place a few rolls at a time in the oil and fry both sides until crisp and golden brown—about 5 minutes in all.

Drain on paper towels and keep them in a 200-degree oven with the door ajar while you fry the remaining rolls.

You can freeze the spring rolls after frying them. To reheat, put them on a rack set in a pan in a preheated 450-degree oven for about 10 minutes.

To serve, cut the spring rolls in half crosswise and serve hot with vinegar and chili pepper oil as dips.

Variation: Substitute ground pork or turkey for the beef.

Cantonese Spring Rolls with Shrimp and Pork

广
东
春
卷

GUANGDONG CHUN JUAN

Before Shanghai spring rolls appeared, these were the only spring rolls Americans knew. When well made, they are very tasty, and this classic filling of pork, vegetables, and shrimp makes one or two spring rolls a meal in itself. Fry the spring rolls twice; the wrapper will be crisp and the filling moist. The first frying can be done 2 or 3 hours ahead of time, and the second just before serving.

Yield: 16 spring rolls

2 cups peanut oil or corn oil
½ pound ground pork
1 tablespoon dry sherry
1 tablespoon soy sauce
½ teaspoon sugar
½ pound raw shrimp, shelled, deveined, and chopped
4 large fresh mushrooms, thinly sliced, about ½ cup
4 cups finely chopped celery
2 teaspoons coarse salt or to taste

½ teaspoon five-spice powder
½ pound fresh bean sprouts, or 3 cups shredded cabbage
1 tablespoon cornstarch dissolved in 2 tablespoons water
16 Cantonese Spring Roll Wrappers (page 95)
1 egg, lightly beaten

MAKING THE FILLING

Heat a wok over moderate heat for 30 seconds. Add 1 tablespoon of the oil, swirl, then add the pork and stir-fry for 2 minutes or until it loses its reddish color. Then add the sherry, soy sauce, sugar, shrimp, and mushrooms and stir-fry for another minute, or until the shrimp turn pink. Scoop contents out into a bowl and set aside.

Heat the wok again over moderate heat for 30 seconds. Add 2 tablespoons of oil, swirl, then add the celery and stir-fry for 5 minutes, or until the celery is very dry. Add the salt, five-spice powder, and bean sprouts or cabbage and toss lightly for 2 more minutes. Return the pork and shrimp to the pan and stir until all the ingredients are well combined. Cook over high heat, stirring, until the liquid starts to boil—there should be about 2 tablespoons of liquid remaining in the center when you push the food to the side. If there is more, spoon it out and discard.

Give the cornstarch mixture a big stir to recombine it and dribble it in the center of the wok. Stir until the liquids have thickened; then stir to coat all the ingredients with the light glaze. Scoop the filling out into a bowl and let it cool. Cover and refrigerate if you are making the spring rolls hours later or even up to a day later.

FILLING THE WRAPPERS AND
FRYING THE SPRING ROLLS
Lay one spring roll wrapper at a time on a flat surface. Place ¼ cup filling a little lower than the center at the corner nearest you. Shape it with your fingers into a narrow mound about 4 inches long. Lift the lower corner over the filling and tuck the point under it, leaving the upper corner of the wrapper exposed. Bring each of the side corners, one at a time, up to the top of the enclosed filling and press the points down. (Do not wrap too tightly; you want only two layers of dough around the filling, if possible.) Brush the exposed corner of the wrapper with beaten egg and then loosely finish rolling the wrapper. The beaten egg will seal the edges.

Place the filled spring rolls on a tray and cover them with a dry towel. You could refrigerate them for a few hours if you need to or put them in the freezer, but you don't need to defrost them completely before frying them. They are best made shortly after being wrapped, however.

Heat a large skillet, about 12 inches in diameter, and add the remaining oil (over 1½ cups). When it reaches 350 degrees, slip in five or six spring rolls. The oil should be at least halfway up the sides of the spring rolls. Fry on both sides until a light golden brown—a total of about 4 minutes. Remove with a slotted spoon. Let the oil heat up again, then refry the rolls for another minute, or until golden brown.

You can freeze the fried spring rolls when they are at room temperature. To reheat them, set them on a rack in a pan in a preheated 450-degree oven for about 10 minutes.

Serve the spring rolls hot with small individual dishes of a dipping sauce made of 1 tablespoon vinegar and a few drops of the chili oil on top of Hot Chili Bean Paste Sichuan- or Hunan-Style (page 302) or a touch of the paste itself.

Vegetarian Spring Rolls (Egg Rolls)

  SU CHUN JUAN

These meatless spring rolls contain a delicious meat substitute that is high in protein—seasoned pressed bean curd. This store-bought food is fresh bean curd that has been pressed into a firm piece, then simmered with soy sauce, star anise, and sugar. It is available in Chinese markets.

Yield: 20 spring rolls

8 **large dried black Chinese mushrooms**	1 **teaspoon coarse salt or to taste**
4 **3 × 3 × ⅓-inch squares ready-to-eat seasoned pressed bean curd (*Wu Xiang Dou Fu Gan*) (page 311)**	1 **teaspoon sugar**
	1 **tablespoon sesame oil**
	1 **tablespoon cornstarch**
4 **cups finely shredded celery**	20 **Shanghai Spring Roll Wrappers, square or round (page 98), at room temperature**
1 **cup finely shredded carrots**	
1½ **cups peanut oil or corn oil**	
1 **tablespoon light soy sauce**	1 **egg, beaten lightly**

PREPARE THE FILLING

Wash and then soak the mushrooms in 1 cup of warm water for 30 minutes, or until soft. Cut off and discard the stems, then finely shred the caps. Reserve the soaking water.

Cut the seasoned pressed bean curd into slices about ⅛ inch thick and cut again into shreds. You should have about 4 cups. Set aside on a platter with the celery, carrots, and mushrooms.

Heat a wok over moderate heat for 30 seconds, or until very hot. Add 2 tablespoons of the oil, swirl, then add the bean curd, and ½ cup of the mushroom liquid, and stir-fry for 2 minutes. Add the soy sauce, mix well, then scoop the contents into a bowl and set aside.

Heat the wok again over medium-high heat, add 2 more table-spoons of the oil, swirl, then add the carrots and celery and stir-fry for 5 minutes, or until the vegetables are soft and dry but not brown. Add the salt, sugar, and sesame oil; then return the bean curd and mushrooms to the pan and stir to mix well; then push the food to the side. Mix the cornstarch with 3 tablespoons of the reserved mushroom liquid and pour into the center of the wok (still on medium-high heat), stirring until the sauce thickens; then stir to coat all the ingredients. Transfer the contents to a bowl and let them cool before you use as filling. Cover and refrigerate if you aren't going to make the spring rolls for a few hours or even the next day.

FILLING THE WRAPPERS AND FRYING THE SPRING ROLLS

Carefully separate the room-temperature spring roll wrappers by gently pulling off two or three together, then peeling them apart one by one. To make them soft and pliable, stack them, wrap them in a damp cloth, and steam them over low heat for 10 to 20 minutes. Check them after 10 minutes, rearranging them if necessary so they soften evenly. Keep them covered with a dish towel as you do the next step: the filling and shaping.

Lay one wrapper at a time on a flat surface. Put about 2 tablespoons of filling at one side if round or near one corner if square. Shape the filling with your fingers into a thin mound about 3 inches long. Lift the near corner over the filling and begin to roll, tucking the edge or point under the filling and rolling in to the center. Bring the two side corners up over the enclosed filling. Brush the exposed far edge of the wrapper with the beaten egg. Continue rolling to the end. Cover the finished spring rolls with a dry dish towel until ready to fry them. They can be refrigerated or frozen, but you don't need to defrost them completely before frying them.

Heat the remaining oil in a 12-inch skillet or a wok over medium heat to about 350 degrees. Put in five to six rolls and fry for about 2 to 3 minutes on each side, or until golden brown and crisp. Drain on paper towels. Repeat until all are done. The fried spring rolls can be frozen once they have cooled. Reheat them on a rack set in a pan in a preheated 450-degree oven for about 10 minutes.

Serve the fried egg rolls whole or cut in half, accompanied by small individual dishes of vinegar with a few drops of chili oil added.

Amoy Popia with Filling and Condiments (Amoy Spring Rolls)

 XIAMEN POPIA

Popia, literally translated, means a "thin pancake"; it is a specialty of Amoy, a coastal city in the south of Fukien province, and it is eaten only on special occasions such as the New Year and big birthday celebrations. The people of Amoy build a whole meal around these wrappers. This recipe is a legacy of my late husband's family, natives of Amoy.

Popia is actually made from the same ingredients as a Shanghai spring roll wrapper, but it is steamed rather than fried. The manner in which it is served is also different. The wrappers are served hot, with an abundant selection of accompaniments—ground peanuts, coriander, bean sprouts, and scallions, to name a few—and with a long-simmered filling of shrimp, pork, and vegetables. The diners wrap whatever delicacies they choose to create their own Amoy *popia.* This recipe is a lot of fun for a party with family and friends.

Yield: 6–8 servings as a full meal; 24 wrappers

THE FILLING

- 8 tablespoons corn oil or peanut oil
- 1 pound boneless pork butt, cut into matchstick strips (about 2 cups), semi-frozen for easy slicing
- 2 tablespoons dry sherry
- 4 tablespoons light soy sauce
- ½ teaspoon sugar
- 1 pound raw shrimp, shelled, deveined, and coarsely chopped
- 1½ teaspoons coarse salt or to taste
- 1 cup winter bamboo shoots cut in matchstick shreds
- ½ cup carrots cut in matchstick shreds
- 4 pieces plain (white) pressed bean curd, cut in matchstick shreds
- 1 pound snow peas, strings removed and cut in matchstick shreds

THE SIDE DISHES

- ½ pound fresh bean sprouts, heads and roots removed, blanched in boiling water for 15 seconds, rinsed in cold water and drained well
- 2 eggs, well beaten, made into 4 very thin 8-inch Egg Crepes and cut into slivers (page 74)
- ½ cup roasted peanuts, finely ground

1 cup coarsely chopped fresh
   coriander
¼ cup finely shredded scallions,
   white part only
2 tablespoons Hot Chili Bean
   Paste, Sichuan- or Hunan-
   Style (page 302) combined
   with 2 tablespoons sweet bean
   sauce or hoisin sauce
½ cup dried green seaweed
   (available in Chinese
   markets), stir-fried in 2
   teaspoons corn oil or peanut
   oil over very low heat until
   dark green and crisp, about 1
   minute (optional)

½ cup dried flat fish fillets (no
   salt added), cut with scissors
   into tiny bits and stir-fried in
   2 tablespoons corn oil over
   medium heat until crisp,
   about 2 minutes (optional)
24 Shanghai Spring Roll
   Wrappers (page 98), heated in
   a steamer

MAKING THE FILLING

Place a large heavy pot near the cooking area. Heat a wok over moderate heat for 30 seconds, or until hot. Add 3 tablespoons of the oil to the wok and swirl, then add the pork and stir-fry for 2 minutes. Splash on 1 tablespoon of the sherry and 2 tablespoons of the soy sauce and add the sugar. Stir to mix, then remove the contents of the wok and place in the large pot. Wash the wok.

Heat the wok again over moderate heat and add 2 more tablespoons of the oil. Stir-fry the shrimp for 1 minute. Splash on the remaining 1 tablespoon of sherry and add 1 teaspoon of the salt. Stir briefly, then transfer the contents of the wok to the same large pot. Heat the wok a third time over moderate heat, add the last 3 tablespoons of oil and heat, then stir-fry the bamboo shoots, carrots, and pressed bean curd for 2 minutes. Add the remaining ½ teaspoon salt and 2 tablespoons soy sauce and cook for another 2 minutes. Transfer the contents of the wok to the pot with the pork and shrimp.

Heat the large pot with all the partially cooked ingredients over low heat and bring it to the boiling point. Add the shredded snow peas, stir to mix well, and bring back to the boil. Cover and simmer for about 2 hours, stirring every 15 minutes or so. Make sure the heat is low enough so that the ingredients don't burn. When the filling is done, it should be moist but with very little sauce. It can be reheated over very low heat (this takes about 30 minutes). The filling should be served piping hot.

Heat the Shanghai Spring Roll Wrappers in a steamer (page 98).

**SERVING THE PANCAKES WITH
ACCOMPANIMENTS**

A round dining table or a large lazy Susan would be perfect for this meal. Whatever you arrange, make it easy for all your guests to reach the pancakes (wrapped in a cloth napkin to keep warm or a small steamer), filling, and accompaniments, since it is a meal of choices.

Each guest takes a wrapper and puts it on his or her own plate. Then he or she takes a few shredded scallions, dips them in the chili bean paste mixture, and places them in the center of the wrapper. Each guest then adds a little of each of the side dishes, then takes 3 to 4 tablespoons of hot filling and wraps the *popia* up around the filling and condiments, egg-roll fashion, with one end tucked in, and eats it with his fingers.

≡
Wontons
≡

Fried or Boiled Filled Wontons

馄
饨　HUNTUN

While the north is famous for its *jiao zi*, a dumpling with a thick wrapper, the south is justifiably proud of its *huntun*, or wontons, dumplings with a light, thin wrapper.

Wonton wrappers are widely available nowadays and can even be found in many non-Chinese supermarkets. I prefer the ones of medium thickness—there are about eighty of them in a one-pound package. You can also make them at home—follow the wrapper recipe on page 95.

This recipe, which has a succulent pork and spinach filling, details two popular ways of serving wontons—in a light chicken broth and shallow-fried. You could also boil them in water and serve them with the Scallion and Dried Shrimp Sauce (page 62), or with a dip of soy sauce with a little sesame oil stirred in. This recipe can be doubled or more.

When you are making the wontons, it is crucial that the wrapping be securely closed during the cooking so that the tasty filling is sealed in.

Yield: 80 wontons

> **Half of a 10-ounce package frozen chopped spinach**
> 1 **pound ground pork**
> 1 **tablespoon dry sherry**
> ½ **teaspoon coarse salt**
> ⅛ **teaspoon white pepper**
> 2 **tablespoons light soy sauce**
>
> 2 **tablespoons corn oil or peanut oil**
> 1 **pound (about 80) commercial wonton wrappers or 1 recipe homemade wonton wrappers (page 95)**

PREPARING THE FILLING AND FORMING THE WONTONS

Thaw the spinach and squeeze out most of the water. Put the pork in a mixing bowl, add the sherry, salt, pepper, and soy sauce, and stir in one direction with a spoon or chopsticks until the meat holds together. Add the spinach and oil and stir until well incorporated. Transfer the filling to a plate.

Have ½ cup cold water ready in a bowl. Cover the stack of wonton wrappers with a damp towel while wrapping to prevent them from drying out.

Take a wrapper in your hand and, using a butter knife, scrape 2 teaspoons of filling from the plate to the center of the wrapper. Fold the two corners at one end of the wrapper over the filling, making a partial triangle at the bottom; then lift the bottom over the filling and roll up almost to the far edge. Dip your finger in the water and moisten the

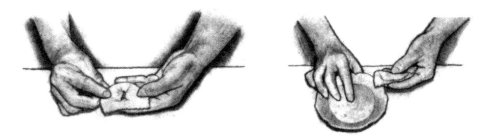

rolled edge of the wrapper. With both hands take the two ends of the rolled edge and pull them toward each other, overlapping them a tiny bit. Press the ends firmly together to seal. As each wonton is finished,

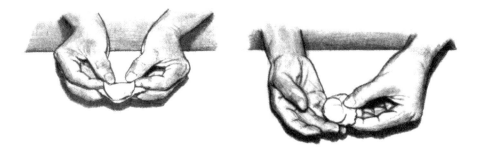

place it on a tray and cover with a cloth until ready to cook. You can keep them in the refrigerator for up to 3 hours, or freeze them at this point. They should be frozen still on the tray. When they are frozen solid, knock the tray on the edge of a table to loosen them, put them into a tightly closed plastic bag, and return to the freezer. They will keep for a month.

Wontons in Broth

This is the most common family recipe for wontons. For a light meal, plan on 10 wontons per person; the recipe calls for 20 in a pot, so you can calculate from that.

Yield: 2 servings

4 teaspoons light soy sauce
2 teaspoons sesame oil
Black or white pepper

1 teaspoon finely chopped
   whole scallions (optional)
1½ cups light chicken broth
20 wontons, fresh or frozen

Over moderate heat bring 1 quart of water to a boil. Meanwhile, put in each of two large soup bowls 2 teaspoons light soy sauce, 1 teaspoon sesame oil, a dash of black or white pepper, and ½ teaspoon finely chopped whole scallions if desired.

Bring the chicken broth to a boil and turn the heat down. Drop the wontons into the quart of boiling water. Gently stir a few times. When the water boils again, add ½ cup cold water. When it boils a third time, the wontons are ready.

Turn off the heat and scoop out the wontons with a slotted spoon and put them in the soup bowls—10 to each. Stir to coat them with the sauce. Add about ¾ cup broth to each bowl. You now have soup, meat, vegetables, and starch all in one bowl—a simple and very satisfying meal.

Shallow-Fried Wontons

Heat a well-seasoned large skillet (a heavy iron or nonstick one is fine) over moderate heat. Add 2 to 3 tablespoons of oil to cover the pan and heat. Put as many fresh or frozen wontons close together in the pan as you can, including the center of the pan. When the bottoms of the wontons turn light brown, add about 6 to 8 tablespoons of water. Cover and cook until the water evaporates—about 3 minutes.

Uncover and let the wonton bottoms fry some more, until a dark-brown crust forms and the wontons start to puff—about 1 to 2 minutes. Do not overcook them. Transfer them from the pan to a plate with the brown side up.

Serve hot with chopsticks or a fork, accompanied by a vinegar-and-chili pepper sauce as a dip (page 138).

Fried Wontons with Curry Filling

酥
炸
馄

SU ZHA HUNTUN

Deep-fried wontons are very popular with Americans. They like them served with a sweet-and-sour sauce on top or dipped in duck sauce, which also has a sweet-and-sour taste. The Chinese prefer them without sauce but with a strong-flavored filling. This curry filling is liked by both Americans and Chinese. It is moist and very exotic tasting.

For this recipe buy the thin wrappers (about 120 per pound). Have ½ cup of cold water ready in a dish. Cover the stack of wonton wrappers with a damp cloth while forming the wontons so they won't dry out. You could also use the recipe for homemade wonton wrappers, the thin variety (page 95), or store-bought wontons, the thin variety.

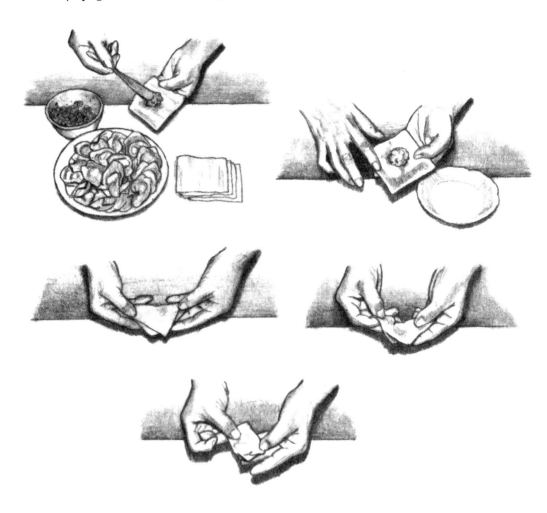

Yield: 80–120 deep-fried wontons

120 wonton wrappers   **About 2 cups of oil**
1 recipe curry puff filling
(page 191)

FORMING THE WONTONS
Place the filling on a plate. Using a butter knife, scrape 1 teaspoon of filling from the plate to the center of a wrapper. Dip your fingers in the cold water and moisten two adjacent sides. Fold the wrapper from one corner a little beyond the diagonal corner, leaving a little of the edge exposed. Dip your fingers in the water again and wet the side ends. With both hands pull the two ends together until they meet and overlap. Press the ends firmly together to seal. As each wonton is finished, place it on a tray and cover with a damp cloth, wrung out well, until you are ready to deep-fry them. They can stay refrigerated for a few hours, or you can freeze them uncooked, but you must take them out of the freezer 30 minutes before cooking them.

DEEP-FRYING THE WONTONS
Heat a wok, add at least 2 inches oil, and heat until the oil reaches 350 degrees. Fry the wontons a few at a time on both sides—about 2 minutes in all, or until the wontons are crisp and light golden. Keep in a 200-degree oven with the door ajar while you fry the remaining wontons. Serve hot.

Fried wontons can be cooked hours ahead of time and reheated in a 450-degree oven for 2 to 3 minutes, until they are hot and crisp.

Shao Mai (Open-Faced Steamed Wontons or Dumplings)

烧
卖
SHAO MAI

Dumplings in central and southern China are smaller than those made in the north, and the wrapper is much thinner. They are usually served as a snack instead of as a meal. This very thin homemade wrapper is delicate in texture, and the rice in the filling is quite unusual—a specialty of Shanghai. The Cantonese prefer a meat filling or meat with shrimp. The wonton filling on page 119 would also be very good.

The very thin commercial wonton wrappers may be used. Cut out rounds with a cookie cutter about 2½ inches in diameter. Form the same way you would homemade shao mai. Apply some water to the edges before steaming.

Yield: 60 shao mai, 1 inch wide × 1½ inches high

THE FILLING

1 cup glutinous rice
⅞ cup chicken broth, preferably homemade
4 dried black Chinese mushrooms
½ pound finely chopped Chinese Roast Pork with some fat attached (page 208)

¼ cup finely chopped bamboo shoots
2 tablespoons corn oil or peanut oil
1 teaspoon coarse salt or to taste
½ teaspoon sugar

THE WRAPPERS

2 cups all-purpose flour

About ⅔ cup hot water (about 150°, hot to the touch but not scalding)

MAKING THE FILLING

Wash the rice and drain it. Put it in a heatproof bowl, add the chicken broth, and let it soak for 30 minutes. Wash the mushrooms and soak them in ½ cup warm water for 30 minutes.

Place the bowl containing the rice in a pot with cold water about 1½ inches below the bowl's rim. Cover the pot and bring the water to a boil; steam over medium-high heat for 30 minutes. After cooking, the rice looks shiny, with the grains stuck together; it is soft but slightly chewy.

Drain the mushrooms, reserving the soaking water. Cut off and discard the stems, then finely chop the caps. You should have about ¼ cup. Set aside with the chopped roast pork and bamboo shoots.

Heat a wok for 30 seconds. Add the oil and swirl, then add the bamboo shoots and mushrooms and stir-fry for 2 minutes. Add the roast pork, steamed rice, salt, sugar, and reserved mushroom water; scoop and toss gently but thoroughly. Remove and set aside.

MAKING THE WRAPPERS

Put the flour in a large mixing bowl. Add the hot water and stir to mix well, forming a pliable but firm dough. You may need more water. Add it one tablespoon at a time. Knead the dough on a lightly floured work surface for about 3 to 4 minutes, or until very smooth; then cover with plastic wrap and let sit for 15 minutes.

Divide the dough in half. Keep one half covered and knead the other for 1 minute on a lightly floured work surface; then shape it with your hands into a cylinder about 15 inches long. Cut into thirty ½-inch pieces. Dust the cut sides lightly with flour. Press each piece with the palm of your hand to flatten it. Cover the disks with plastic wrap while you do the final shaping.

Take one disk at a time and press it with the heel of your hand to flatten it some more. Using a small rolling pin, roll it on a lightly floured work surface into a paper-thin (almost transparent) circle about 2½ inches in diameter. As you roll the pin with one hand, feed and turn the wrapper with the other to keep the shape round and make the edges like a ruffle, much thinner than the center. Stack the finished disks overlapping and cover them with a dry cloth to prevent them from drying out. It is better to fill these and then shape wrappers from the other half of the dough than to do all of them now, so that the wrappers will still be soft and pliable enough to work with.

SHAPING AND STEAMING THE DUMPLINGS
Place 1 tablespoon of filling in the center of a disk. Gather up the edges of the wrapper to hold in the filling, letting the wrapper form small pleats. Squeeze the middle gently to make sure the wrapper sticks firmly

to the filling. Holding the sides with both hands, press the bottom down on a flat surface so that the dumpling can stand, with the filling exposed at the top. Leave a narrow ruffled border of the wrapper at the top unattached to the filling. Place the filled dumplings on an oiled plate 1 inch smaller in diameter than your steamer. Cover with plastic wrap and form the rest of the dumplings from the other half of the dough.

You could refrigerate the dumplings covered with plastic for a few hours, or freeze them. In that case put them on a tray and freeze them until solid; then hit the tray on the edge of a table to loosen them, and put them in a tightly closed plastic bag, and return them to the freezer. They will stay fresh in the freezer for up to one month.

Put the oiled plate with fresh or frozen dumplings on it on top of a steamer rack or, if you have a bamboo steamer, place them on individually cut-out squares of aluminum foil or on a damp oiled cloth and put them on the rack. Cover the pot tightly and steam over medium-high heat for 5 minutes (1 minute longer for frozen dumplings). Serve hot.

Variation: Substitute cooked Smithfield ham for the Chinese roast pork if you like a saltier taste.

Wonton Duck Soup in Casserole

全
鸭
沙
锅
馄
饨 QUAN YA SHA GUO HUNTON

Here is an elegant and utterly delicious wonton soup from the eastern provinces of Zhejiang and Jiangsu, featuring a whole duck as well as wontons, Smithfield ham, and snow peas.

I like to make more wontons than I need for this recipe and keep the rest in the freezer for other meals to serve with sauces (see the two sauces for boiled dumplings, page 139; they are the sauces from Beijing and from Hunan province that are most often served with dumplings). This recipe calls for 40 wontons, but the filling here is sufficient for 80.

Yield: Serves 4 as a meal in itself

1 duck, fresh or frozen, about 4–4½ pounds
2 quarter-size pieces peeled fresh ginger, lightly crushed with the flat of a knife
2 teaspoons coarse salt
2 tablespoons dry sherry
1 large stalk scallion

1 pound very thin wonton wrappers (about 120)—you'll make about 80 wontons. Freeze the remaining in foil.
Salt and pepper, to taste
10 very thin slices cooked Smithfield ham 1 × 1½ inches (page 324)
20 snow peas, strings removed
4 tablespoons light soy sauce

THE FILLING FOR THE WONTONS

½ pound raw shrimp
1½ teaspoons coarse salt
1 small egg white
4 dried black Chinese mushrooms, soaked in warm water till soft, stems removed and caps finely chopped
2 tablespoons finely chopped bamboo shoots

1 teaspoon finely chopped fresh ginger
1 pound ground veal or pork
½ teaspoon sugar
1 tablespoon dry sherry
1 tablespoon light soy sauce
1 teaspoon cornstarch
⅛ teaspoon white pepper
2 tablespoons sesame oil

PREPARING AND COOKING THE DUCK
Remove the duck's neck and giblets and save for another use. Trim the excess skin around the neck and the cavity. Remove all fat from the

cavity and along the neck, if any. Rinse and drain the duck and set it on a large plate. Rub the crushed ginger over the outside and inside of the duck and then discard it. Sprinkle the salt inside and outside and rub some more. Set the duck aside for at least 30 minutes or for as long as 2 hours.

Rinse the duck with cold water, put it in a 4-quart casserole, add about 2 quarts of cold water, and bring to a boil. Remove any foam, then add the sherry and scallion. Reduce the heat to low and cover so that the water simmers gently. Cook for 2 hours, or until the meat of the duck can be lifted easily with chopsticks. Remove and discard the scallion and all the fat that has floated to the top (to do this very easily, let the duck soup cool completely). If you want to remove the duck bones and cut the meat into small pieces, this is the best time to do so. Up to this point this dish may be prepared ahead of time. The duck, boned or still whole, should remain in the broth.

MAKING THE WONTON FILLING

While the duck is cooking, make the filling: Shell and devein the shrimp. Rinse, drain, and dry the shrimp with paper towels. With a cleaver, coarsely chop the shrimp and put it in a bowl. Add ½ teaspoon of the salt and the egg white, and with your fingers or chopsticks, mix them in until they coat the chopped shrimp evenly. Set the shrimp in the refrigerator. Put the prepared mushrooms, bamboo shoots, and ginger on a plate.

Put the veal in a mixing bowl. Add the remaining 1 teaspoon of salt and the sugar, sherry, soy sauce, cornstarch, and pepper. Stir in one direction until the meat holds together. Add the mushrooms, bamboo shoots, ginger, shrimp, and sesame oil and mix until completely combined, then transfer the filling to a plate, where it will be easy to scoop onto a wrapper with a butter knife.

FILLING THE WONTONS

Cover the wrappers with a damp dish towel to prevent them from drying out while you make the wontons. Take one wonton wrapper at a time in the palm of your hand and, with a butter knife, put 1 heaping teaspoon of filling—about the size of a large grape—in the center. Using a chopstick, push the edges of the wrapper up to the center to adhere the wrapper to the meat; then squeeze gently. The filled wonton should look like a little ball about 1 inch wide. Set the wonton, closed side down, on a tray.

Continue making wontons until all the filling is used up—you'll have about 80 wontons. If you aren't cooking the finished wontons right away, cover them with plastic wrap and refrigerate them for a few hours. They can also be frozen on the tray; when solid, transfer them to a plastic bag and keep them in the freezer. In this recipe you will need 40 wontons; the remaining can be frozen. Do not defrost frozen wontons before boiling them; simply cook them 1 minute longer.

FINISHING THE CASSEROLE AND SERVING IT

Bring the duck casserole to a boil. Lower the heat to medium so the broth is gently simmering. Add salt and pepper to taste, then scatter in the ham, snow peas, and wontons. Cover and simmer for 5 minutes. Take the casserole to the table. Ladle some soup, wontons, duck, ham, and snow peas into individual bowls; if the duck is whole, pull the meat away with chopsticks and put some in each bowl.

Serve the soup with 1 tablespoon of light soy sauce in individual small sauce dishes for each person, so he or she can season the soup and wontons as desired.

Yan Pi Wontons and Dragon's Beard Wontons

燕皮馄饨、龙须燕丸 YAN PI HUNTUN AND LONG XU YAN WAN

Yan pi, a specialty of Fujian province in the southeast of China, is a wrapper made from ground pork that is pounded into a paste and combined with wheat flour and liquid to make a dough. The dough is rolled into a thin sheet, which is then dried. Because of this complex process, Chinese families do not make these wrappers at home. You can purchase them in boxes at Chinese markets. When very fresh, they are slightly damp and give off the marvelous smell of fresh dough.

Uncooked *yan pi* is grayish white; after cooking it becomes translucent and the texture is somewhat crisp. There are two ways to use this kind of wrapper: One is to cut the sheet into 2½-inch squares, to use as wrappers; the other is to cut it into very fine shreds. These strips are pressed around small meatballs, which are steamed and then added to chicken broth.

Since *yan pi* is essentially a meat product, the sheets should be stored, tightly wrapped, in the refrigerator, where they will keep for months.

Yield: 30 yan pi *wontons, serving 4 as a light meal*

¼ **cup dried shrimp, covered with cold water and soaked for 15 minutes**	1 **tablespoon light soy sauce**
4 **large dried black Chinese mushrooms, soaked in ¾ cup warm water until soft, about 30 minutes**	20 *yan pi* **sheets, each 3 × 6 inches**
1 **pound finely ground pork, about 2 cups**	4 **cups Best Chicken Broth (page 77)**
1 **teaspoon coarse salt**	1 **cup watercress leaves or ½ cup fresh coriander leaves with tender stems**
	Salt and pepper to taste

MAKING THE SHRIMP AND PORK MIXTURE

Drain the shrimp and mushrooms, reserving the mushroom liquid (½ cup); finely chop the shrimp and mushrooms without stems and set aside.

Combine the pork with the reserved mushroom liquid, add salt and soy sauce, and stir in one direction until the meat holds together. Add the shrimp and mushrooms and stir some more. Set aside. Lightly oil two 8-inch plates and set aside.

USING *YAN PI* STRIPS WITH MEATBALLS

Using a water sprayer, lightly spray one side of each *yan pi* sheet (do not overspray). Stack them in one pile, cover with a dish towel, and let them rest for 10 minutes. Then cut the damp sheets into strips 1 inch long and ⅛ inch wide. Toss to loosen them; you should have about 2 cups. Scatter the strips on a baking tray.

With a teaspoon and your hands, scoop up a spoonful of meat mixture and then form 15 balls 1 inch in diameter (about half the mixture); put them on top of the shredded *yan pi*. Roll each meatball around in the *yan pi* shreds so they adhere to the meat as much as possible; then let the coated ball bounce along on your palm so that it becomes round. Put the coated meatballs on a lightly oiled plate as you finish them, 15 to a plate. Scoop up, form, and coat the rest of the meatballs; you should have about 30 of them.

USING *YAN PI* WRAPPERS WITH MEATBALLS

If you prefer using the *yan pi* as wrappers, cut a dampened sheet into thirty 2½-inch squares. Spray a little more water on one side of each square. Form thirty small meatballs. Put a meatball in the center of the square and gather up the edges over the meat as neatly as possible. Put the meatballs, closed side down, on a lightly oiled plate, fifteen to a plate.

STEAMING COATED OR WRAPPED
MEATBALLS AND MAKING THE SOUP
Put the two plates of wontons on two tiers of a 10-inch bamboo steamer, or do them one plate at a time in a large pot. Steam them over high heat for 8 minutes. The coated shreds or the wrappers may be dry in some places, but do not worry about this.

Bring the chicken broth to a boil in a large pot. Add the coriander or watercress, reduce the heat to low, then add the steamed meatballs and cook for 1 minute. Add salt and pepper to taste. You can coat or wrap the meatballs and steam them hours ahead of time; keep them in plastic wrap until you're ready to heat them in the broth.

Miniature Firecrackers (Date Wontons)

 ZAO NI HUNTUN

枣
泥
馄
饨

Twenty-five years ago, on my first out-of-town demonstration of Chinese cooking, the class I was teaching modified these classic date-and-walnut wontons. They formed them into small firecracker shapes rather than the traditional "nurse's cap" wontons and added grated orange rind to the filling and a sprinkling of powdered sugar on top.

These elegant dessert wontons are traditionally served with hot tea, either after a meal or as a sweet snack. They can be kept in a covered container for up to two weeks.

If you don't have the time to make homemade wrappers, buy the commercial ones, but cut them into smaller squares, 2 by 2 inches.

Yield: 140 miniature firecrackers

THE FILLING

8 ounces pitted dates
½ cup finely chopped walnuts
2 teaspoons grated orange rind
Orange juice (optional)
1 recipe homemade Cantonese
Spring Roll Wrappers, rolled
very thin and cut into 2-inch
squares (page 95), or 1 pound
very thin commercial wonton
wrappers, cut into 2-inch
squares (about 140)

2 cups corn oil or peanut oil
2 tablespoons confectioner's
sugar

MAKING THE FILLING AND FORMING THE WONTONS

Chop the dates fine and combine with the walnuts and orange rind.
Add a little orange juice if the filling is too dry. Squeeze the filling with
your hands to make it smoother. The filling can be made days ahead of
time; refrigerate it wrapped in plastic. To form the filling, wet your
hands with some water and shape the filling into tiny sausage shapes
about 1 inch long and ⅓ inch thick. Set on plates and cover with wax
paper.

Cover the cut wrappers with a damp dish towel while you work so
they don't dry out. Place one roll of filling at one corner of a wrapper
and roll the wrapper up around it; pinch to seal, dabbing the far edge
with water if you are using commercial wrappers. Twist both free ends
to enclose the filling but leave the outer edge open, like ears. Cover the
finished wontons with a damp dish towel. You will be making about 140
"firecrackers."

DEEP-FRYING THE WONTONS

Heat the oil in a wok to 350 degrees and slip in about 20 wontons at a
time; deep-fry until crisp and golden brown—about 3 to 4 minutes.
Scoop out with a slotted spoon and drain on paper towels, allowing
them to cool completely. Arrange them on a platter lined with paper
doilies. Sift some confectioner's sugar on top.

☰ Dumplings ☰

Boiled Dumplings, Beijing-Style, with Three Fillings and Two Sauces

饺
子 JIAO ZI

About one-third of all Chinese daily meals consist of wheat noodles and/ or buns accompanied by a simple meat-and-vegetable dish, or *jiao zi* alone (the Chinese equivalent of tortellini or ravioli) filled with meat and vegetables. *Jiao zi* can become a whole meal in themselves. The Chinese almost always eat them during the holidays, when the entire family is around to pitch in to wrap them. In the north of China everyone knows how to make *jiao zi*. When I was young I could eat thirty *jiao zi* at one meal, and I never tired of them.

Although the wrappers can be bought, a true northerner wouldn't consider that option. I am one of them.

Jiao zi aren't difficult to make; in fact, after a few tries you will probably want to double the recipe, or even triple and quadruple it. In that case put the uncooked *jiao zi* you don't need on a baking sheet and let them freeze until they are solid. Hit the baking sheet on a table to loosen the *jiao zi,* then put them in an airtight bag and return them to the freezer— for up to a month. Cooking frozen *jiao zi* takes only 30 seconds to 1 minute longer than cooking fresh ones.

I have included three fillings for boiled dumplings, Beijing-style: The first is the most popular and the most traditional—the meat and vegetable; then there is the vegetarian filling (page 140), and finally the fish filling (page 139). You can also use the Beijing-style fried filling (beef and scallions, page 141) or steamed filling (shrimp and pork, page 145).

Yield: 30 large or 40 small jiao zi

THE DOUGH FOR BOILED DUMPLING WRAPPERS

2 cups all-purpose flour   **¾ cup cold water, approximately**

Meat and Vegetable Fillings

ROU JIAO

2 cups hand-chopped or food processor pulse-chopped celery cabbage, Chinese cabbage (bok choy), or green cabbage

4 large dried black Chinese mushrooms, washed, soaked 30 minutes in warm water, stems discarded and caps finely chopped

1 teaspoon minced fresh ginger (optional)

2 tablespoons chopped whole scallions or ½ cup chopped Chinese chives

1 pound ground pork

¼ cup chicken broth or water

1 teaspoon coarse salt or to taste

2 tablespoons light soy sauce

1 tablespoon dry sherry

1 tablespoon corn oil or peanut oil

2 tablespoons sesame oil

2 teaspoons coarse salt for boiling the dumplings

MAKING THE DUMPLING DOUGH IN A FOOD PROCESSOR

I find that the easiest way to mix and knead the dumpling dough is with a food processor. Put the flour in the bowl fitted with the steel blade. Because of its gentle pulse action, the dough will be less "tight" than if processed without interruption. Press "pulse" twenty or thirty times while gradually adding the water. Stop the machine and pinch the texture of the dough to see whether it is soft but holds its shape firmly. When you have this texture, continue processing for 1 minute to knead it. Then take it out, including the bits that remain at the bottom of the bowl. With the heel of your hand, gently knead these into the dough on a lightly floured work surface. Cover the dough with plastic wrap and let it rest at room temperature for 30 minutes.

MAKING THE DUMPLING DOUGH BY HAND

Put the flour in a large mixing bowl. Slowly add the water while you mix with your fingers or chopsticks until the dough just holds together. Knead the dough in the bowl to gather up any bits of dough into a ball. The dough should be soft but not sticky. Place it on a lightly floured work surface and knead for at least 5 minutes, or until it is very smooth. Cover with a damp dish towel and let rest for 30 minutes.

MAKING THE MEAT-AND-VEGETABLE FILLING

If you are chopping the cabbage in the food processor, you needn't wash the bowl. Cut the cabbage into large chunks and put these in the bowl. Using the pulse action, chop the cabbage with about eight to ten pulses—do not chop too fine. Then parboil the cabbage for 2 minutes. Drain and press most of the water out; there should be about ½ cup. Set the cabbage on a plate with the chopped mushrooms, minced ginger, and scallions or chives.

Put the ground pork in a large mixing bowl and gradually add the chicken broth or water while stirring with chopsticks in one direction until the meat holds together. Add the salt, soy sauce, sherry, cabbage, mushrooms, ginger, scallions or chives, and corn and sesame oil, mixing until completely combined. The filling should be shiny, fragrant, and light, but it should hold together. Transfer it to a plate, cover with plastic wrap, and refrigerate while you make the wrappers.

FORMING THE WRAPPERS AND MAKING THE DUMPLINGS
Divide the dumpling dough in half. Keep one half under plastic wrap while you knead the other for a few turns; then roll it with your hands into a cylinder about 12 inches long and 1 inch wide. Break or cut this into fifteen pieces. Sprinkle some flour on the pieces and move them around so that the cut side is lightly coated (this will prevent them from sticking together), then press with the palm of your hand to flatten each piece. Cover the disks with plastic wrap.

Taking one disk of dough, press it with the heel of your hand to flatten it some more; then, with a small rolling pin, roll it into a circle 3 inches in diameter. To make the circle as perfect as possible, the rolling pin should be rolled with the palm of one hand while you feed and turn the disk of dough counterclockwise with the fingers of the other hand. Try to roll from the edges to the center, so the edges are thinner than the center. Stack the wrappers so they overlap. If you have a noodle-making machine, roll out the dough by machine at the next-to-last setting and then cut the sheet with a cookie cutter into 3-inch rounds. When you have formed these fifteen wrappers, fill them before working the other half of the dough.

Taking one wrapper at a time, scoop 1 heaping tablespoon of filling from the plate with a butter knife and put it in the center of the wrapper. Fold the edge over to make a half-moon shape. Then, with your forefinger and thumb, press and twist the edge into small pleats.

The finished *jiao zi* will be crescent-shaped, with pleats on the back side.

Arrange the *jiao zi* on a floured tray and cover with a dry cloth if you aren't cooking them right away (they can rest for a few hours if refrigerated). You can also freeze them on the tray at this point. When they are frozen solid, hit the tray on the edge of a table to loosen them; then put them in a tightly closed plastic bag and return them to the freezer.

Make and fill wrappers from the other half of the dough.

USING STORE-BOUGHT WRAPPERS

The round, frozen Japanese *jiao-zi* wrappers are very high quality. Completely defrost before using. Put 1 heaping tablespoon of filling in the center of each wrapper. With your fingers, smear the edges with water, fold the dumpling over, then pleat and press tightly to seal. As you work, keep the wrappers covered with a damp cloth so they don't dry out.

BOILING THE DUMPLINGS

Bring 3 quarts of water to a rolling boil in a large pot over high heat. Add 2 teaspoons of salt, which will seal the dough. Then add the fresh or frozen *jiao zi* and gently stir a few times with a wooden spoon—enough to make sure they don't stick to the pot. Bring the water back to the boil and then slowly add 1 cup of cold water. Let the water come back to the boil, and slowly add another cup of cold water. When the water boils again and the *jiao zi* are slightly puffy, scoop them out with a strainer and place on a plate. (The cooking time for store-bought wrappers depends on their thickness; they are usually thinner than home-made ones and will generally need a minute or so less time. Homemade fresh *jiao zi* are done in about 5 minutes total. Frozen ones take a minute or so more to cook.)

SERVING THE DUMPLINGS

Serve the *jiao zi* hot with a simple dip of Zhejiang or red wine vinegar and hot chili sauce: 1 tablespoon of vinegar to ½ teaspoon of chili sauce for each person, in individual dishes. You can use tabasco sauce, which has vinegar and hot chili in it, or one of the two following sauces. The first is pungent; the second is peppery.

Scallion and Ginger Sauce

Yield: ½ cup

2 tablespoons sesame oil
2 teaspoons minced fresh ginger
2 tablespoons chopped whole
   scallions

3 tablespoons light soy sauce
2 teaspoons red wine vinegar
¼ cup chicken broth
1 teaspoon sugar

Heat the sesame oil in a small saucepan over low heat. Add the ginger and scallions, and let them sizzle for 10 seconds. Add the remaining ingredients and heat for another 10 seconds, stirring. Divide the sauce into individual dip dishes.

Black Bean Chili Sauce

Yield: ½ cup

1 tablespoon light soy sauce
1 tablespoon dry sherry
2 teaspoons sugar
¼ teaspoon coarse salt or to taste
2 tablespoons chicken broth or
   water
2 tablespoons chopped whole
   scallions

2 tablespoons corn oil or peanut
   oil
2 tablespoons salted black beans,
   rinsed and drained
1 teaspoon chili pepper flakes
1 clove garlic, finely chopped

Put into a small bowl the soy sauce, sherry, sugar, salt, chicken broth, and scallions and mix well. Set aside.

Heat the oil in a small saucepan. Add the black beans and chili pepper and cook for 1 minute. Stir in the garlic and cook for 30 seconds. Remove from heat, add the bowl of ingredients, and stir to mix well. Adjust seasonings with salt if you wish. Divide the sauce into individual dishes.

Fish Filling

鱼 YÜ JIAO

饺 About ten years ago six young couples who were Orthodox Jews asked me to teach them Chinese cooking in their own homes, using kosher ingredients. The lessons were very satisfying and successful; and

I never had to use the second sink or second set of dishes, because Chinese cooking does not use dairy products. All I had to do was substitute chicken, turkey, beef, veal, or fish for any pork or shellfish. This fish-filled dumpling or wonton was one of the most popular of my lessons.

1 pound fillet of scrod, cod, or other white fish, such as sea bass, red snapper, sole, or flounder, cut into 2-inch pieces
2 tablespoons chicken broth or water with a pinch of msg
1 egg white
1 tablespoon dry sherry

1 teaspoon coarse salt or to taste
3 tablespoons corn oil or peanut oil
2 tablespoons sesame oil
¼ teaspoon white pepper
1 cup chopped Chinese chives or regular leeks

Using a food processor fitted with the steel blade, put the cut-up fish in the bowl and add the broth or water. Make pulse action twenty or thirty times. Add the remaining ingredients and continue with ten more pulses, or until the filling is fairly smooth. Dish it out onto a plate, cover, and refrigerate for 30 minutes to firm it.

If you hand-chop the fish, do the job with one or two cleavers, dribbling water on the fish periodically. Chop until the fish becomes fairly smooth. Put it in a bowl and stir in the remaining ingredients.

Vegetarian Filling

 SU JIAO

3 cups finely chopped green cabbage
1 cup finely chopped hearts of celery
10 large dried black Chinese mushrooms, soaked in warm water till soft, or 12 ounces fresh mushrooms, chopped by hand or in a food processor

6 tablespoons corn oil or peanut oil
2 tablespoons light soy sauce
¼ teaspoon sugar
2 teaspoons minced fresh ginger
1 teaspoon coarse salt, or to taste

PREPARING THE FILLING

If you have already mixed and kneaded the dumpling dough in a food processor, there is no need to wash the bowl. Cut the cabbage into chunks and toss them into the bowl. Using the pulse action, chop the cabbage for eight to ten pulses. Transfer to a bowl. Chop the celery the same way and add to the cabbage. Squeeze the mushrooms over the soaking bowl and reserve the liquid. Cut off and discard the stems and finely chop the mushroom caps. Set aside in a small bowl.

COOKING THE FILLING

Heat a wok over moderate heat. Add 2 tablespoons of the oil, swirl, then stir-fry the mushrooms for 1 minute. Add the soy sauce and sugar, stir to mix, then add the reserved mushroom water and cook until the liquid dissipates and the mushrooms are fairly dry. If you use fresh mushrooms you may have to cook them longer—about 5 minutes. Dish them out.

Using the same wok, add the remaining 4 tablespoons oil and heat, then add the ginger, celery, and cabbage and stir-fry for about 4 minutes or until the vegetables are dry. Add the salt and stir to mix. Return the mushrooms to the wok and toss briefly. Taste and correct the seasoning with salt if needed. Scoop the filling out onto a plate and let it cool before you use it. The filling is enough for one recipe of dough. It can be used for boiled, fried, or steamed dumplings.

Variation: Add a 3 × 3 × 1-inch piece of fresh mashed bean curd to the filling, with 2 tablespoons of sesame oil. Increase sugar to ½ teaspoon and add more salt if necessary.

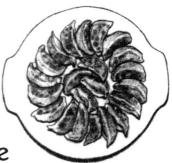

Fried Dumplings, Beijing-Style

锅
贴 GUO TIE

Guo tie literally means "pot stickers." These dumplings are fried *jiao zi*. They are first pan-fried and then steamed with a little water in the pan, during which they take on a crisp golden brown texture on the bottom and a soft one on top, bursting with juice inside. The best way to eat these juicy dumplings is to pick one up with chopsticks and immediately transfer it to a soup spoon, so that when you bite into it, you lose none of the delicious juice.

Guo tie may be prepared ahead of time and frozen. The beef filling here is very tasty, but you could also use the meat-and-vegetable filling for Boiled Dumplings, Beijing-Style (page 135) or the shrimp-and-pork filling for Steamed Dumplings, Beijing-Style (page 145). For a first course or a snack, serve them with the vinegar-and-chili pepper paste as a dip (page 138) or the two sauces for *jiao zi*—Boiled Dumplings, Beijing-Style (page 139). Accompanied by the Yangzhou Noodle Soup in Casserole (page 82) or the Brown Bean and Meat Sauce on Noodles (page 59), they make a delicious, nourishing meal.

Yield: 30 guo tie

THE *GUO TIE* DOUGH

2 cups all-purpose flour

¾ cup boiling water, approximately

THE BEEF FILLING

1 pound ground round steak
6 tablespoons chicken broth or water
3 tablespoons light soy sauce
1 teaspoon coarse salt or to taste
⅛ teaspoon white pepper
1 tablespoon dry sherry

3 tablespoons corn oil or peanut oil
2 tablespoons sesame oil
1 tablespoon finely minced fresh ginger
1 cup loosely packed chopped whole scallions

2–3 tablespoons corn oil or peanut oil

MAKING THE *GUO TIE* DOUGH
WITH A FOOD PROCESSOR
If you are making the dough in a food processor, put the flour in the bowl fitted with the steel blade. Make the pulse action about twenty or thirty times while you gradually add the water. Turn the machine "on" until a soft but not sticky dough forms—about 10 seconds. Do not let it spin more than this or it will stick to the work bowl. Take the dough out and knead it on a lightly floured work surface until it is smooth—about 1 minute. Put the dough in a tightly closed plastic bag and let it rest for 15 minutes or longer.

MAKING THE DUMPLINGS BY HAND

If you are making the dough by hand, put the flour in a large mixing bowl. Slowly add the boiling water while you stir with chopsticks until the flour is all damp and has separated into small pieces of soft dough. Gently knead the damp dough in the bowl. If the dough seems too dry, add a little boiling water—about 1 tablespoon. The dough should be soft-firm but not dry. Put it on a lightly floured work surface and knead it until very smooth—about 3 minutes. Put the warm dough in a tightly closed plastic bag and let it rest for 15 minutes or longer.

MAKING THE BEEF FILLING

Put the beef in a mixing bowl and gradually add the broth or water while stirring in one direction until the meat holds together. Add the soy sauce, salt, pepper, sherry, corn and sesame oils, ginger, and scallions and stir some more. The filling should be shiny, fragrant, and light, but it should hold together. Scoop it onto a plate and refrigerate until ready to use.

SHAPING THE WRAPPERS AND
MAKING THE DUMPLINGS

Divide the dough in two; leave one part in the plastic bag and roll the other with your hands into a cylinder about 12 inches long. Cut it into fifteen pieces. Sprinkle some flour on them and move them around so the cut side is lightly coated with flour, preventing the pieces from sticking together. Press each piece with the palm of your hand to flatten it. Cover the disks with plastic wrap.

Taking one piece of dough, press it with the heel of your hand to flatten it some more; then, with a small rolling pin, roll it into a circle 3 inches in diameter. To make the circle as perfect as possible, roll the pin with the palm of one hand while you feed and turn the disk of dough with the fingers of the other. Try to roll from the edges to the center, so the edges are thinner than the center. Stack the wrappers overlapping.

Working one wrapper at a time, scoop 1 heaping tablespoon of filling from the plate with a small spreader and put it in the center of the wrapper. Fold the edge over to make a half-moon shape. Then, with your thumb and forefinger, press and twist the edge into pleats. The finished dumpling will be crescent-shaped, with pleats along the back side. Arrange the *guo tie* on a floured tray and cover with a dry cloth if you aren't cooking them right away (they can rest refrigerated for a few hours), or freeze them uncovered on the tray until solid. At that point hit the tray on a table to loosen the *guo tie,* put them in a tightly closed plastic bag, and return them to the freezer.

Make the other half of the dough into wrappers and fill as described.

FILLING STORE-BOUGHT WRAPPERS

The Japanese round frozen wrappers are very high quality. Completely defrost them before using. Put 1 heaping tablespoon of filling in the center of each wrapper. With your fingers smear the edges with water, fold the dumplings over, then pleat and press tightly to seal. As you work, keep the remaining wrappers covered with a damp dish towel to prevent them from drying out.

FRYING THE DUMPLINGS

Use a 10-inch skillet for fifteen dumplings or a 14-inch skillet for thirty dumplings; the skillet should preferably be nonstick, so that if the dumplings aren't properly sealed, they can easily be removed when done. Heat the skillet over high heat until hot, add 2 tablespoons of oil (3 for a 14-inch skillet) and swirl, then turn the heat to medium-high. Place the dumplings in a winding circle in the pan. When the bottoms of the dumplings turn light brown—in about 1 minute—add 6 tablespoons of water. Cover and cook until the water evaporates—about 5 minutes. Uncover and let the dumplings fry a little more—about 2 to 3 minutes—until a dark-brown crust forms on the bottom and the dumplings start to puff up. Transfer the dumplings from the pan to a serving plate, setting them browned side up. Serve with either of the two sauces that accompany the Boiled Dumplings, Beijing-Style, page 135.

Steamed Dumplings, Beijing-Style

 蒸 饺 CHENG JIAO

These delicate steamed dumplings, a specialty of Beijing, are usually served right from a bamboo steamer, which not only is very attractive but also has the advantage over a metal steamer that it won't retain excess moisture on the cover, which then drips on the food during steaming.

To prevent the dumplings from sticking to the steamer rack, place the traditional parboiled bok choy leaves on the rack and arrange the dumplings on top, or cut 1½-inch squares of aluminum foil for each dumpling (don't use a sheet of it or it will block the heat). A third method, the easiest of all, is to oil the rack right before arranging the dumplings for steaming, but you must remember to wash the steamer with soap and water right afterward, so the oil doesn't remain and turn rancid when you store the steamer.

Since these dumplings have a delicate, subtle taste, you should accompany them with something hearty, such as Shredded Pork and Red-in-Snow Noodle Soup (page 87) and Scallion Pancakes (page 162).

Yield: 30 large dumplings

1 recipe Fried Dumplings,   Beijing-Style dough (page 141)

THE FILLING

½ **pound raw shrimp**
6 **large dried black Chinese mushrooms, soaked in warm water until soft**
½ **cup finely chopped bamboo shoots**
2 **teaspoons minced fresh ginger**
½ **pound ground pork, with some fat**

¼ **cup chicken broth**
1 **teaspoon coarse salt or to taste**
1 **tablespoon light soy sauce**
1 **tablespoon dry sherry**
2 **tablespoons corn oil or peanut oil**
1 **tablespoon sesame oil**

MAKING THE FILLING

Shell and devein the shrimp. Wash and drain, then pat them dry with paper towels. Chop them fine and set them on a large plate. Finely chop the soaked mushroom caps, discarding the stems, and put them on the same plate with the shrimp, adding the bamboo shoots and the ginger.

Put the pork in a large mixing bowl and gradually add the broth while stirring in one direction until the meat holds together. Add the salt, soy sauce, sherry, shrimp, ginger, bamboo shoots, mushrooms, and the corn and sesame oils. Stir thoroughly; the filling should be shiny, fragrant, and fully combined. Transfer the filling to a plate, cover with plastic wrap, and refrigerate until ready to use.

SHAPING THE WRAPPERS AND MAKING THE DUMPLINGS

Do this as described in the recipe for Fried Dumplings, Beijing-Style (page 141).

STEAMING THE DUMPLINGS

If you are using a bamboo steamer, cut out a small square of foil for each dumpling and place on two racks. Place the dumplings on the racks ½ inch apart. Cover and steam over high heat for 8 minutes. Serve immediately.

If you are using a large pot, arrange them on an oiled plate sitting on top of a tin can with its ends removed. Pour in boiling water around the can to within 2 inches of the plate. Bring the water to a boil before you put the plate on. Cover the pot and steam over medium-high heat for 8 minutes. Serve immediately.

Steamed dumplings will contain a lot of juice. The best way to eat them is to pick one up with chopsticks and immediately transfer it to a soup spoon, so that when you bite into it, no juice is lost. Serve the dumplings hot with very fine shredded or grated fresh ginger in Zhejiang vinegar: ¼ teaspoon ginger to 1 tablespoon vinegar per person in individual dipping dishes.

Variation: Ground turkey or chicken can be used instead of pork.

Steamed Dumplings, Canton-Style in Two Shapes and with Two Fillings

虾 HAR GAW AND FUN GOR

饺
粉
菓

Cantonese *har gaw* (steamed shrimp dumplings) and *fun gor* (steamed meat dumplings) have a very delicate taste; the wrappers, made from a mixture of wheat starch and tapioca flour, are extremely light because there is no gluten in the dough, and the traditional fillings are subtly seasoned. The shrimp dumplings are always made in the shape of a pouch and the meat dumplings are always crescent-shaped. Unlike the northern dumplings, which are hearty and eaten as a meal in themselves, these southern dumplings are served as *dim sum*, food for snacking or a light meal. If you want to make a full meal of them, serve them with Stir-Fried Rice Noodles, Singapore-Style (page 227).

Store-bought Cantonese wrappers aren't yet available in this country, so you must make them. I use a tortilla press, both sides covered with plastic wrap, to shape the wrappers, making the whole job not very difficult at all. You could also use one side of a Chinese cleaver that you keep greased with a lightly oiled cloth. Then press the dumpling dough down on a flat surface. The dumplings can be made ahead of time and frozen.

Yield: 40 shrimp or meat dumplings

THE SHRIMP FILLING

1 pound raw shrimp	1 teaspoon salt
2 tablespoons minced parboiled pork fat or fatty bacon	1 teaspoon cornstarch
	Dash white pepper
¼ cup finely chopped bamboo shoots	½ teaspoon sugar
	1 teaspoon dry sherry
1 small egg white	2 teaspoons sesame oil

MAKING THE SHRIMP FILLING

Shell and devein the shrimp. Chop the fat and bamboo shoots and set them on a plate. Rinse and drain the shrimp and pat them dry with paper towels. Chop them fine, then put them in a bowl and add the egg white and the 1 teaspoon of salt. Stirring with chopsticks, make sure the shrimp is completely coated. Then add the cornstarch, pepper, sugar, sherry, and sesame oil and mix some more until the coating is smooth. Add the bamboo shoots and fat and mix well.

Cover with plastic wrap and refrigerate for at least 30 minutes, so the shrimp will absorb the egg whites, making the filling tender-crisp.

THE MEAT FILLING

½ cup finely chopped bamboo shoots	½ teaspoon sugar
	1 tablespoon soy sauce
4 dried black Chinese mushrooms, soaked in water until soft, stems removed and caps finely chopped	1 tablespoon dry sherry
	2 tablespoons corn oil or peanut oil
2 tablespoons finely chopped whole scallions	1 teaspoon coarse salt or to taste
	⅛ teaspoon white pepper
½ pound ground lean pork	½ tablespoon oyster sauce
1 teaspoon cornstarch	1 tablespoon cornstarch mixed with 2 tablespoons water

MAKING THE MEAT FILLING

Put the chopped bamboo shoots on a plate with the mushrooms and scallions. Put the pork in a mixing bowl, add the cornstarch, sugar, soy sauce, and sherry, and mix thoroughly.

Heat a wok, add 1 tablespoon of the oil, and swirl, then stir-fry the pork for 1 minute, or until the pork separates into bits; do not overcook. Dish out to a bowl. Heat the wok again, add 1 tablespoon of oil and swirl, then stir-fry the bamboo shoots, mushrooms, and scallions for 1 minute. Add the salt and pepper and mix well.

Return the cooked pork to the pan, stir and toss briefly to heat through. Add the oyster sauce and stir briefly. Stir the cornstarch-and-water mixture, add it to the pan, and stir until it coats the contents with a clear glaze.

Transfer the filling to a bowl and let it cool. It can be made ahead of time and refrigerated, covered with plastic wrap.

THE DOUGH FOR THE SHRIMP AND MEAT DUMPLING WRAPPERS

½ pound wheat starch, about 1½ cups
⅓ cup tapioca flour
¼ teaspoon coarse salt

1½ cups boiling water
2 tablespoons corn oil or peanut oil

MAKING THE DUMPLING WRAPPERS

Combine the wheat starch, tapioca flour, and salt in a large mixing bowl. Make a well in the center and pour in the boiling water all at once. With chopsticks, stir to incorporate the dry flour on the sides of the bowl; then add the oil. Continue to stir until a ball forms. Turn the hot dough onto a work surface and knead the ball of dough until it is very smooth—about 2 to 3 minutes. Put it in a tightly closed plastic bag and let it rest for 5 minutes.

Divide the dough into four pieces. Keep three of them in the plastic bag while you roll the first with your hands into a sausage shape about 6 to 8 inches long. Cut it into ten pieces. Smear a tiny bit of oil on the plastic wrap covering both sides of the tortilla press and a tiny bit on the dough pieces themselves. Place one piece cut side down on the press and press it into a 3-inch round. Put the circles of dough aside, overlap-

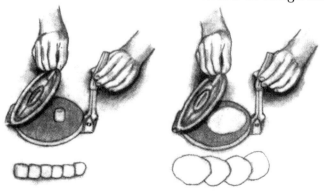

ping, while you press the others. It is better to fill these ten wrappers first than to make wrappers out of the remaining dough, because you want the wrapper dough to remain soft and pliable.

For Shrimp Dumplings: Take one wrapper and press and pinch four to five ¼-inch pleats, thus making a small pouch. Put 2 teaspoons of shrimp filling in the pouch and press the edges together to close.

For Meat Dumplings: Put 2 teaspoons of filling in the center of a wrapper. Fold over the edge to make a half-moon shape. Set the dumpling upright and press and push the curved edges together so the dumpling will be upright when being steamed and then served.

Continue making and then filling ten wrappers at a time. Both meat and shrimp dumplings may be made ahead of time: Either freeze them on an oiled tray first, then put them in a plastic bag, and keep frozen until ready to use, or refrigerate on an oiled plate tightly wrapped with plastic wrap for a few hours.

Steam the dumplings as described in Steamed Dumplings, Beijing-Style (page 145); the cooking time will be 4 to 5 minutes.

The Cantonese often use oyster sauce as a dip for the shrimp dumplings, and they eat the meat dumplings plain or with a little light soy sauce as a dip.

Pancakes

Pancakes with Beef and Scallion Filling, Taiwan-Style

牛　NIU ROU XIAN ER BING

肉
馆　The texture of these pancakes resembles *guo tie* (fried dumplings, page
儿　141). In this recipe, broth is added to a delicious meat filling and stuffed
饼　inside the pancakes. They are very popular in Taiwan, where they are
sold in noodle shops and at small roadside stands. They are fried with a
little oil in the skillet. They are very juicy, and the way to eat them is to
cradle one in a soup spoon and then bite and suck it, so you don't lose a
drop of the luscious juice.

If you are serving them as a main course, give each person two pancakes and accompany them with a soup, such as the Drop Noodles in Two
Soup (page 90). They also go well with congee, either plain or with
chicken (page 294).

Yield: 20 pancakes 3 inches in diameter

THE FILLING

1 pound ground beef, about 2
  cups
1 tablespoon finely minced fresh
  ginger
½ cup finely chopped whole
  scallions

½ teaspoon coarse salt or to taste
⅛ teaspoon white pepper
2 tablespoons dark soy sauce
2 tablespoons sesame oil
¼ cup Best Chicken Broth
  (page 77)

THE PANCAKE DOUGH

2 cups all-purpose flour

¾ cup cold water

Oil for pan-frying

MAKING THE FILLING

Combine the filling ingredients in a mixing bowl. Stir with a spoon in
one direction until the meat holds together. Set the filling in the refrigerator for at least 30 minutes so that it firms and is easier to put into
the pancakes.

MAKING THE DOUGH

Put the flour in a large mixing bowl. Slowly pour in the water while stirring with chopsticks or a wooden spoon until all the flour is damp. (If some dry flour remains, add more water 1 tablespoon at a time.) Pat the dough with your hands until it is soft and smooth. Then put it on a lightly floured surface and knead it until soft and elastic—about 2 minutes. Cover the dough with plastic wrap and let it rest for 30 minutes.

SHAPING THE PANCAKES

After the dough has rested, divide it in two pieces. Keep one half in the plastic wrap while you break the other into ten pieces on a lightly floured surface. Flatten each piece slightly with your palm and then roll each with a rolling pin to make a circle 3 inches in diameter, with the edge thinner than the center. Cover these ten circles with a dry dish towel.

Scoop out 2 tablespoons of the filling into the center of a circle. Then, as you push down the filling with the thumb of one hand, gather the edges of the circle with the thumb and forefinger of the other, taking up as little dough as possible. With your fingers, pinch and twist to seal the opening. Put the finished pancake on a surface seam side down and gently press it into a round 3 inches in diameter. Set it aside and cover with the towel. Continue to work the remaining circles in the same way, and then work the other half of the dough.

COOKING THE PANCAKES

Heat two 12-inch skillets over medium heat until hot (each will hold ten pancakes) or heat one large cast-iron griddle that can hold all twenty pancakes. Grease the pan with about 2 tablespoons of oil. Place the pancakes close together and fry for 1 minute. During that time dribble 2 to 3 drops of oil with a spoon on top of each pancake. When the bottoms are lightly brown, turn the pancakes with a spatula and fry the other side for 2 minutes. Turn them over and fry the first side for another minute. When the dough and meat are fully cooked, the pancakes will puff up slightly. Transfer them to a serving plate and serve immediately, with chopsticks and a soup spoon to eat them with.

Leftover pancakes can be reheated over medium-low heat in a dry covered skillet for 2 minutes. They won't be quite as juicy as freshly made ones, however.

Vegetarian Pancakes, Beijing-Style

 SU XIAN ER BING

These vegetable-filled pancakes are often served as a complete meal, along with millet congee in northern Chinese homes; they are healthful and mouth-watering. The mushrooms give the filling a rich, nutty edge. This pancake is unusually tender because it is made from a very soft cold-water dough. It requires mastering a few special techniques, and produces an extremely smooth and velvety pancake.

Yield: 4 pancakes; 4 servings for a light meal

THE DOUGH

2 cups all-purpose flour

⅞ cup cold water, approximately

THE FILLING

2 cups finely chopped tender green cabbage, about ½ pound

12 ounces finely chopped fresh mushrooms

1 cup finely chopped celery hearts

2 teaspoons coarse salt plus ¼ teaspoon

4 tablespoons peanut oil or corn oil

2 teaspoons finely minced fresh ginger

2 tablespoons light soy sauce

Oil for pan-frying

MAKING THE DOUGH

Put the flour in a large mixing bowl. Slowly pour in the water while stirring with a wooden spoon until all the flour is mixed in and the dough is *very soft* and smooth; add a little more water, 1 tablespoon at a time, if the dough is too firm. Cover the dough with plastic wrap and let it rest for 30 minutes.

MAKING THE FILLING

The cabbage, mushrooms, and celery should be chopped to the size of ¼-inch dice. If you do this in a food processor, using the pulse action, chop each vegetable separately. Put the chopped cabbage in a bowl and the chopped mushrooms and celery on a plate. Add 2 teaspoons of salt to the cabbage and stir to mix; let the cabbage sit for 20 minutes. Then put it in cheesecloth or a dish towel and squeeze out the water. Return the cabbage to the bowl and set aside.

Heat a wok, add the 4 tablespoons of oil, swirl, and heat. Add the ginger and stir; then add the celery and mushrooms and stir-fry for 3 to 4 minutes. Add the ¼ teaspoon salt and the light soy sauce. Stir and toss a little longer, or until the vegetables are fairly dry. Scoop them out into the bowl with the cabbage and mix well.

SHAPING AND FRYING THE PANCAKES

Put the soft dough on a generously floured surface. Sprinkle some more flour on top of the dough. With a dough scraper, divide the dough into four pieces. Form each piece into a disk with your fingers and then, with a rolling pin, roll each into a circle 6 inches in diameter. Put one-quarter of the filling in the middle of each circle and gather the edges to seal the package. Then set the pancakes, sealed side down, on a lightly floured

surface and press them out on the smooth side so they are 6 inches in diameter. Set them aside.

Heat a small skillet over medium-low heat with 1 tablespoon of oil swirled around the bottom. Put a pancake in the pan and fry it, covered, on one side for 3 minutes. With a spoon, dribble a little oil on top of the pancake, turn it over, and fry the other side for another 3 minutes, or until lightly brown and puffy. Transfer to a plate and cover with the lid of a pot. Cook the other three pancakes and cover them. If you can't serve them right away, they can be reheated in a covered skillet without oil for 2 minutes on each side.

To serve, cut each pancake into four wedges and eat with your fingers.

Variation: If you would like some meat with the vegetables, add ¼ pound ground pork, beef, or turkey, seasoned with 1 tablespoon soy sauce and ¼ teaspoon salt, to the filling after it has cooled. You can cook the meat as you fry the pancakes.

Mandarin Pancakes

 BAO BING

 A few years before the Second World War, my good friend Peng-fei invited me to spend summer vacation at her home in Luoyang Henan province, in the far north. It was my first experience eating authentic northern food, and in no time I became very fond of scallions and doughs made from wheat. I was served noodles and buns almost every day. I also had a lot of what I've called Mandarin pancakes (a term I came up with for the Time-Life Chinese cookbook). Mu Xi Pork was the usual filling, consisting of meat, lily buds, and tree ears. The servants' portions contained very little meat but an abundance of bean sprouts and cellophane noodles. My friend and I preferred the servants' version, and after we finished our meal we usually had another one or two Mandarin pancakes filled with this vegetable mixture.

The pancake dough for Mandarin pancakes is a hot water dough, and it will make very tender pancakes.

As fillings for the Mandarin pancakes, I've included the classic Mu Xi Pork, *He Cai Dai Mao* (Cellophane Noodle and Mushroom Filled Pancakes with a Hat), and Ants on a Tree (Ground Beef with Cellophane Noodles). A hot-and-sour soup would be an excellent accompaniment for all these fillings.

Yield: 26–28 pancakes

2 cups all-purpose flour　　　　　　**¾ cup boiling water**
2 tablespoons peanut oil or corn
oil

FORMING THE PANCAKES

Put the flour in a large mixing bowl, make a well in the center, and add 2 teaspoons of the oil. Pour the hot water into the well all at once, and immediately stir with a pair of chopsticks or a fork until the flour is damp and in small pieces. If some dry flour remains, add more hot water 1 teaspoon at a time. Pat the dough into a ball. It is slightly firm at this point but will soften in the plastic bag later. Transfer the dough to a floured surface and gently knead it until smooth.

The dough can be made in a food processor fitted with the steel blade. Make the pulse action while you gradually add the water. Turn the machine "on." As soon as the dough forms a ball, remove it and knead it on a floured surface for a few turns.

Put the dough in a tightly closed plastic bag and let it rest for at least 15 minutes. Then divide it in two, keeping one half covered in the plastic bag while you roll out the other to a thickness of about ¼ inch. Using a 2½-inch cookie cutter, cut out as many circles as possible and stack them overlapping in two or three piles. Put the scraps into the other portion of dough. Roll that out the same way and cut more pancakes; then stack the remaining scraps unevenly, roll the dough swiftly, and cut out more. You don't want to overwork the dough. You should be able to make about twenty-six to twenty-eight of them.

With a pastry brush, spread a little oil evenly over the top of all the pancakes and then lay one on top of another. Sprinkle both sides of a double pancake with a little flour and, working from the center out, roll it out, forward and back only, on both sides. Each time you roll, give the double pancake a quarter-turn. Continue until the circle is about 6 inches in diameter. Stack the finished ones and cover them with a cloth while you work with the rest of the dough.

COOKING THE PANCAKES

Preheat a dry heavy frying pan over medium heat. Fry each double pancake until it begins to bubble and tiny light brown spots appear on the bottom; then turn it over briefly, until bubbles appear. This takes less than 1 minute for both sides. (If the spots are too large, the heat is too high and the pancake will be dry and hard. It isn't necessary to have the brown spots, but they do give the pancake a better flavor.)

Remove the double pancake from the pan, smack it down on a

table to loosen it, and look for an opening along the edge; then pull the two pancakes apart while they are still hot. Stack them fried side down while you cook the rest. When finished, keep the pancakes wrapped in a damp dish towel until ready to serve. (They can be kept in a steamer over low heat for up to one hour.) They should be served hot; fold them in quarters and arrange them on a plate to accompany the filling you choose.

The stacked pancakes can be wrapped in aluminum foil and frozen for up to two months. After they have defrosted, remove the foil and wrap the pancakes with a damp dish towel; steam them over low heat for 15 minutes (for ten pancakes) or until they are hot and pliable.

Cellophane Noodle and Mushroom Filled Pancakes with a Hat

 HE CAI DAI MAO

This is the vegetarian filling I loved when I was a child (see page 157), with the addition of meat here. You can easily substitute 1 cup of shredded seasoned pressed bean curd (page 311) for the pork. The "hat" in the title refers to the egg sheet that is placed on top of the dish after it is cooked.

This recipe amply fills twenty-four Mandarin Pancakes (page 157). It is also delicious served alone, accompanied by a hot soup such as Sichuan Spicy Beef Sauce and Noodle Soup (page 80) or a hot-and-sour soup.

Yield: Serves 4 as a light meal

6 **dried black Chinese mushrooms**
2 **ounces cellophane noodles**
1 **pound fresh mung bean sprouts**
4 **whole scallions, cut in 2-inch sections and shredded**
½ **pound pork tenderloin or flank steak, semi-frozen for easier slicing**

2 **tablespoons soy sauce**
1 **teaspoon cornstarch**
½ **teaspoon sugar**
1 **tablespoon dry sherry**
6 **tablespoons peanut oil or corn oil**
1 **teaspoon coarse salt**
3 **eggs**

PREPARING THE VEGETABLES AND PORK

Rinse the mushrooms, then soak in warm water to cover; soak the cellophane noodles in a separate bowl with hot water for 30 minutes. Drain the mushrooms, and reserve ¼ cup of the liquid. Cut off and discard the stems. Shred the mushrooms finely. Drain the cellophane noodles and cut them into 2-inch lengths. Set both aside on a large plate with the bean sprouts and shredded scallions. Thinly slice the pork wih the grain; then cut again into matchstick strips about 2 inches long. Put the pork in a bowl and add the soy sauce, cornstarch, sugar, and sherry; mix well. If you are making this filling ahead of time, cover the vegetables and the pork with plastic wrap and refrigerate.

COOKING THE FILLING

Heat a wok until hot, then add 2 tablespoons of the oil and swirl. Over moderate heat stir-fry the pork, separating the shreds. Then add the mushrooms and toss well for 1 minute. Scoop out and set aside on a plate. Clean the wok and heat 3 tablespoons of the oil over high heat; add the scallions, bean sprouts, mushrooms, cellophane noodles, salt and the reserved mushroom liquid; stir and toss for 2 minutes. Return the pork to the wok for another 2 minutes and stir-fry with the vegetables for 2 more minutes. Transfer the wok contents to a serving platter and keep them warm, covered, in the oven while you make the egg sheet.

Heat a 10-inch skillet over medium heat until very hot. Add the last 2 tablespoons of oil and swirl. Then beat the eggs well, pour them into the skillet and swirl; then let them sit till very lightly browned on the bottom—1 to 2 minutes. Then carefully turn the sheet over with a spatula and cook for a few seconds more. Remove the egg sheet and cover the *He Cai* dish with it.

Mu Xi Pork
(with Mandarin Pancakes,
Sesame Bread, or Steamed Buns)

木
犀
肉

MU XI ROU

Mu xi in Chinese means "sweet osmanthus." According to the famous twentieth century Chinese philosopher Lin Yutang, Mi Xi Pork is defined in his dictionary as Scrambled Eggs with Pork. The scrambled eggs do resemble the tiny yellow flowers that are sweet osmanthus, but the real origin of this title comes from the imperial court's desire to avoid using the word *dan* ("egg"), out of deference to the many eunuchs who held powerful positions there.

This recipe will fill twenty-four Mandarin Pancakes (page 157). It also makes a marvelous stuffing for Sesame Seed Bread (page 167) or goes beautifully served with steamed buns (page 199).

Yield: 6 servings

60 dried lily buds
½ cup dried tree ears
4 whole scallions, cut in 2-inch sections and shredded
1 pound pork tenderloin or fresh pork butt, semi-frozen for easier slicing

6 tablespoons peanut oil or corn oil
6 large eggs
1 teaspoon coarse salt
1 tablespoon sesame oil

THE MARINADE FOR THE PORK

2 teaspoons cornstarch
1 teaspoon sugar
2 tablespoons soy sauce

1 tablespoon dry sherry
1 tablespoon peanut oil or corn oil

PREPARING THE VEGETABLES AND PORK
Soak the lily buds and tree ears in separate bowls with plenty of hot water for 30 minutes. Drain and squeeze dry. Then pick off and discard the hard ends of the lily buds, if any. Pile the buds together and cut them in half, to make about 1 cup. Rinse the tree ears under cold water several times. Drain and squeeze dry; then cut or break them into small pieces and place them with the lily buds on a plate. Add the shredded

scallions. Cover with plastic wrap and set aside if you are cooking the filling later.

Cut the pork with the grain into very thin slices, then cut again into matchstick strips 1½ inches long; there should be about 2 cups. Put the pork strips in a bowl, add the marinade, and mix well. Cover and set in a refrigerator for a few minutes, or longer if you are going to cook the filling later.

COOKING THE FILLING

Heat a wok over medium heat until very hot. Add 2 tablespoons of the oil and swirl. Beat the eggs well with a whisk and pour them into the wok. With a spatula, slowly push the eggs back and forth until they are dry—about 1 minute. Then break them up into pieces—the eggs should be dry so that they will absorb the sauce later. Scoop the eggs out onto a plate.

Clean the wok and heat the remaining 4 tablespoons of oil in it at medium-high heat. Add the scallions and toss, then add the marinated pork and stir-fry until the pork whitens a little and separates into shreds—about 2 minutes. Add the lily buds, tree ears, and salt. Stir and toss over high heat for 2 minutes. Add the egg pieces and stir just to mix. Add the sesame oil, stir to blend well, and put in a hot serving bowl. Serve with twenty-four hot Mandarin Pancakes (page 157).

Scallion Pancakes

CON YU BANG

Scallion pancakes originated in the north but then became popular throughout most of China as a breakfast or snack food. The Chinese often make a meal from these pancakes, rice, or millet congee (a hot gruel), pickles, and fried peanuts. They are also good with a light soup, such as the Drop Noodles in Two Soups (page 90) or Shredded Pork and Red-in-Snow Noodle Soup (page 87), or served in their own right as an appetizer. When I was a student in Sichuan province, a scallion pancake was a great treat for me—sold in roadside shops, it was crisp and succulent and inexpensive.

When making this pancake be sure to observe the rest periods after kneading the dough and forming the pancakes. These times are crucial, because they allow the dough to give up its springiness. It is also very important to roll out the pancakes just before you cook them, so that you can create a crisp crust and a tender (not chewy) inside.

Yield: Four 6- or 8-inch pancakes

2 cups all-purpose flour
¾ cup boiling water, approximately
1½ teaspoons coarse salt

2 tablespoons finely chopped whole scallions
½ cup corn oil or peanut oil, for brushing and cooking

MAKING THE DOUGH BY HAND

Put the flour in a large mixing bowl and make a well in the center. Slowly pour the boiling water into the well as you stir with a pair of chopsticks or a wooden spoon until the flour becomes damp. If some dry flour remains, add 1 to 2 tablespoons more water. Then, with your hands, pat and knead the dough into a ball while it is still in the bowl, the dough should be soft but not sticky.

Transfer the dough to a floured work surface and gently knead with a little flour until the dough is smooth—about 2 minutes. Divide the dough into four portions and cover with plastic wrap. Let them rest for at least 15 minutes.

MAKING THE DOUGH IN A FOOD PROCESSOR

The processor should be fitted with the steel blade. Use the pulse action, about twenty pulses while you add the boiling water. Check the flour by pinching the dough. It should be soft but firm. Turn the machine on and process 30 seconds—turn it out onto a lightly floured work surface and knead it just a few turns. Divide the dough into four portions, cover with plastic wrap, and let them rest for 15 minutes.

FORMING THE PANCAKES

Roll one portion of the dough into a sheet about 6 by 8 inches. Pour about ½ tablespoon of the oil on the sheet and spread it evenly all over with a pastry brush. Then sprinkle the sheet with ½ tablespoon of chopped scallions and a little less than ½ teaspoon of salt. From the longer side, loosely roll the dough into a cylinder with your hands and pinch the edge to seal. Coil the cylinder into a circle, like a hair bun, with the pinched edge inside but slightly overlapping as you turn. Tuck the ends underneath and gently press with your fingers to flatten the coils a little. Cover with plastic wrap and let the coils rest for at least 30 minutes. If you aren't cooking the pancakes for several hours, refrigerate them, but bring to room temperature before cooking.

Repeat the process with the other three portions of dough.

Just before cooking, roll the coiled bun flat into a pancake about 6 inches in diameter if you are serving them as an entrée. Repeat with the other three coils of dough. If you are making these as a first course or appetizer, roll the coils into pancakes about 8 inches in diameter.

FRYING THE PANCAKES

Heat a 10-inch skillet over medium-high heat until very hot. Pour in enough oil to cover the bottom of the pan—about 3 tablespoons—and then heat. Put a pancake in and move it around as it sizzles. With a spatula, loosen the edges of the pancake all around to make sure it fluffs up as it cooks. Then cover it and let it fry for 2 minutes. It should have a crisp crust to it. Uncover and dribble a few drops of oil on the top, and with a spatula, turn the pancake over. Loosen the edges again, cover, and fry this side for 2 minutes. Scoop it out onto a platter and

keep warm in a 200-degree oven with the door ajar. Cook the other pancakes, adding more oil each time and dribbling a little oil on top before turning them.

Scallion pancakes are best when freshly made, but you can prepare them ahead of time. Stack them and keep them at room temperature. Reheat them in a covered dry skillet or in a preheated 450-degree oven for 5 minutes, or until crisp.

To serve, cut each pancake into four or eight wedges.

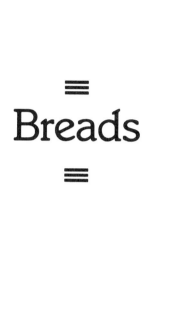

Breads

Sesame Seed Bread

 SHAO BING

When I was a child one of my favorite pastimes was watching professional bakers work their magic. Sesame seed bread and deep-fried devils were usually made in the same shop. I would watch for a long time, then buy some bread for breakfast or a snack.

The sesame seed bread was baked in a large barrel-shape oven with a hot charcoal fire inside, at the bottom. The baker slapped the oblongs of dough against the inside wall of the oven, and in 4 to 5 minutes they puffed up. Then the baker slightly loosened one at a time with a long spatula and scooped it up swiftly with his other hand. The bakers had to be very deft to do this under the very hot conditions, and I was mesmerized by their actions.

This hot layered pan-fried bread is a little like pita bread, only richer because of the roux inside. Slit horizontally almost all the way around, it becomes the traditional "pocket" for Deep-Fried Devils (page 172) as well as for numerous other fillings, such as the sharp-tasting Sesame Seed Pockets with Pork and Cabbage Filling (page 171).

Yield: Ten 3-by-6-inch breads

**2 tablespoons white sesame
seeds, on a large plate**

THE OIL-AND-FLOUR ROUX

**¼ cup corn oil or peanut oil,
approximately**

**¾ cup unsifted unbleached flour
½ teaspoon coarse salt**

THE DOUGH

**2 cups all-purpose flour
½ teaspoon coarse salt**

**¾ cup boiling water
2 tablespoons cold water**

MAKING THE ROUX

Heat the oil in a small frying pan over moderate heat. When it is very hot, gradually add the flour and salt, stirring to mix well. If the mixture is too dry and lumpy, add some oil 1 teaspoon at a time and stir it in; then keep stirring until the roux turns a light nut brown and is fragrant—about 5 minutes; the consistency should be like that of softened butter.

MIXING THE DOUGH

Pour the flour and salt into a large mixing bowl and make a well in the center; pour into it the boiling and cold water all at once and mix with chopsticks or a wooden spoon until the flour is totally damp. Rub a little flour on your hands and pat the dough into a ball. Knead it on a lightly floured surface until it is smooth—about 1 to 2 minutes, and cover with plastic wrap.

FORMING THE BREAD

Place the dough on a lightly oiled surface. Shape and roll it with a rolling pin into a strip 16 inches long and 4 inches wide. For 2 inches all along the long edge, leaving a little dough free at the edge, spread 5 tablespoons of the roux; then roll the strip over to cover the roux, letting the far edge overlap a little. Pinch the edge to the strip to seal in the roux. (Refrigerate the extra roux in a covered bowl; it will stay fresh for weeks.)

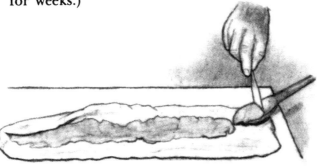

Cut the long roll into ten pieces. Smear a little oil on the work surface. Roll out one piece of dough, the cut side facing you and the folded seam up, back and forth from the center out, until it's 5 to 6 inches long. Use dough scraper to pick up the ends and fold into thirds crosswise, overlapping the folds completely. Turn the piece of dough so

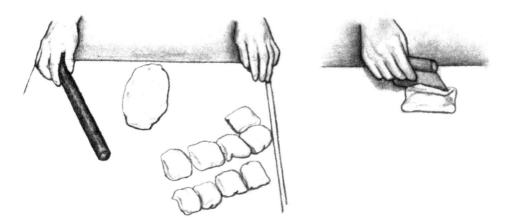

an open end is facing you and roll the piece out again until it's 8 inches long. Press the near end hard with the rolling pin so that the edge becomes very thin. Then, from the other end, roll the dough up into a cylinder, pressing the thin edge into the rest of the dough. Set the cylinder smooth side down on the plate of sesame seeds.

Repeat the process with the other pieces. Press the smooth side of each in the sesame seeds. The cylinders can rest under plastic wrap for several hours. Roll each cylinder, sesame seed side down, into a 3-by-6-inch oblong, doing it crosswise and then lengthwise. You can stack them overlapping and let them rest, covered, for an hour or cook immediately.

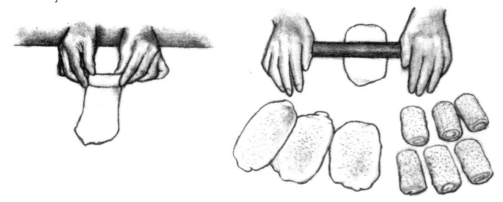

COOKING THE BREAD

Heat a 12-inch skillet over medium heat until hot. Fry two breads at a time on both sides (sesame seed side down first, then the other side, then the seed side again) until they are lightly browned and have started to puff up—about 3 minutes in all.

SERVING AND STORING THE BREAD

Sesame seed bread is best eaten hot, when it has just been made, but it can be covered and eaten later in the day. Reheat it in a preheated 400-degree oven for about 5 minutes.

In China this bread is traditionally used as a sandwich pocket. With scissors or a small knife, cut each open horizontally along one length, but not all the way through. Fill with Deep-Fried Devils (page 172). Or, if you are filling the bread with chopped ingredients, cut the bread into two pieces crosswise to make smaller horizontal pockets.

Sesame seed bread keeps for up to one week in the refrigerator or for one month in the freezer, wrapped tightly in plastic.

Sesame Seed Pockets with Pork and Cabbage Filling

肉　ROU MO SHAO BING
末
饦　In this simple, delicious recipe ground pork is put into a pocket of sesame
饼　seed bread. The preserved vegetable that gives the filling its special bite is
Tianjin dong cai, a northern specialty—celery cabbage that has been preserved in a mixture of salt and garlic. It is sold in Chinese grocery stores
coarsely chopped and packed in earthenware jars marked Tientsin dong
cai (page 321). After opening, transfer the celery cabbage to a tightly
covered glass jar. It will keep for months.

To accompany these "sandwiches," try Cellophane Noodle Soup with
Pork Omelets (page 277).

Yield: 4–6 servings as a light meal

½ **pound ground pork**
¼ **cup minced bamboo shoots**
3 **tablespoons minced** *Tianjin*
　dong cai
1 **tablespoon minced scallion**

1 **recipe Sesame Seed Bread**
　(page 167)
2 **tablespoons peanut oil or corn**
　oil

THE MARINADE

1 **tablespoon light soy sauce**
2 **teaspoons sugar**
2 **teaspoons cornstarch**

1 **tablespoon chicken broth or**
　water

Put the ground pork in a mixing bowl. Add the marinade and stir
well. Set in the refrigerator for a few minutes, or longer if you wish.

Put the minced bamboo shoots, *dong cai,* and scallions on a plate.
Cover with plastic if you are cooking the dish later.

Before cooking the pork, heat the sesame seed bread in a preheated 400-degree oven for 5 minutes. Cut each bread crosswise in two.
Cover with a dish towel and keep warm while you prepare the filling.

Heat a wok over medium heat until hot. Add 2 tablespoons oil and
swirl, then add the pork. Stir-fry, tossing and turning the meat constantly, until it changes color and separates into bits—about 2 minutes.
Do not overcook, since the meat will exude its oil and become dry. Push
the meat to the side, add the bamboo shoots, *dong cai,* and scallions and

stir for 10 seconds; then toss with the pork and cook a few seconds more. Transfer to a bowl.

To serve, open the cut side of the bread to make a pocket. Put about 2 tablespoons of filling in each half.

Variation: Beef may be used instead of pork. If it is very lean, add 1 tablespoon of oil to the marinade. *Zha cai,* a specialty of Sichuan province that is made from celery knobs, can be used instead of *dong cai;* chop fine before using. *Zha cai* is flavored with salt and chili peppers, but no garlic.

Deep-Fried Devils

 YOU ZHA GUI OR YOU TIAO

You zha gui are deep-fried strips of dough that are puffy and crisp on the outside and soft on the inside. They are popular throughout China as a breakfast or snack dish and are traditionally served wrapped inside sesame seed bread and accompanied by soybean milk. They are also delicious served with congee (rice gruel, page 296), stuffed with shrimp or meat, or cut up in broth soups.

The origin of the name comes from the Sung dynasty, around A.D. 1200. A great general, Yoh Fei, who was very loyal to the emperor, was holding the line of defense against invaders who had overrun northern China. A minister in the government, Zhen Gui, had forged a secret deal with the invaders, so he issued fake imperial orders to have General Yoh Fei imprisoned in the name of the emperor. Later, after Yoh Fei was dead and the territories lost, the people realized that Zhen Gui had been the traitor, not the general. In Chinese the word *gui* sounds like the word for "devil"; hence the cooks were deep-frying ("*you zha*") the man who had betrayed the people's hero.

This recipe has two pharmaceutical ingredients in it—alum and ammonium carbonate—which are essential, though they may seem unusual to Westerners. Alum makes the dough harder and therefore very crisp when fried. The ammonium carbonate gives the dough air, making it puff up. The small amounts will not harm you at all; I grew up eating these deep-fried devils every morning for breakfast, and they were magnificent!

Yield: Twenty 8-inch pieces

2 teaspoons coarse salt
1 teaspoon alum (available at pharmacies)
1 teaspoon ammonium carbonate powder (available at pharmacies)
1 teaspoon baking soda
1 teaspoon baking powder

1¼ cups water at room temperature
3½ cups unbleached flour, approximately
6 cups or more peanut oil or corn oil for deep-frying, preferably in a wok

MAKING THE DOUGH

Put the salt, alum, ammonium carbonate, and baking soda and powder in a large mixing bowl. Add the water and stir until all the powders are dissolved. Add 3 cups of the flour and use your hands in a pressing and pushing motion to mix the dough. Add the remaining flour if the dough is too soft. It should be firm enough to handle.

Transfer the dough to a floured surface and knead it until smooth, with no lumps. The kneading should take no more than 2 to 3 minutes.

Divide the dough into two pieces, and with a little flour shape them into two oblong loaves, then coat with oil and wrap tightly in plastic. Let them sit at least 4 hours and up to 8 hours at room temperature.

MAKING THE DEEP-FRIED DEVILS

Sprinkle a large cutting board with flour and place it near the stove. Stretch the loaves so that each measures 14 inches long and 3 inches wide. Lay them on the board at least 4 inches apart. Sprinkle some flour on top. With a small rolling pin, roll one loaf lengthwise till it is about ¼ inch thick, 4 inches wide, and about 16 inches long. Do the same with the other loaf. Cover both with a slightly damp dish towel and let them rest for 10 minutes.

Meanwhile, set a 12- or 14-inch wok over medium-high heat and pour in at least 3 inches of oil. Line a tray with paper towels and place three chopsticks alongside.

When the oil is about 350 degrees, you can begin the final cutting and cooking.

Using a sharp knife, cut four crosswise strips ⅔ inch wide from one of the loaves. Brush the top of two with water, then lay the other two on top. Press a chopstick lengthwise on top of a pair of strips—this makes the two stick together. Hold the ends of the two-strip piece and gently pull until it is 8 to 10 inches long. Then lower the dough pieces into the

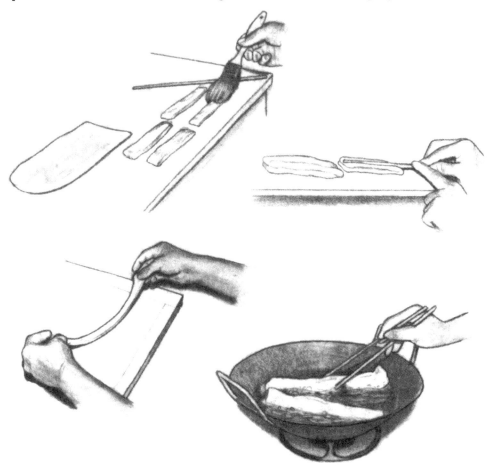

oil, immediately turning them with the chopsticks gently, without squeezing them, so that all sides become lightly browned. This takes about 2 minutes. Drain on the paper towels.

Repeat the cutting and frying process with the rest of the dough.

STORING AND REHEATING
Deep-fried devils keep well, wrapped in plastic, for one week in the refrigerator and one month in the freezer. Reheat them in a preheated 450-degree oven for about 2 minutes, until they are crisp but not dry.

Prune Crepes

 ZAO NI BING

This prune version of a famous Chinese sweet is much easier to make than the original. The recipe was developed by Chef Seventh Uncle at the Sun Luck Imperial restaurant in New York, who demonstrated it in my cooking class. It is not a fragrant or as intensely sweet as the classic jujube date filling, but it is absolutely delicious.

If you want to be totally authentic, use dried jujube red dates for this recipe. First soak 8 ounces of dried red dates in warm water for 10 minutes. Wash them several times and drain. Cook them with water to cover until just soft and the skins are smooth and there is little liquid left—about 15 minutes. Remove and discard the skins and pits. Use this pulp and the liquid to cook with the sugar and flour-and-oil mixture. You can also use pitted jujube red dates (page 315) instead of dry jujube. (They are less fragrant and sweeter than the dried kind.) Reduce the sugar to ¼ cup or to taste.

If you do not have the time to make the filling, you can use Hungarian lekvar of prune or apricot, which has a more tart flavor. Red bean paste (page 181) is a favorite of the Chinese, and another wonderful substitute. It is smooth and not as sweet as the prune filling; use ⅓ cup for each crepe.

Yield: Four 4-by-6-inch crepes; 8 servings for dessert

¼ cup corn oil for making the crepes

THE FILLING

12 ounces pitted prunes	**⅔ cup flour**
2 cups water	**½ cup sugar or to taste**
⅔ cup corn oil	

THE BATTER

1½ cups all-purpose flour	**1 large egg**
2 cups water	

MAKING THE FILLING
In a heavy saucepan combine the prunes and water and cook over medium-low heat for about 30 minutes. Mix the oil and flour together until smooth and set aside.

Use a wooden spoon to stir and mash the cooked prunes while still over heat until they are smooth. Add the sugar and cook, stirring, for about 5 minutes. Slowly add the oil-and-flour mixture to the prunes while stirring constantly. When the mixture is shiny and doesn't stick when touched, it is ready—this will take about 2 minutes. Remove from the heat and stir to cool.

You will need about half the filling for this recipe; refrigerate or freeze the other half; it will keep for weeks.

MAKING THE BATTER AND COOKING THE CREPES

Mix all the batter ingredients with a wire whisk or in a blender or food processor; this can be done ahead of time. Stir well before making the crepes.

Heat a 10-inch crepe pan or skillet over medium-low heat. Lightly grease the pan with oil. Pour about ⅓ cup batter in, tilting the pan slightly, to make a 9-inch crepe. When lightly browned on the bottom—in about 1 minute—turn it over and cook for 30 seconds; then transfer to a plate and continue making seven more.

Spread ¼ cup filling in the center of two crepes lightly pressed together, and fold the four sides of the two crepes into the center as though making a 4-by-6-inch envelope. Seal the exposed and in-between edges with a little of the remaining batter. Set aside and make three more in the same fashion. (If you want a sweeter dessert, use a single crepe to wrap the filling.)

Now add 2 teaspoons of oil to the pan and fry the crepe envelope on medium-high heat for 2 minutes on each side, or until brown and crisp. Keep in a low oven with the door ajar while making the remaining three crepes. Add more oil as needed. Cut each crepe into four pieces and serve hot.

The crepes can be made ahead of time, cooked till lightly browned, and reheated in a frying pan or 400-degree oven for 5 minutes. They are best when freshly made, however.

Flaky
Pastry

Flaky Pastry, Master Recipe

酥
饼
皮

SU BING PI

Su bing, Chinese flaky pastry, is a northern specialty usually reserved for banquets. There are many traditional fillings, giving the pastry different names, such as Flaky Pastry Filled with Red Bean Paste (page 181), Flaky Pastry Filled with White Turnips and Ham (page 185), Flaky Pastry Egg Custard Tarts (page 190), as well as Flaky Pastry Baby Chicks and Daisies (page 188), but the basic dough is always the same.

There are two ways to cook the pastry: The first is deep-frying, the oil being mildly hot (300 degrees) in the beginning but higher to finish. The color of deep-fried pastry is pale yellow—almost white—and it has an extremely flaky texture and a very rich flavor. The second method is baking. In China this is usually done in a shop or restaurant, where ovens are available. In this country, of course, there are ovens in everyone's home. Baked pastry is also flaky but drier and not as rich as the deep-fried version. Nevertheless, it tastes just as scrumptious.

There are three ways of cutting the dough. You can make horizontal layers if you are baking the pastries, or vertical, or spiral layers for both baking and frying.

THE WATER DOUGH

2 cups all-purpose flour
2 tablespoons chilled lard or shortening such as Crisco

⅞ cup warm water, approximately

THE OIL DOUGH

1½ cups all-purpose flour

¾ cup chilled lard or shortening such as Crisco

MAKING THE WATER DOUGH
Put the flour in a mixing bowl and make a well in the center. Add the lard. Mix with your fingers as you pour in all but 2 tablespoons of the warm water. Add the rest of the water if you need it. The lard will stiffen a bit at first if it is cold, but eventually, when mixed with the flour, it will become damp and soft. Stir the mixture into a very soft dough in the bowl and then put it on a lightly floured surface. Gently knead it until it is very soft, elastic, and smooth—about 2 minutes. Divide the dough into two equal balls and cover these with plastic wrap while you work with the oil dough.

MAKING THE OIL DOUGH

Put the flour in the same mixing bowl and make a well in the center. Add the lard, and with the back of a wooden spoon or your fingers, mash it into the flour until the dough is well blended and there isn't any dry flour left in the bowl. The dough will be soft. With a little flour on your hands, pat the dough into a ball (do not knead) and put it on a lightly floured surface. Divide the dough in two and pat and roll the pieces into balls. Cover them with plastic wrap.

MAKING THE FINAL DOUGH

Take one piece of water dough and roll it into a circle 6 to 7 inches in diameter. Put one ball of oil dough in the center of this circle and pull and push the edges of the water dough up around the oil dough to enclose it.

Put the dough, enclosed side down, on a lightly floured surface. Press it with your fingers in the center to make it flat, and also push the inner dough to the sides so that the oil dough will be evenly around it.

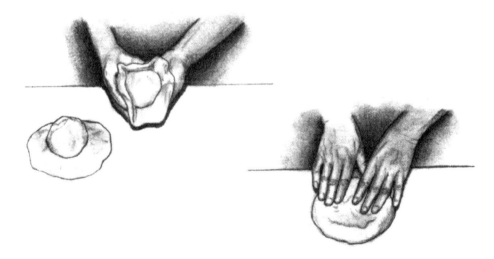

Gently roll it with a large rolling pin into an oblong approximately 8 to 12 inches, rolling both sides from the center, away from you, then toward you, and use as little dusting flour as possible during the process. Try to square off the corners. Fold the oblong in thirds so you have a piece 4 by 8 inches. Roll this piece out to 8 by 12 inches and fold again into thirds. These two folds are enough for most of the pastry recipes that follow. Cover the dough with plastic wrap and let it rest in the refrigerator while you create the other sheet of dough from the two remaining balls.

You could refrigerate the dough at this point for a few days or freeze it for a month. Form the pastry when it is slightly chilled. This is the basic flaky pastry dough, ready to shape into different forms and fill with various fillings.

Flaky Pastry Filled with Red Bean Paste

 DOU SHA SU BING

This sweet pastry is reserved for special occasions and served at a special tea lunch or as dessert after a banquet. The filling can also feature Jujube Red Date and Nut Filling (page 215) or lotus seed paste (page 316)—both classic favorites. In this recipe you make horizontal layers to bake the pastry. You can also shape vertical or spiral layers for a flakier texture and fry them for a richer flavor (see Flaky Pastry Filled with White Turnips and Ham, page 185). These filled pastries are the Chinese equivalent of puff pastry and they are so richly flaky, I urge you to make them.

Yield: 24 oval pastries 2 inches wide and 3 inches long

1 recipe flaky pastry dough
  (page 179)
2 cups red bean paste (page 184)

½ cup white sesame seeds
1 tablespoon sugar dissolved in
  2 tablespoons water

SHAPING THE PASTRY IN
HORIZONTAL LAYERS

With a large rolling pin, gently roll one of the 4-by-8-inch folded dough rectangles into a 14-inch square. Roll toward both sides from the center, away from you, then roll back toward you; use as little dusting flour as possible during the process. From the one side roll the dough up into a cylinder about 2 inches thick. Roll the whole cylinder a little to make it even and a little longer—about 16 inches. Cut the cylinder into twelve portions. Cover them with plastic wrap.

On a surface very lightly dusted with flour, flatten each piece of dough, smooth side down, with your palm; then, with a small rolling pin, roll each into a 3½-inch round disk, the edges thinner than the center. As you finish the disks, stack them overlapping and cover them with plastic wrap.

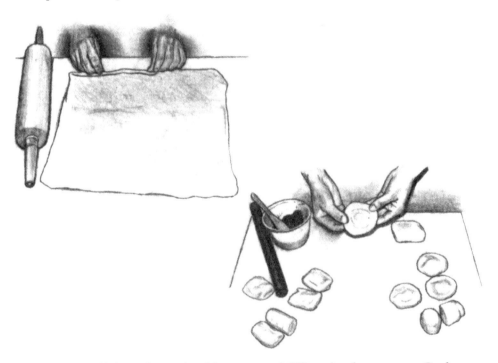

Take a disk and put 1 tablespoon of filling in the center. Gather as little dough as possible at the edges and pinch and pleat it, then twist to close, making sure it is sealed well. Shape the pastry into an oval and press it on a surface to flatten it a little. Cover the finished pastry with a slightly damp dish towel while you make twelve more disks with the other half of the dough.

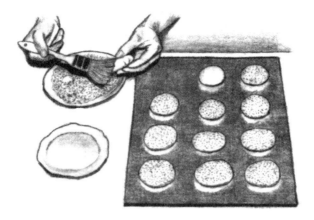

BAKING THE PASTRY

Preheat the oven to 400 degrees. Set a plate of sesame seeds and the sugar water near the work area.

Brush the top and sides of each pastry with sugar water, then press the sides and top with sesame seeds so that the seeds stick; do not treat the bottom. Set the pastries, sesame seed side up, on a baking sheet 1 inch apart; arrange the twenty-four pastries on two baking sheets. Bake at 400 degrees for 15 minutes; then reduce the heat to 350 degrees and continue baking for 15 minutes. The pastry will have puffed up and the top layer will be slightly cracked in places. Serve warm or at room temperature.

The cooked pastries can be kept in the refrigerator for one week or in the freezer for one month. Reheat the refrigerated ones in a 350-degree oven for 15 minutes, the frozen ones for 2 minutes more.

Red Bean Paste Filling

红 HONG DOU SHA
豆
沙 This is a wildly popular filling frequently used in Chinese flaky pastry and
steamed buns, cakes, and wontons. It is really the equivalent of chocolate
in China. In fact, it resembles a very thick chocolate sauce. Homemade
red bean paste is much better than the kind that comes in a can. It isn't
hard to make and it is also inexpensive. You can, of course, use canned
products to begin the paste; the instructions follow.

Yield: About 6 cups

1 pound dried Chinese or Japanese red beans, or small red chili beans	**1½ cups sugar or to taste** **1½ cups peanut oil or corn oil**

MAKING FRESH RED BEAN PASTE

Pick over the beans, discarding any that are bad. Put them in a 3-quart
saucepan, wash them under cold running water several times, and drain
off the water. Pour in 6 cups of water and bring to a boil, cover, turn off the
heat, and let the beans sit in the water for 30 minutes. Then bring to a boil
again and cook over low heat at a gentle boil for about 1 hour, or until the
beans are very soft and there is practically no liquid left in the pan.

Put the cooked beans in a food processor fitted with the steel blade
(do this in two batches if you have a small processor). Grind the beans
for 2 to 3 minutes, or until they are puréed. If you don't have a
food processor, use a food mill to make a purée as lump-free as possible.

Scrape the bean paste into the saucepan, add the sugar, and bring
to a boil. Over medium-low heat cook the bean paste, stirring constantly, for about 10 minutes, or until it is quite dry. Then turn the heat
down to low and slowly add the oil while stirring, until it is completely
blended and the paste is smooth, or until the paste does not stick to the
pot. This takes about 15 minutes. Remove from the heat and stir the
paste to cool it and keep it smooth; it is then ready to be used as a
filling. You will have about 6 cups. Leftover bean paste can be stored in
the refrigerator for months or in the freezer for a year.

**MAKING BEAN PASTE FROM
CANNED PRODUCTS**

Canned puréed red beans, jujube red dates, or lotus seeds may be used instead of dried beans. They are usually very sweet and sticky, because the manufacturers use more sugar and water to make the paste. You can recook them with an oil-and-flour mixture to reduce the sweetness and make the mixture a drier paste that isn't sticky. (If you prefer a sweeter filling, use any of these directly from the can.)

For an 18-ounce can of red bean paste or an 11-ounce can of jujube red dates jam, use ¼ cup flour mixed with ¼ cup corn oil.

For a 7-ounce can of lotus seed paste, use 2 tablespoons of flour mixed with 2 tablespoons of corn oil.

Heat either of the canned pastes in a saucepan until hot. Mix the flour and oil well and slowly add this mixture to the paste, stirring constantly until it is fully heated through and is shiny and nonsticky—this will take about 5 minutes. Remove from the heat and stir to cool, so that the paste will be smooth.

Flaky Pastry Filled
with White Turnips and Ham

 LUOBO SI SU BING

This savory flaky pastry is a classic banquet dish, usually offered after or with a serving of a clear exotic soup, such as shark fin, bird's nest, or fish maw. It is also marvelous as an appetizer all by itself. It also makes a tasty light meal, accompanied by Steamed Dumplings, Canton-Style (page 147) and Drop Noodles in Two Soups (page 90), followed by Flaky Pastry Filled with Red Bean Paste (page 181).

If you cannot find *luobo*, the Chinese white turnip, substitute grated tender carrots (see the variation at the end of the recipe). The filling will be less pungent, but you could add 2 tablespoons soaked chopped dried shrimp for a little bite.

In this recipe you shape vertical or spiral layers of dough for either baking or frying; frying the pastries in oil gives them a flakier texture and a richer flavor. You could also use this savory filling in the horizontal layers of Flaky Pastry Filled with Red Bean Paste—for baking only.

Yield: Twenty-four 2½-inch pastries

1 recipe flaky pastry dough
(page 179)
½ cup white or black sesame
seeds

1 egg, well beaten
4 cups peanut oil or corn oil (for
frying, optional)

THE FILLING

2 pounds *luobo* (Chinese white
turnip)
1 tablespoon coarse salt, for
salting the turnips
½ cup minced Smithfield ham or
other salty ham

½ cup finely chopped whole
scallions
2 teaspoons sugar
4 teaspoons sesame oil or corn
oil
½ teaspoon coarse salt, or to taste

MAKING THE FILLING

Peel the turnip and grate it in a food processor or with a hand grater. The shreds shouldn't be more than 1 inch long, and you should have about 8 cups, loosely packed. Put the grated turnips in a bowl, add the 1 tablespoon of salt (or 2 teaspoons if the ham is salty) and mix well, then press the mass down and let it stand for 10 minutes to macerate.

Put the salted turnips in a cloth towel and twist to squeeze out all the water you can. Return the turnips to the bowl and fluff them. Mix in the ham, scallions, sugar, and sesame oil. Add ½ teaspoon salt, or to taste, and set aside.

**SHAPING THE PASTRY IN VERTICAL OR SPIRAL LAYERS
(FOR BAKING OR FRYING)**

With a large rolling pin, gently roll the 4-by-8-inch folded dough into a 14-inch square, rolling away from the center toward both sides and then back toward you; use as little dusting flour as possible during the process. From one side roll the dough into a cylinder about 2 inches thick. *For vertical layers*, cut the cylinder into six pieces. Cut each piece lengthwise in two. Cover all the pieces with a damp cloth.

Put one piece at a time, cut side down, on a surface very lightly dusted with flour. Flatten it gently with your palm. Then roll it with a small rolling pin into a 3½-inch round disk, rolling the edges thinner than the center. Cover the finished disk with a slightly damp dish towel while you roll out the remaining eleven pieces.

For spiral layers, cut the cylinder crosswise into twelve pieces. Roll each disk, cut side down, into a 3½-inch round disk.

Take a disk and put 1 tablespoon of filling in the center. Gather as little dough as possible at the edges and pinch and pleat it; then twist to close, making sure the pastry is well sealed. Shape the pastry into a round, put it on a work surface, and press with your hand to flatten it a little. Cover the finished pastries with a slightly damp dish towel while you make twelve more disks with the other half of the dough and then fill them.

BAKING THE PASTRIES

Preheat the oven to 400 degrees. Set a plate of sesame seeds and the beaten egg near the work area.

Brush each pastry bottom with beaten egg and press it down flat in the sesame seeds. Set the pastries, bottoms down, on a baking sheet about 1 inch apart. When all twenty-four pastries are on two sheets, brush the tops with beaten egg. Bake at 400 degrees for 15 minutes, then reduce the heat to 350 degrees and continue baking for another 15 minutes. Serve warm or at room temperature.

FRYING THE PASTRIES

For extra rich, flaky pastries, deep-fry them. Set a plate of sesame seeds and the beaten egg near the work area.

Brush each pastry bottom with beaten egg and press it down flat in the sesame seeds. Set aside on a tray. Do not brush the tops with beaten egg (the egg would burn in the oil). Heat 4 cups of peanut oil or corn oil in a 12-inch wok or a deep fryer to 300 degrees. Slip pastries into the oil

four to six at a time and let them fry for about 3 minutes; then raise the heat to about 350 degrees and fry them for another 2 minutes, or until they start to bubble and float. The fried pastries should be a light brown

color, and they should be puffed and flaky. Carefully scoop them out with a small strainer and let them drain on paper towels.

The fried pastries can be kept in the refrigerator for one week and in the freezer for one month. Reheat refrigerated ones in a 350-degree oven for 15 minutes, frozen ones for 2 minutes more.

Variation: Use 4 cups of grated tender carrots instead of the *luobo*. After macerating them with the 1 tablespoon of salt and squeezing them dry, stir-fry them in 2 tablespoons of oil for 2 minutes. Add the remaining ingredients, but omit the sugar. Add 2 tablespoons of soaked chopped dried shrimp, if you wish, for a sweeter taste.

Another tasty filling is a combination of 1 cup of chopped cooked bacon, 1 cup of chopped scallions, 2 teaspoons of salt, and 1 teaspoon of sugar. Use 2 teaspoons of filling for each pastry.

Flaky Pastry
Baby Chicks and Daisies

小 XIAO JI SU BING

鸡

酥 In 1981 a group of Beijing chefs visited the United States in order to
attend a trade fair. During their stay here they cooked an elaborate din-

饼 ner at the China Institute in New York, and I witnessed their preparations. These filled "baby chicks" and "daisies" were served as part of the
dessert course. They are fun to make, not at all as difficult as they might
sound.

Yield: 14 chicks and 14 daisies

1 recipe flaky pastry dough (page 179)	1 egg, separated in 2 dishes, beaten till frothy
1 cup red bean paste (page 184)	1 teaspoon black sesame seeds

Prepare the bean paste, and with your hands lightly floured, take half of it and roll it into a long cylinder; break this into twenty-eight pieces about the size of cherries. Roll each piece with your palms to make little balls. Set aside.

With a rolling pin, roll one of the 4-by-8-inch folded pastry dough portions into a 12-by-16-inch oblong, rolling toward the sides from the center and then back toward you; use as little dusting flour as possible during the process. From the long side roll the dough into a cylinder about 1 inch thick. Cut the cylinder into fourteen portions and cover them with plastic wrap.

MAKING BABY CHICKS

On a lightly floured surface, flatten each piece of dough, smooth side down, with your palm. Then, with a small rolling pin, roll each into a 2½-inch round disk with the edges thinner than the center. Wrap a ball of filling inside a circle of dough, then gently shape the ball into a chick, squeezing it a little off-center to form a small head with beak and then a larger body, and make a slight depression on the bottom so the chick can sit securely. Using a small wavy metal clip or your fingers, pinch and stretch the filled dough to make wings, beak, comb, and tail. Set the chick on a baking sheet and repeat with the other thirteen pieces of dough. Dot a little egg white on each cheek and press on two black sesame seeds for eyes. Brush a little egg yolk on the wings, beak, tail, and comb. Bake in a preheated 350-degree oven for 15 minutes, or until slightly yellow and flaky.

MAKING DAISIES

After breaking the other piece of dough into fourteen pieces as described in the beginning of the recipe, cover them with a damp dish towel.

On a lightly floured surface, flatten each piece of dough, smooth side down, with your palm. Then, with a small rolling pin, roll each into a 2½-inch disk. Wrap one of the balls of filling inside and gently shape into a ball; then flatten the ball with your fingers, pressing from the center to the sides so the filling is evenly distributed. Then press with your palm to make the filled disk about 3 inches in diameter—take care not to break the wrapper.

With a small sharp knife make about eight evenly spaced slits all around the disk almost to the center. Gently turn and twist each cut section up 90 degrees to show the filling. Carefully push the petals close together, forming a daisy with the filling showing. Brush a little egg yolk on the uncut center and bake in a preheated 350-degree oven for 15 minutes, or until slightly yellow, puffed, and flaky.

Flaky Pastry Egg Custard Tarts

 DAN TART

The egg custard is definitely Western in origin, as is the word *tart*, used even in Chinese. These tarts are a favorite snack or dessert among the Chinese, particularly in Cantonese tea houses. The flaky pastry dough is excellent for this tart shell, although you could substitute your own favorite pie crust recipe.

Yield: Sixteen 3-inch tarts

½ recipe flaky pastry dough (page 179)	16 3-inch tart tins, metal or aluminum

THE CUSTARD FILLING

1 cup sugar	6 eggs
¾ cup water	2 teaspoons vanilla extract
¾ cup milk	

FORMING THE TART SHELLS
Roll out the folded flaky pastry dough into a sheet 8 by 12 inches. Fold the sheet into thirds, so you have a sheet 4 by 8 inches. Then roll out the dough on a lightly floured surface into a 16-inch-square piece. With a 4-inch round cutter or an empty can, cut out circles 4 inches in diameter. Fit each round into a tart tin. Press firmly, making sure the bottom

and sides fit snugly. Stack the finished tart shells with wax paper in between and refrigerate them wrapped in plastic. You can make them ahead of time and freeze them for as long as a month.

**MAKING THE CUSTARD AND
COOKING THE TARTS**
Dissolve the sugar in the water in a small saucepan over low heat. Let it cool completely. Preheat the oven to 300 degrees. With an electric mixer or food processor, mix the sugar water, milk, eggs, and vanilla until they are well combined. Pour through a fine strainer. Place the tart shells on a baking sheet and pour in the egg mixture almost to the brim. Place the sheet on the lowest rack of the oven and bake for about 40 minutes. Turn off the heat and let the tarts remain in the oven 10 minutes more.

The custard tarts may be served warm or at room temperature. They will keep fresh in the refrigerator, covered with plastic wrap, for two to three days. To serve, reheat them in a preheated 350-degree oven for 10 minutes.

Curry Puffs

咖 GAI LI JIAO
哩
饺 These little crescent-shaped pastries have been a favorite of mine for years. In 1965, after I had been teaching for five years, I was interviewed by Craig Claiborne of *The New York Times,* the subject being my *dim sum* class at the China Institute in New York. This curry puff was featured in the article, and after that I made and sold the puffs, frozen, at a gourmet shop. Had I continued to do it, I'd probably be very wealthy today, for they are so good, and they were very popular.

I use pie crust as the wrapper in this recipe, since it is easy to work with. The mashed potatoes in the filling, a secret imparted to me by my good friend Pao-G Shen, make the filling extremely moist. You can make these puffs ahead of time and freeze them for up to several months without danger of them drying out.

Curry puffs make excellent appetizers. They are also marvelous as a light meal with a soup dish such as Clam, Pickled Vegetable, and Noodle Soup (page 89) or Wontons in Broth (page 121).

Yield: 60 puffs 2½ inches wide

THE FILLING

2–3 tablespoons peanut oil or corn oil

1 pound ground pork or beef

1½ tablespoons light soy sauce

2 teaspoons coarse salt or to taste

1½ teaspoons sugar

1 cup hand-chopped minced onion

1 tablespoon Madras curry powder

½ cup packed mashed potatoes

THE CRUST

2 cups all-purpose flour

1½ sticks (¾ cup) margarine

⅓ cup ice water, approximately

1 egg, well beaten, for the glaze

MAKING THE FILLING

Heat a wok until hot; add 1 tablespoon of oil if using pork and 2 table-spoons if using lean beef. Swirl, and heat. Then add the ground meat and stir-fry until it separates into bits—about 2 minutes. Do not over-cook or it will exude too much oil. Add the soy sauce, salt, and sugar; stir well. Transfer to a bowl.

Heat the same pan with another tablespoon of oil. Add the onion and stir-fry until it is translucent, then add the curry powder. Cook with the onion for 1 minute, stirring constantly. Then add the cooked meat and the mashed potatoes and mix thoroughly. Taste and add more salt if you wish. Let the mixture cool and then put it in the refrigerator, covered with plastic wrap, to chill.

MAKING THE PUFFS

In a large mixing bowl combine the flour with the margarine and work with your fingertips until the margarine is evenly mixed in and most of the flour has the consistency of cornmeal. Stir in the ice water, mix and knead the dough until smooth (1 minute). Shape into two balls. Flatten the balls and cover with plastic wrap.

Roll the dough one ball at a time on a lightly floured surface into a

6-by-12-inch piece; then fold into thirds so you have a sheet 6 by 4 inches. Roll the dough again into a sheet approximately 12 inches square and 1/16 inch thick. Using a cookie cutter, cut out circles about 2½ inches in diameter. Stack them in two or three piles. Combine the scraps into the remaining dough and roll out to make more circles. Stack the last scraps unevenly and make more circles (you don't want to overwork the dough, however). Cover with plastic wrap.

FILLING AND COOKING THE PUFFS
Place 1 heaping teaspoon of filling in the center of each round, fold the dough over to make a crescent, and seal the edges by pressing hard;

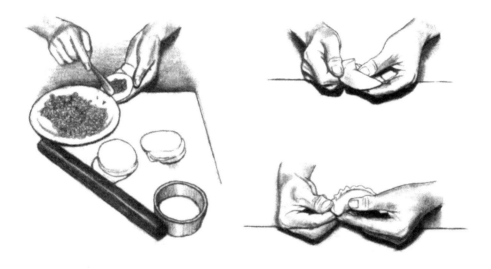

then use your fingertips to make a scalloped edge (you could also use the tines of a fork to press in the lines, sealing it more securely). Place the puffs on an ungreased baking sheet; then brush each one with beaten egg and prick the tops with a fork once. (At this point you could put the baking sheet in the freezer. When the puffs are frozen solid, hit the baking sheet on a table to loosen the puffs and put them in a tightly sealed container. They will keep in the freezer for as long as four months.)

Bake the curry puffs in a preheated 400-degree oven for 20 minutes, or until they are golden brown. The puffs can be frozen before or after baking, though they are better frozen before. Reheat them in a preheated 350-degree oven for 10 minutes if you freeze them already cooked.

Variation: For a chicken filling, use one whole steamed chicken breast. Steam it for 20 minutes and let it cool. (Omit the stir-frying.) Chop the chicken, including the skin, in a food processor, adding some of the chicken juice to produce a fairly soft purée. Season with salt instead of soy sauce. After you stir-fry the onions and curry powder, mix in the chicken with the mashed potatoes. Chill the filling before you put it in the puffs.

Boiled shrimp, chopped, may be used instead of meat or chicken. The mushroom filling would also be excellent.

Mushroom Puffs

 YU SU JIAO

These meatless puffs are absolutely delicious because of the magnificent flavor of fresh mushrooms that have been cooked till their juices disappear.

Yield: 60 puffs 2½ inches wide

3 tablespoons peanut oil or corn oil
1 pound firm fresh mushrooms, thinly sliced (6–7 cups)
1 teaspoon coarse salt or to taste
1 tablespoon light soy sauce
1 recipe curry puff crust (page 191)
1 egg, well beaten, for the glaze

Heat a well-seasoned wok or large skillet over medium-high heat until hot. Add the oil, swirl, then add the mushrooms and stir-fry for about 7 to 8 minutes, or until the liquid has cooked away. Add the salt and soy sauce and stir-fry a little more, until they are dry again. Scoop the mushrooms into a bowl and let them cool; then chop them very fine by hand with a Chinese cleaver or in a food processor, using the pulse action very sparingly. They should be like *duxelles*. Set aside.

Prepare the crust and wrap the puffs the same way as with the curry puffs. You can make them ahead of time and refrigerate or freeze them, as described on page 193. Bake them in a preheated 400-degree oven for 20 minutes, or until golden brown and a little puffed up.

≡

Steamed and Baked Buns and Fillings

≡

Steamed and Baked Yeast Dough Buns

  FA MIAN

Every cuisine has some kind of hot sandwich, and the Chinese is no exception. In fact, yeast dough buns, especially the delicate steamed variety, filled with either a sweet or a savory salty stuffing and always served hot, are enjoyed throughout China. We eat them as a snack or light meal, and in the north they are the daily bread. If the filling is sweet, the buns can be served as a dessert or breakfast pastry.

Until now, however, Chinese yeast dough has been tricky, time consuming, and tiring to make. I used to spend most of the day chopping the ingredients for the filling and worrying whether the dough would rise well. Now, with the food processor method I've devised, the dough is kneaded in seconds, shaped immediately, and with only a half-hour of rising the buns are ready to be steamed or baked. It is easy to make dozens of buns in a short time, which can be frozen for use later.*

Most Chinese prefer the traditional steamed buns—they have a more delicate texture than that of baked buns—but the color is white, a characteristic that doesn't appeal much to Americans. If you consider their other features, however—the succulent filling, and the warmth and softness of the bun—you'll soon love these steamed buns as much as the Chinese do.

Baked bun dough contains milk and eggs, making it richer than steamed bun dough. The additional ingredients probably reflect a European influence, and the baked buns actually are very much like a brioche. Filled with roast pork, they are a popular snack in Cantonese bake shops and tea houses.

Yeast Dough for Steamed Buns

Plain steamed buns are my favorite breakfast bread at home, made with a mixture of whole wheat and white flours. I use 1 teaspoon of salt instead of sugar in the basic recipe. Besides the traditional way of serving the buns steamed, I sometimes slice them in half, toast them, and butter them. The texture and flavor are far better than any baked bread, I think. You could also try a traditional Chinese variation: Cut

---

*For those who want to make these buns the old-fashioned way, by hand, see *Florence Lin's Chinese Regional Cookbook* (Hawthorne/Dutton, 1975), which contains the recipe for steamed, and *Florence Lin's One-Dish Meal Cookbook* (Hawthorne/Dutton, 1977), which contains the recipe for baked buns.

the plain buns (page 203) into ½-inch-thick slices and deep-fry them in 350-degree oil until they are crisp and golden brown outside and soft inside. Sprinkle salt on top and serve the fried slices hot with soup or congee. Finally, try them at room temperature. When I lived in northern China, I used to have a nighttime snack of one plain bun and one hard-boiled cold salted duck egg. They made a wonderful country snack.

Yield: 14 steamed buns 3 inches in diameter

¾ cup warm water (105°–115°)
½-ounce package dry yeast, 2½ teaspoons
2 teaspoons sugar
2 tablespoons corn oil
2½ cups unbleached all-purpose flour

Filling at room temperature (Use 1 recipe of Roast Pork Filling, page 209; or Chopped Pork, Mushroom, and Leafy Green Filling, page 210; or Curried Chicken Filling, page 211; or Red Bean Paste Filling, page 184.)

MAKING THE DOUGH

In a measuring cup, put in ¾ cup warm water, add the yeast, stir to dissolve it, and let it stand for 1 minute or until slightly foamy. Add the sugar and oil and mix well.

Put the flour in a food processor fitted with the metal blade. With the machine running, pour the yeast mixture through the feed tube in a steady stream. A ball of dough will form in about 10 seconds; if it doesn't, add more water, 1 tablespoon at a time. Check the dough; it

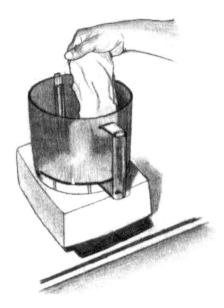

should be soft-firm. Continue to process for another 60 seconds, until the dough is very smooth and does not stick to your fingers.

FORMING AND FILLING THE BUNS

Transfer the dough to a lightly floured work surface and knead it for a few turns. Then roll it with your hands into a cylinder 14 inches long and 1½ inches wide. Cut the cylinder into 1-inch pieces. Turn the pieces on their sides and press with your palm to flatten them. Lightly roll each one with a rolling pin into a 3-inch round, rotating the dough as you roll and rolling the edges thinner than the center. Cover the rounds with a slightly damp cloth as they are finished.

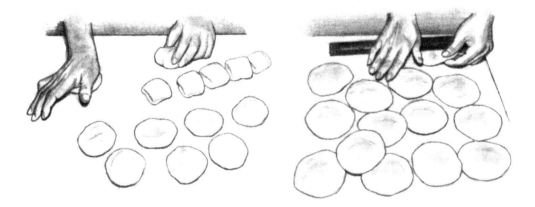

Put about 2 tablespoons vegetarian filling (or 1½ tablespoons meat, chicken, or sweet filling) in the center of each round, keeping the remaining rounds covered with the damp cloth. Use one thumb to push the filling down while you pinch and pleat the edge of the round with the thumb and forefinger of your other hand to enclose the filling. Do this carefully, so the pleats are thin and even, with a professional look.

In China buns with a sweet filling, such as the red bean paste (page 184) or jujube date filling (page 215), are traditionally steamed upside down to identify them as such. First pinch the edge and twist the bun to make sure it is tightly closed, then place the closed end down. After steaming, while they are still hot, these sweet buns may be marked with a spot of red food coloring, if desired, to further identify them as sweet.

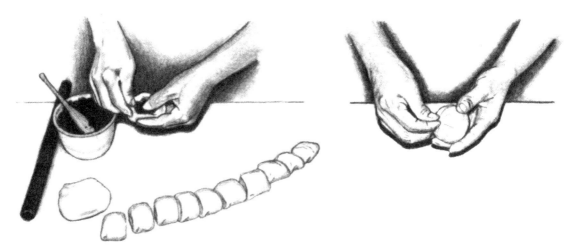

Buns with a salty filling are generally steamed right side up to mark them as salty. To further identify them, you could put a bit of filling in the pocket left at the top of the bun after shaping.

Put each filled bun on a 3-inch square of parchment or wax paper and place on a baking sheet, with a little space between them. Leave them uncovered in a warm place (about 80 degrees), such as a pilot-lit oven, for about 30 minutes, or until they are almost double in size.

STEAMING AND SERVING THE BUNS
Pour 3 to 4 inches of water into the bottom of a steamer or large pot and bring to a boil. Transfer the buns, with the paper, to the steamer rack or a rack elevated above the pot's boiling water with a little rack or a can. The buns should be about 1 inch apart. You can steam two tiers at once if you have such a steamer. Otherwise do the cooking in two pots at the same time. Steam the buns over high heat for 15 minutes.

Serve the buns directly from the steamer or transfer them to a platter. You can make them ahead of time. Remove them from the steamer to cool on a dry towel. In a plastic bag they will keep for two to three days in the refrigerator or for up to two months in the freezer. To reheat, steam the buns for 5 minutes; 2 more minutes if they're frozen.

Plain Steamed Buns

  MAN-TOU

After mixing and kneading the dough, form it with your hands into a cylinder that is 18 inches long and 1½ inches wide. Cut the cylinder into fourteen pieces. Without rolling or filling these pieces, put each on a 3-inch square of parchment or wax paper and place on a tray. Put the tray in a warm place, about 80 degrees, such as a pilot-lit oven, for 45 minutes or until almost double in size. (Lightly spray the buns with water if a crust forms.) Then steam the buns for 20 minutes.

Lotus Leaf Buns

 HE JE JUAN

 These are steamed breads that are shaped in the form of lotus leaves. They resemble a firm-soft bread that is folded into a crescent shape. They might be called a Chinese-style steamed pita bread. The Chinese usually fill them with slices of roast meat and eat them as we would a sandwich. I've suggested Chinese roast pork in this recipe, but these breads go wonderfully well with roast duck, roast chicken, or even roast beef. After mixing and kneading the dough, form it with your hands into a cylinder that is 18 inches long and 1½ inches wide. Cut the cylinder into twenty pieces for use with Chinese Roast Pork (page 208). Roll each piece with a rolling pin into a 3-inch circle. Brush half of the circle with corn oil and fold over into a half-moon shape. With a pastry scraper or knife, make impressions

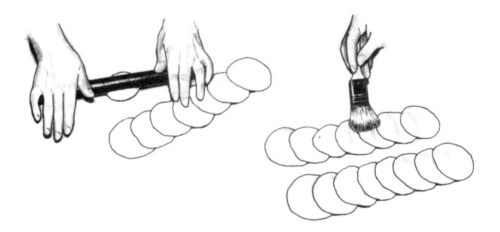

on the dough all the way across at ¼-inch intervals. Placing a chopstick against the center of the rounded edge and your thum'' and forefinger pinching the straight edge, press the dough on the curved edge up toward the center to form a leaf shape.

Let the leaf buns rise on a 3-inch square of parchment or wax paper in a warm place, about 80 degrees, such as a pilot-lit oven, for about 30 minutes, or until almost double in size. Steam the buns for 15 minutes.

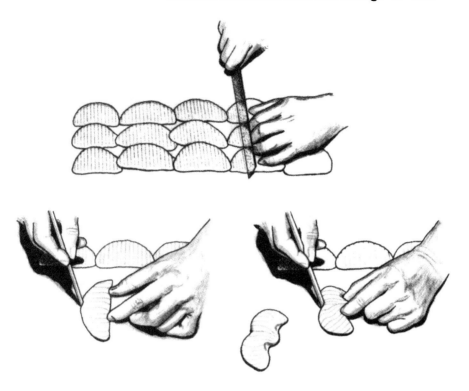

Once the buns are steamed, they are ready to be filled with thin slices of roast pork. Open the rounded side and slip in the pork. The buns can be made ahead of time and resteamed for 3 to 4 minutes, till hot.

Yeast Dough for Baked Buns

I often make these baked buns in small or large brioche molds. For appetizers you could also make tiny buns, 1½ inches in diameter, filled with roast pork. In that case cut the cylinder of dough into thirty pieces.

Yield: 14 baked buns 3 inches in diameter

½ ounce package dry yeast, 2½ teaspoons

2 tablespoons warm water (105°–115°)

⅔ cup warm milk

4 tablespoons of butter, melted, or corn oil

2 eggs, at room temperature, 1 well beaten

1 tablespoon sugar

2½ cups unbleached all-purpose flour

Filling at room temperature (Use 1 recipe of Roast Pork Filling, page 209; or Curried Chicken Filling, page 211; or Jujube Red Date and Nut Filling, page 215.)

MAKING THE DOUGH

In a measuring cup dissolve the yeast in the warm water and let it stand for 1 minute or until slightly foamy. Stir in the milk, the oil, the 1 beaten egg, and the sugar.

Put the flour into a food processor fitted with the metal blade. With the machine running, gradually pour the yeast mixture through the feed tube in a steady stream. A ball of dough will form in about 10 seconds; if the dough doesn't form by then, add more water 1 tablespoon at a time. Check the dough; it should be *very soft*. Continue to process for another 60 seconds, until the dough is very smooth and does not stick to your fingers.

FORMING AND FILLING THE BUNS

Transfer the dough to a lightly floured work surface and form it with your hands into a cylinder 14 inches long and 1½ inches wide. Cut it into 1-inch pieces and shape each into a ball. Lightly roll each ball into a 3-inch round, feeding and rotating the dough with one hand as you roll it with the rolling pin in the center; the edges should be thinner than the center (or use your fingers to push the ball into a 3-inch round).

Put about 1½ tablespoons of filling in the center of a round. Pinch and pleat the edges and bring them up to enclose the filling. Twist the

bun tightly closed. Put it on a baking sheet closed end down, continue with the other rounds, and put them all on a baking sheet with 2 inches between them. Let them rise, uncovered, in a warm place (about 80 degrees) for about 30 minutes, or until they are almost double in size.

For jujube-date-filled buns, make a cigar shape: Spread the filling over the circle of dough to within an inch of the round edge; then roll the dough up like a jelly roll and place the "cigars" seam side down to rise about 30 minutes on the baking sheet.

Preheat the oven to 350 degrees. Beat the remaining egg lightly with a fork and brush the tops of the buns with it. Bake the buns in the

middle level of your oven for 20 minutes, until they have a nice, shiny, golden-brown glaze.

The buns will keep for two to three days in the refrigerator, or they can be frozen for up to two months. Reheat at 350 degrees for 10 minutes, or, if frozen, for 12 minutes.

Chinese Roast Pork

 CHAO SHAO

 Roast pork is a very versatile food in Chinese dishes. It can be used as a main course alone, stir-fried with vegetables and used as a topping for noodles, or made as a filling for buns and dumplings.

This recipe is the classic Cantonese version of roast pork. The marinade can also be used on spare ribs or country-style ribs, to give you an unusual taste treat. The salty brown bean sauce is used in Chinese cooking exclusively for marinades and sauces.

Yield: 6 servings as a main course

THE ROAST PORK

2 **pounds boneless pork butt or loin**
1 **tablespoon brown bean sauce**
1 **clove peeled garlic, lightly flattened with the side of a cleaver**
3 **tablespoons light soy sauce**
1 **tablespoon sweet bean sauce or hoisin sauce**

2 **tablespoons dry sherry**
1 **teaspoon coarse salt**
1 **tablespoon sugar**
1 **tablespoon corn oil or peanut oil**
½ **teaspoon five-spice powder or** ⅛ **teaspoon white pepper**
2 **tablespoons of chicken broth or water with msg**

MARINATING THE PORK

Cut the pork into strips approximately 6 by 1½ by 1½ inches. With a sharp knife make four or five tiny slashes on both long edges of the strips, to prevent the meat from curling during the roasting. In a mixing bowl combine the remaining ingredients. Mix to blend well. Marinate the pork strips at room temperature for at least two hours or as long as 8 hours, turning them once or twice.

ROASTING THE PORK

Preheat the oven to 350 degrees. Put the pork strips on a rack over a roasting pan containing an inch of water; reserve the marinade. Cook the pork in the oven for 1 hour, turning once and brushing on the marinade twice. The edges will be slightly charred. Leave in the oven without heat for 10 minutes before serving.

Slice the pork and serve hot as a filling for Lotus Leaf Buns. (For steamed or baked buns, coarsely chop the pork to make the filling—see page 209.) The roast pork will keep in the refrigerator, covered, for three days or in the freezer for up to one month. To reheat frozen roast pork, thaw it completely and reheat in a 400-degree oven for 5 to 10 minutes.

Roast Pork Filling

 CHA SHAO BAO XIAN

 This is a simple but divine filling for steamed or baked buns (pages 199 and 206). When I make this I always leave a little fat in from the roast pork, to give the filling a rich flavor. I also slice the pork thin first and then chop it, so the filling is smooth. If you do the chopping in a food processor, cut the pork into chunks first and then use the pulse action, so the filling won't be mushy.

Yield: 2½ cups roast pork filling

2 tablespoons cornstarch	1 tablespoon sugar
6 tablespoons water	Pinch salt
1 tablespoon corn oil	Pinch freshly ground white
1 cup hand-chopped onions	pepper
2 cups coarsely chopped Chinese	¼ cup hand-chopped whole
Roast Pork (page 208)	scallions
2 tablespoons light soy sauce	

Stir together the cornstarch and 4 tablespoons of the water and set aside. Heat the oil in a wok or large skillet over moderate heat. Add the onions and cook, stirring constantly, until soft and translucent—about 2 minutes. Stir in the pork, the remaining 2 tablespoons of water, the soy sauce, sugar, salt, and pepper. Push the pork to one side, make a well in the center, and then pour the cornstarch mixture in and stir until it thickens. Then combine with the pork. Add the scallions and mix in. Remove from the heat and set aside to cool to room temperature.

The filling can be made ahead of time and will keep in the refrigerator for a week. Bring it to room temperature before using it.

Chopped Pork, Mushroom, and Leafy Green Filling

  CAE ROU BAO XIAN

I use this filling for steamed buns (page 209) because it is soft and delicate, with a subtlety much appreciated by the Chinese.

For many years when the women's association of the China Institute held its bazaar, steamed buns filled with this delicate pork-and-vegetable combination were sold in the Chinese food section—and they were always gone in half an hour. I made hundreds of them with several friends in my small kitchen, using one of the original Cuisinarts, given to me by Carl Southeimer; and then we'd freeze them.

This recipe can be doubled.

Yield: About 4 cups

6 ounces fresh mushrooms	1 package (10 ounces) frozen
2 tablespoons corn oil	chopped kale or chopped
8 ounces pork, cut into 1-inch	collard greens, completely
cubes, or ½ pound ground	thawed and squeezed very dry
pork	1 teaspoon coarse salt or to taste
1½ tablespoons soy sauce	½ teaspoon sugar
1 tablespoon dry sherry	⅛ teaspoon freshly ground white
1 teaspoon cornstarch	pepper
1 can (5 ounces) bamboo shoots,	
drained, about ¼ cup	

Chop the mushrooms by hand or use a food processor fitted with the metal blade—pulse-chop them about four to six times, until they are coarsely chopped. Heat 1 tablespoon of the oil in a medium skillet over moderate heat. Add the mushrooms and cook, stirring, until their moisture has been released and has completely evaporated—about 5 minutes. Scoop out to a dish and set aside.

Use the metal blade of the food processor to chop the pork, turning the machine on and off four to six times, or until chopped to a medium coarseness; or chop it by hand. Transfer to a mixing bowl, stir in the soy sauce, sherry, and cornstarch, and set aside.

Use the metal blade to chop the bamboo shoots, turning the machine on and off six to eight times, or until coarsely chopped. Or do it by hand with a Chinese cleaver.

Heat the remaining 1 tablespoon of oil in a wok or large skillet over moderately high heat. Add the pork mixture and cook, stirring constantly, just until the pork loses its pink color. Add the bamboo shoots and stir lightly for 1 minute. Add the kale and reserved mushrooms and mix well; then stir in the salt, sugar, and pepper. Taste for seasoning, adding more salt and pepper if needed. Cool the filling to room temperature.

This filling can be made ahead of time and will keep in the refrigerator for two days, covered. Bring to room temperature to use it.

Curried Chicken Filling

咖 GAI LI CHI BOA XIAN

哩
鸡   This curry filling, which is much loved by my students, is to be used with
饱   steamed or baked yeast buns (pages 199 and 206). Its exotic curry flavor
馅   is quite different from the subtlety of the pork and vegetable filling on
     page 210. The recipe can be doubled.

Yield: About 1½ cups

4 teaspoons cornstarch	1 tablespoon dry sherry
1 teaspoon coarse salt	½ cup hand-chopped onions
1 whole chicken breast, skinned and boned, about 6 ounces, coarsely chopped	1½ teaspoons curry powder
	1 teaspoon sugar
	2 tablespoons chopped scallions, green part only
2 tablespoons chicken broth	
2 tablespoons corn oil	

In a mixing bowl stir together 1 teaspoon of the cornstarch and ¼ teaspoon of the salt. Add the chopped chicken breast and stir well.

Stir together the remaining 3 teaspoons of cornstarch and the chicken broth and set aside.

In a wok heat 1 tablespoon of the oil over moderate heat. Add the chicken and cook, stirring constantly, until the pieces have separated—about 1 minute. Sprinkle on the sherry and transfer to a serving dish.

Heat the remaining 1 tablespoon of oil in the wok over moderate heat. Add the onions and cook, stirring, until they are translucent—about 1 minute. Add the curry powder and stir for 30 seconds. Stir in the sugar, the remaining ¾ teaspoon of salt, and the reserved chicken. When heated through, push the chicken to one side and pour the cornstarch-and-broth mixture into the center of the wok and stir until the sauce thickens. Then mix in the chicken. Scatter in the scallions and transfer to a dish to cool to room temperature.

The filling will keep, covered, for a week in the refrigerator; bring to room temperature before using.

Steamed Juicy Buns with Two Fillings

汤 TANG BAO

 These are the famous Yangzhou steamed juicy buns that I mentioned in the recipe for Yangzhou Noodle Soup in Casserole (page 82), which by the way makes an excellent accompaniment.

These buns are not hard to make. Traditionally one should mix two kinds of dough (a yeast dough and a hot-water dough) and combine them into one, so that the dough is tender and yet still has the strength to hold the chicken broth inside the bun. I have simplified the method, putting the leavening in one dough only, and you can achieve the same quality. The recipe can easily be doubled or tripled.

The delicate, juicy meat filling was perfected by my cousin Hsiang Ju Lin, the author of *Chinese Gastronomy*, published by Thomas Nelson. The vegetable filling, also very delicate and easy to make, was perfected by my daughter Flora.

Yield: 20 steamed buns

THE MEAT FILLING FOR THE BUNS

½ pound finely chopped celery cabbage or bok choy (in a food processor, use the pulse action about 10 times), about 2 cups

½ pound ground fresh bacon (pork belly), both fat and lean, with skin removed but reserved, preferably ground in a meat grinder but it can also be hand-chopped

1 teaspoon finely chopped fresh ginger

1 cup Best Chicken Broth (page 77)

1 tablespoon light soy sauce

½ teaspoon coarse salt

¼ teaspoon sugar

⅛ teaspoon white pepper

THE DOUGH FOR THE BUNS

1 cup all-purpose flour

½ teaspoon sugar

1½ teaspoons baking powder

6 tablespoons warm water, approximately

20 pieces aluminum foil, each 1½ inches square

MAKING THE FILLING FOR THE BUNS
Put all the filling ingredients in a 1-quart saucepan, including the bacon skin cut into four pieces. Bring to a boil, cover, and simmer for 1 hour. Remove and discard the bacon skin. The juice and solids should measure about 2 cups. Push the solids down and let the filling cool; then cover and place in the refrigerator. It will set like a jelly in about 4 hours. This can be done a day ahead of time.

MAKING THE DOUGH
In a large mixing bowl combine the flour, sugar, and baking powder and mix well. Make a well in the center and gradually pour about 4 tablespoons of warm water into the well while you stir with chopsticks, out from the center, to incorporate the flour. There will probably be some dry flour remaining in the bowl, so add the remaining 2 tablespoons of warm water 1 tablespoon at a time and continue to stir until all the flour is damp. With some flour on your hands, pat and knead the

dough in the bowl just enough to make it soft but not sticky; then place it on a floured surface and gently knead it for 2 minutes, or until it is smooth. Cover the dough with plastic wrap and let it rest for 30 minutes.

When you're ready to use the filling, remove and discard any solid fat around the edge of the saucepan. Then stir the filling and transfer it to a plate.

FILLING AND STEAMING THE BUNS
Set up a 10- to 12-inch bamboo steamer, and set the foils on the rack ½ inch apart. Have the filling ready on a plate.

Roll the dough with your hands on a lightly floured surface into a rope about 14 inches long and less than 1 inch thick. Break or cut this into twenty pieces. Sprinkle some flour on the disks and move them around so that the cut sides are lightly coated; this will prevent them from sticking together. Press each with the palm of your hand to flatten it. Cover the disks with a dry dish towel.

Take one disk of dough, press it with the heel of your hand to flatten it some more, and then, with a small rolling pin, roll it into a circle 3 inches in diameter. To make the circle as perfect as possible, roll the pin with the palm of one hand while you feed and turn the disk of dough counterclockwise with the fingers of the other. Try to roll from the edges to the center, so the edges are thinner than the center. Stack the wrappers overlapping.

Take one wrapper at a time in the palm of your hand, scoop 1 heaping tablespoon of filling from the edge of the plate with a butter knife, and put it in the center of the wrapper. Push the filling down with the thumb of the hand holding the wrapper while you pinch and pleat the edge of the round with the thumb and forefinger of your other hand to enclose the filling. Try to make these pleats as thin and even as possible. When you make the last pleat, lift all of them slightly so the bun has a topknot look.

Put the finished buns on the foil doilies. They can be covered with a dry dish towel and kept in the refrigerator for up to 4 hours at this point.

Bring the steamer water to a rolling boil and steam the buns over high heat for 8 minutes. Serve immediately with individual dips of 2 tablespoons Zhejiang vinegar combined with 1 teaspoon very finely shredded fresh ginger. Give your family or guests chopsticks and a Chinese soup spoon so that the broth will be caught by the spoon when they bite into the bun.

THE VEGETABLE FILLING FOR THE BUNS

1 **pound finely chopped bok choy or watercress, cut into 1-inch sections and put in a food processor. Use the pulse action, about 20 to 30 pulses. You should have 3 cups.**

2 **pieces seasoned pressed bean curd, thinly sliced. Put in the food processor and chop for 1 minute. Scrape down 2 or 3 times during processing. You should have ½ cup.**

4 **large soaked black mushrooms. Chop same as the bean curd, about ¼ cup**

3 **tablespoons sesame oil Salt and pepper to taste**

Cook the chopped bok choy with 2 cups water for 5 minutes. Let cool, then drain and squeeze most of the water out and put in a mixing bowl. Add the chopped bean curd, mushrooms, and sesame oil; mix well. Add salt and pepper to taste. Use this in place of meat filling but use 2 tablespoons for each bun.

Jujube Red Date and Nut Filling

  ZAO NI

This is a very popular filling for baked buns, and the small frankfurterlike shape signals to the Chinese that these buns contain a sweet filling. If you want to make steamed buns with this filling, steam them closed-end down to denote a sweet bun. (See the description of steamed buns, page 199, and baked buns on page 206.)

Yield: 2 cups

8 **ounces red jujube dates, pitted**
½ **cup walnut meats**

¼ **cup sesame seeds, toasted in a dry skillet till fragrant**
¼ **cup corn oil**

Put the dates in a 2-quart saucepan with 2 cups of water. Boil for 30 minutes, or until the water has almost evaporated. Set aside.

To make the filling in a food processor, put the dates, walnuts, and sesame seeds in the bowl fitted with the metal blade. Use the pulse action about ten times; then scrape down the bowl. Then pour the oil through the feed tube and continue to process with the pulse action about ten to twenty times, or until finely chopped.

To make the filling by hand, first chop the dates, walnuts, and sesame seeds until they are a fine mince. Scoop into a bowl and mix in the oil with a spoon.

The filling will keep, covered, for a week in the refrigerator or in the freezer for up to three months.

Steamed Open Buns Filled with Mushrooms and Dried Shrimp

 NUO MI JUAN

 These yeast-dough buns wrap a plush filling of glutinous rice, mushrooms, and bamboo shoots flavored with dried shrimp. The dough here is coiled around the filling and then sliced thickly. Each serving is like a piece of the filling encircled with a layer of the steamed bun. You could substitute for the shrimp ½ cup of minced roast pork, ham, or steamed sausage if you wish. These buns are good as a breakfast or brunch dish, a snack, or an accompaniment to a meal. Best of all, they can be made ahead of time. Resteam them and serve hot.

Yield: 10 servings as a snack, 6 as part of a meal

1 recipe basic yeast dough (page 199)

THE FILLING

1½ cups glutinous rice (sweet rice)
1½ cups Best Chicken Broth (page 77)
2 tablespoons corn oil or peanut oil

2 cups chopped fresh mushrooms (see *Variation* at end of recipe)
¼ cup minced bamboo shoots
2 tablespoons finely minced dried shrimp

2 tablespoons dry sherry
1 tablespoon oyster sauce or
light soy sauce

1 teaspoon coarse salt
⅛ teaspoon white pepper

MAKING THE FILLING

Wash the rice until the water runs clear; then drain. Put the rice in a heatproof bowl, add 1½ cups of the broth, and let the rice soak for at least 30 minutes. (Soaking softens the rice and shortens the steaming time.)

Set the rice bowl in a large pot. Add water around the bowl until it comes to 2 inches below the rim. Cover the pot and bring the water to a boil. Steam the rice over high heat for 30 minutes. Turn off the heat and let the rice sit for 10 minutes.

Heat a wok for 30 seconds, add the oil and swirl, then add the mushrooms and stir-fry over medium-high heat until almost all the liquid has cooked away—about 3 minutes. Then add the bamboo shoots and shrimp and stir-fry for 2 more minutes. Add the sherry, oyster sauce, salt, and pepper, and stir and toss to mix well. Turn off the heat.

Fluff the rice with chopsticks, stir in the cooked ingredients, and taste for seasoning, adding more salt if needed.

Divide the filling into three portions and put each on a piece of plastic wrap; then fold the plastic over to cover the filling. Press and shape the filling into a tube shape about 7 inches long and 1½ inches wide. Set aside, but do not refrigerate.

FORMING AND STEAMING THE ROLLS

Follow the yeast dough recipe to make the dough. Divide it into three pieces. Roll each piece with a rolling pin into a 7-inch square. Put one oblong of rice filling in the center of this dough and wrap the dough around it to make an oblong shape, pinching the edges to seal it, including the two ends. Put each oblong roll seal side down on a 4-by-8-inch piece of parchment or wax paper on a tray. Set the tray in an unheated oven (about 80 degrees) to let the dough rise for 30 minutes.

Set up a bamboo steamer in a large wok or improvise a steamer from a large pot with a rack set on top of a can with both ends removed or a heatproof bowl with water in it. Pour in 3 to 4 inches of water and bring to a boil. Then cover and set the rolls on the steamer rack (you could steam two tiers at once in a bamboo steamer). Steam the rolls over high heat for 15 minutes.

Transfer the rolls to a dry towel to cool, or serve them immediately. Cut the rolls into slices about 1 to 2 inches thick. When they are cold, the rolls, uncut, can be stored in the refrigerator for a week and in the freezer for a month; wrap them well in plastic. Cut the rolls while still cold and reheat them in a steamer for 5 minutes before serving.

Variation: Instead of fresh mushrooms, use 8 dried black Chinese mushrooms in the stuffing. Wash, then soak them in hot water till soft, remove and discard the stems, and chop the caps, about ½ cup.

Pan-Fried Pork Scallion Buns

生
煎   SHENG JIAN BAO ZI
饱
子

This is a tasty bun of quick yeast dough stuffed with a scallion and ginger infused pork filling. It is often found on restaurant menus and reserved for special occasions at home. The method of cooking—a combination of pan-frying and steaming—makes the bottom a crisp brown and the rest of the bun pale and very juicy. Preferably the pan should be nonstick so that if the buns aren't properly sealed, they can easily be removed when done.

I sometimes make thirty-two tiny ones rather than the sixteen called for here. They are a wonderful finger food for an appetizer, but you should warn your guests how juicy they are.

This recipe recalls the steamed buns sold in a tiny shop behind my middle school. Often I couldn't wait till class ended to run outside and purchase them, so I'd slip out early to get them, piping hot, filled with pork or beef. I was caught only once by the headmaster, and he didn't scold me very severely, such was the reputation of those steamed buns!

Yield: Sixteen 2½-inch buns or thirty-two 1½-inch buns

THE FILLING

1 pound ground pork or beef, about 2 cups
2 teaspoons finely minced fresh ginger
½ cup finely chopped whole scallions

½ teaspoon coarse salt
2 tablespoons light soy sauce
1 tablespoon sesame oil
¼ cup Best Chicken Broth (page 77)

THE QUICK YEAST DOUGH

1 package dry yeast, ¼ ounce

¾ cup lukewarm water, approximately

2 teaspoons sugar

2 tablespoons peanut oil or corn oil

2 tablespoons peanut oil or corn oil

2½ cups unbleached all-purpose flour

MAKING THE FILLING

Combine the filling ingredients in a mixing bowl, stirring in one direction with a spoon until the meat holds together. Refrigerate for 30 minutes or more.

MAKING THE DOUGH

Dissolve the yeast in the warm water and let it set for 1 minute or until it is slightly foamy. Then add the sugar and oil to the yeast mixture and mix well. Put the flour in a food processor with a metal blade in the bowl. Turn the machine on and begin processing; then pour the yeast mixture through the food tube in a fast stream until a dough ball forms (about 10 seconds after all the liquid has been added). If the dough does not form, add a little more water 1 tablespoon at a time. The dough should be medium-firm at this point—check it. Continue processing for 1 minute, or until the dough is very smooth and not sticky; this is the equivalent of kneading the dough by hand for 10 minutes.

Place the dough on a lightly floured surface and knead for a few turns; then roll into a long roll on the surface with your hands to make a thick rope about 16 inches long. Cut the dough into sixteen or thirty-two pieces. Flatten each piece with your palm and then quickly roll each piece with a rolling pin into a 2- or 3-inch round (depending on whether you are making the very small buns or the larger ones). The edges should be thinner than the center. Stack the rounds overlapping.

FILLING THE BUNS

Put 2 tablespoons of the filling (or 1 tablespoon for the small buns) in the center of each circle and cradle the dough in the palm of your hand. Then, as you push the filling down with the thumb of that hand, with your other thumb and forefinger pleat the edge of the dough so that the filling is enclosed, being careful to pleat just a little of the dough so that the little bun looks professional. The pleats should close over the top of the bun but they should be upright, not flat. Make the other rounds, setting the finished buns on a floured surface. The buns are best fried right away, but you can freeze them at this point and cook them, still frozen, later.

FRYING THE BUNS

Heat a 14-inch skillet or two 10-inch skillets over medium-high heat until very hot. Add 2 tablespoons of oil to coat the pan. Arrange the finished buns 1 inch apart in the pan, pleats up, and fry them until they are lightly browned on the bottom. Add 1 cup of water for the large skillet or ½ cup for each of the smaller ones and cover immediately. Cook for about 8 minutes, or until the water has cooked away. (If the buns are frozen, cook for about 10 minutes.) Remove the cover and continue cooking until a crust forms on the bottom of the buns. Serve them hot, crust side up.

The buns can be reheated in a skillet. First fry them for 2 minutes; then add 2 teaspoons of water, cover the pan, and steam them for 2 to 3 minutes, or until the water has cooked away and the bottoms of the buns are crisp.

Doughs Made from

Rice
Flour

≡

Rice
Noodle
Dishes

≡

Rice Flour

Rice or rice flour can be divided into two types: long grain and short, or oval, grain. The short-grain variety is also called glutinous (or sweet) rice, because it is stickier than the long-grain. Japanese rice has a texture between these two.

Rice flour is an important ingredient in making both sweet and salty noodles or cakes. The Chinese and the Japanese are particularly fond of sweets made with rice flour. Glutinous rice dumplings or cakes, for instance, are symbolic of family happiness. During the Chinese New Year, many regional variations on these delicacies appear, such as Ningbo Glutinous Rice Dumplings Filled with Sesame Seed Paste or Stir-Fried Rice Cake (Savory) (page 243), but the main ingredients are always glutinous and long-grain rice flours.

Rice Noodles (or rice sticks) are a popular pasta in the south of China; they are made from ground long-grain rice, and they are light, fluffy, and white when cooked. They are used in soups, soaked and then stir-fried, or deep-fried while still dry to make a crisp garnish.

Rice Noodles (Rice Sticks)

 PAI MI FEN

Dried rice noodles, also referred to as rice sticks, are available at most Chinese and Oriental markets. They keep for a long time without refrigeration, and their quality is very good. They are an off-white color and come in various thicknesses, from ¼ inch wide to about ⅟₃₂ inch wide. They are usually sold in 1-pound packages with four wads of them inside cellophane. For most dishes the noodle that is slightly thicker than ⅟₁₆ inch is suitable.

If you are using precooked dried rice noodles as a main course, you need to put them first in water (the thick kind in boiling water; the very thin kind in cold water) until they are light and soft. If you are using dried rice noodles as a garnish in salads or with very spicy food, you need to deep-fry them first in very hot oil.

Fresh rice noodles are not as versatile as dried. Their texture tends to be much softer and consequently they absorb less sauce. I'm including the recipe here primarily for those who cannot get the dried kind. Just remember that for any rice noodle dish calling for the soaking-in-water step first, you can eliminate that procedure with fresh rice sticks. To make fried rice noodles, you have to dry the fresh noodles thoroughly.

Yield: 1¼ pounds

2 cups rice flour, preferably water-ground (page 322)
1¾ cups boiling water, approximately

1 tablespoon corn oil
Cornstarch for dusting

Put the rice flour in a mixing bowl and stir in the boiling water with a fork or pair of chopsticks to make a firm dough. While the dough is still warm, knead it for about 2 minutes on a work surface, until it's smooth and soft. Pat the dough down flat to a piece about 6 by 4 inches, put it on a plate, and steam over high heat for 20 minutes.

Put the steamed hot dough in a food processor fitted with the steel blade. Add 1 tablespoon of oil. Turn the machine on for about 30 seconds, or until a ball forms. Remove the dough, smear a little oil on your hands, and knead the dough for 2 minutes. (The dough can also be kneaded entirely by hand. Smear a little oil on your hands and knead the dough until it is very smooth—about 4 minutes. The kneading must be done while the dough is hot.)

Divide the dough into two pieces, keeping one hot in the covered steamer. Roll the other into a sheet about ¹⁄₁₆ inch thick, sprinkling the dough with a little cornstarch as you roll. When the sheet is made, dust it on both sides with cornstarch, smoothing it in with your hands, to prevent it from sticking. Then fold from the two ends to the center in 3-inch folds. With a sharp knife cut across the folds to make strips about ¹⁄₁₆ inch wide. Unroll the noodles by tossing loosely. Roll out, fold, and cut the other piece of dough.

For a main dish, keep the noodles in a plastic bag until you are ready to cook them. For a garnish, dry them completely if you are going to deep-fry them. Fresh rice noodles will keep in the refrigerator for up to a week, and for a month in the freezer.

Stir-Fried
Rice Noodles, Singapore-Style

 XING ZHOU MI FEN

Here dried rice noodles are boiled briefly and then added to a mélange of meat, shrimp, and vegetables flavored with curry powder and chicken broth. (If you have fresh rice noodles, the boiling step should be eliminated.)

The "Singapore-Style" refers to the curry, which the Cantonese and Amoy Chinese living in Singapore add to a favorite dish. It is a well-known dish by this name, even in mainland China.

This recipe can easily be doubled; if you do so, keep the first portion hot in the oven while you prepare the second amount.

Note: If you use very thin rice noodles soak them in cold water for 5 to 10 minutes; do not boil them.

Yield: 4 servings as a light meal or a starch dish

½ **pound dried rice noodles slightly thicker than ¹⁄₁₆ inch**
1 **cup shredded roast pork, ham, or cooked chicken**
¼ **pound raw shrimp, shelled and cut into small pieces**
½ **cup shredded onion**
1 **cup shredded celery or mung bean sprouts**
5 **tablespoons peanut oil or corn oil**

1–2 **teaspoons curry powder, to taste**
1 **teaspoon coarse salt, or to taste (more if using chicken)**
1 **teaspoon sugar**
1 **tablespoon light soy sauce**
1 **cup Best Chicken Broth (page 77)**

PREPARATIONS

Bring 2 quarts of water to a boil in a large pot. Set a large colander in the sink. Add the dried rice sticks to the boiling water and loosen the layers with chopsticks. As soon as the noodles get soft—in 30 seconds—drain them in the colander. Then put them on a clean counter or tray and cover with the colander so they cool gradually and stay soft. Fluff them with chopsticks. They should be soft, but dry.

The noodles can be kept in a plastic bag to be used later in the day. You needn't refrigerate them.

Prepare the meat, shrimp, and vegetables and put them in separate piles on a large plate.

THE COOKING
Heat a wok over high heat until hot. Add 1 tablespoon of the oil and stir-fry the shrimp until it changes color—not more than 30 seconds. Set aside.

Heat the remaining 4 tablespoons of oil in the wok and add the onion; stir-fry until translucent. Push aside and stir the curry powder into the oil for about 10 seconds. Then add the celery or bean sprouts, salt, and sugar and stir to mix. Add the meat and the soy sauce, mix well, then add the shrimp and chicken broth. Bring to a boil.

Put the rice sticks on top without stirring them in. Cover and cook over medium-high heat for about 3 minutes to steam the rice noodles; there should be some sauce remaining. With a spatula, stir and lift gently from the bottom of the wok so that the sauce is absorbed by the noodles.

The dish can be kept in a steamer or in a low oven (about 200 degrees) for several minutes until you are ready to serve.

Stir-Fried
Rice Noodles with Ham and Cabbage

火 HUO TUI MI FEN
腿
米 This is one of the lunches or light meals that I serve most often for my
粉 family. It's a great everyday meal because it's so easy to make. This dish is
   Chinese home cooking at its best. Dried rice noodles are a staple in my
   house. The soft, fluffy cooked noodles are soothing and filling.

Note: If you use very thin rice noodles, soak them in cold water for 5 to 10 minutes; do not boil them.

Yield: 4 servings as a light meal or as a starch dish

½ **pound dried rice sticks (rice noodles), slightly thicker than ¹⁄₁₆ inch**

1 **cup shredded ham or Chinese Roast Pork (page 208)**
¼ **cup shredded whole scallions**

2 cups shredded green cabbage, or bean sprouts	1 cup Best Chicken Broth (page 77)
3 tablespoons corn oil	1 tablespoon light soy sauce

PREPARING THE NOODLES

Bring 2 quarts of water to a boil in a large pot. Set a large colander in the sink. Drop the dried rice sticks into the boiling water and loosen the layers with chopsticks. As soon as they become soft—within 30 seconds—drain them in the colander, then put them on a work surface or tray and cover with the colander so they cool gradually. Fluff the noodles with chopsticks.

If you are going to use them hours later, put them into a plastic bag after they cool. You needn't refrigerate them.

MAKING THE TOPPING

Put the meat and vegetables on a plate. Heat a wok or large skillet over medium-high heat. Add the oil, heat, then stir-fry the scallions and cabbage for 1 minute; add the meat and stir-fry together for another minute. Pour in the broth and soy sauce, bring to a boil, then put the noodles on top without mixing them in. Cover and cook over medium-high heat for 3 minutes to steam the noodles. There should be some sauce remaining. With a spatula, stir and toss from the bottom of the pan up, so that the remaining sauce will be absorbed by the noodles. Serve hot, immediately.

To double, prepare the dish twice and keep the first portion in a low-temperature oven or a steamer until the other is done.

Spicy Beef with Fried Rice Noodles

干 GAN BIAN NIU ROU SI
煸
牛 This is a typical Sichuan dish; it should be dry and spicy-hot. It can be
肉 served straight from the wok or at room temperature. Dish out small
丝 portions for an appetizer or serve it with boiled rice or rice congee as the
main course. I first had it at the home of my best friend in China, Peng-
fei, and she perfected this recipe.

After I left China in 1947 for the United States, I "lost" my friend for thirty-two years, unable to discover where she was living. But in 1979 relatives of mine found her, and when I returned to China in 1980, I visited Peng-fei and her husband and grown-up daughter. They lived in a one-room walk-up apartment, with the stove in the doorway and the only running water in the courtyard below. That night she cooked a twenty-course dinner, and this favorite recipe of ours was among them. So, once again after all these years, we were enjoying food together—and we cried many times that night.

Yield: 8 to 10 servings as an appetizer; 6 servings with rice or rice congee

1 **pound flank steak or sirloin, semi-frozen for easier slicing**
2 **ounces dried rice noodles or rice sticks, slightly thicker than 1/16 inch**
2 **cups peanut oil or corn oil for deep-frying and stir-frying**
1½ **cups matchstick-strip carrots (a mandolin produces the best cut)**
½ **cup fresh hot chili peppers, seeded and cut into matchstick strips**

1 **teaspoon chili pepper flakes or to taste**
2 **teaspoons minced fresh ginger**
½ **teaspoon minced fresh garlic**
1 **teaspoon sesame oil**
24 **lettuce leaf cups 5 inches in diameter, from iceberg or Boston lettuce**

THE MARINADE

¼ **teaspoon coarse salt**
3 **tablespoons soy sauce**
2 **teaspoons sugar**

2 **teaspoons cornstarch**
1 **tablespoon dry sherry**
1 **tablespoon oil**

PREPARATIONS

Cut the steak diagonally with the grain into thin slices, stack them overlapping, and cut again with the grain into 2-inch-long matchstick strips. Put the steak strips in a bowl, add the marinade and mix well, then refrigerate for a few minutes or up to eight hours if you wish.

Break 1 wad of rice noodles in half lengthwise to give you 2 ounces. Pull the wad into two or three very loose nests and set aside.

Pour 2 cups of oil into a wok. Heat the oil till very hot—about 375 degrees. The oil must be very hot so that the rice noodles will puff up immediately without soaking up the oil. Drop one nest of rice noodles in at a time. It will fluff up instantly. Turn it over with the help of a spoon and a small strainer and then scoop it out with the strainer to drain on paper towels. When all the rice noodles have been deep-fried, crush them with a spatula or your hands into short pieces about 2 inches long. This step can be done days ahead of time; the rice sticks keep well in a jar, can, or plastic bag. The oil can be reused.

Put the carrots, fresh hot peppers, chili pepper flakes, ginger, and garlic on a plate.

THE COOKING

Heat a wok or large skillet and add 2 tablespoons of oil. When it is hot, add the carrots and fresh hot peppers and stir-fry for 2 minutes over medium heat; then scoop them out onto a plate. Reheat the pan; then add 3 tablespoons of oil and the ginger, garlic, and chili pepper flakes; fry for 5 seconds or until light brown and fragrant. Then add the beef, stir-frying over high heat for about 2 minutes, or until the meat is dry and there is no more liquid. Lower the heat and stir-fry for another minute. Add the cooked vegetables, stir together for 1 minute, and add the sesame oil. Mix well.

Scoop out the ingredients and mound them on a large serving platter; put the rice noodles around the beef or scatter them on top. Mix lightly at the table before serving.

Each diner should put 1 to 2 tablespoons of the beef-and-noodle mixture in a lettuce leaf and then roll it up to eat it.

Variation: Deep-fried cellophane noodles may be used instead of rice noodles; they will be snow white in color. They must be used the same day they are fried, however, since they lose their crispness quickly. Chicken or pork can be substituted for the beef, using the same marinade.

Cold Crabmeat Salad with Fried Rice Noodles

 LIANG BAN XIA ROU

 This is an elegant and scrumptious dish made in the famous Tse Yang restaurants in Paris and New York. The chef uses pimento, but when tomatoes are in season you might try them instead. Dip one ripe tomato in boiling water, then peel and seed it. Dry with paper towels and cut into fine strips.

Yield: 4 servings

½ **pound fresh lump crabmeat**
3 **cups shredded iceberg lettuce**
⅓ **cup pimento cut into fine strips**

2 **cups deep-fried rice noodles, about 2 ounces (see instructions for frying the noodles in Spicy Beef with Fried Rice Noodles, page 229)**
2 **cups peanut oil or corn oil**

THE DRESSING

2 **tablespoons red wine vinegar**
1 **tablespoon light soy sauce**
1 **teaspoon sugar**

¼ **teaspoon white pepper**
1 **tablespoon sesame oil**

Break the crabmeat lumps into smaller pieces if they're large. Put the shredded lettuce and pimento strips in a salad bowl and put the crabmeat on top without mixing it. Cover with plastic wrap and chill in the refrigerator if you are making the salad ahead of time.

Fry the rice noodles in the oil and crumble them now; of course, you could have prepared them days in advance. Set aside.

Combine the dressing ingredients in a small cup. Just before serving, pour the dressing over the salad and toss well. Sprinkle the fried rice sticks on top and toss again.

This recipe can easily be doubled.

Sha He Noodle Sheet

沙　SHA HE FEN
河
粉

Sha He is a small town in Guangzhou (Canton) province. It is well known for its velvety-soft, shining white noodle sheets, made with a locally milled rice flour. They can be homemade (see the following recipe), but most Chinese prefer to buy them. Bean curd factories in major-city Chinatowns here usually make these noodle sheets. They come in large squares, 2 feet by 1½ feet, weighing about 1 pound. They are already cooked, oiled on both sides to prevent them from sticking together, and usually folded for easy handling. If they're not folded properly, you must refold them while they are still soft, before you refrigerate them.

If you are making wrappers, cut the sheets into 4-by-5-inch pieces; for noodles, cut ½-inch-wide strips about 8 inches long. They are traditionally served stir-fried with meat and vegetables as a main course, in a soup, or sprinkled with granulated sugar and honey and eaten as a cold dessert.

The texture is moist and pliable when the sheets are used the same day they're bought. Even after just a few hours in the refrigerator, they lose their softness. If you do store them in the refrigerator (for up to a few days) or the freezer (for up to a month), you must restore their freshness through brief cooking. Either take them out of the plastic and steam them until they are soft and pliable, or let them come to room temperature still tightly closed in plastic and submerge them in very hot water, bag and all, until soft.

Because you cannot buy the special rice flour needed for these sheets, I have substituted cake flour.

Yield: About 1 pound: in a 10-inch skillet, about 12 sheets 8 inches in diameter; in a 6-inch skillet, about 20 sheets 5 inches in diameter

1 cup cake flour
½ cup tapioca starch
½ cup cornstarch
¼ teaspoon coarse salt

1½ tablespoons peanut oil or corn oil
2 cups water

Put the flour, tapioca starch, cornstarch, salt, and oil in a mixing bowl. Since the dough won't mix well if you add all the water at once, pour in 1 cup and beat with a wire whisk until you have a smooth batter. Add the remaining cup of water and whisk well. Set aside.

Pour a thin layer of oil over a large tray. Heat a nonstick skillet over medium-low heat until it is hot (a 10-inch one if making noodles, a

6-inch one if making wrappers). Pour in just enough batter, tilting the pan, to cover the bottom of the pan; then cover and let it cook for about 2 minutes, or until the top is no longer sticky when touched. Turn it over, cook for a few seconds, and transfer it to the oiled tray, brushing the top with oil, too.

Continue making the noodle sheets, each time stirring the batter, because the flour will settle to the bottom. Pour more oil on the tray when needed. The cooked noodle sheets can be stacked as long as both sides of the sheets are liberally oiled. When the noodle sheets cool, put them in a plastic bag, and do not refrigerate if used the same day.

For noodles, cut the sheets while still soft into ½-inch-wide strips. For wrappers, leave them whole.

Sha He
Noodle Sheet Chicken Roll

JI SI ZHENG FEN CHANG

Here shredded chicken, bamboo shoots, and Chinese mushrooms, delicately flavored with oyster sauce and soy sauce, are wrapped inside Sha He noodle sheets, and the rolls are then steamed. They resemble egg rolls with two ends open. They are perfect for a light meal.

Yield: 24 rolls

2 small whole chicken breasts, semi-frozen for easier slicing
8 dried Chinese mushrooms
2 cups winter bamboo shoots, cut into matchstick strips
1 whole scallion
6 tablespoons peanut oil or corn oil

2 pieces commercial Sha He noodle sheets or 2 recipes homemade sheets
Fresh coriander or watercress leaves as garnish

THE MARINADE

½ teaspoon salt
2 teaspoons cornstarch

2 tablespoons water
1 tablespoon oil

THE SAUCE

2 tablespoons light soy sauce	1 teaspoon sugar
2 tablespoons oyster sauce	2 tablespoons cornstarch
½ teaspoon coarse salt	5 tablespoons chicken broth

MAKING THE FILLING

Cut the semi-frozen chicken breasts diagonally into very thin slices. Stack them overlapping and cut again into matchstick strips. Put them in a bowl, mix in the marinade, and set in the refrigerator for a few minutes or longer if you wish.

Rinse the mushrooms, then soak them for at least 30 minutes in warm water. Remove and discard the stems and cut the caps into matchstick strips. Cut the bamboo shoots and the scallion the same way; then put all the vegetables on a plate.

Combine the sauce ingredients in a small bowl.

Heat a wok over medium heat until hot. Add 4 tablespoons of the oil and let it heat for 30 seconds. Add the chicken and stir-fry until it changes color and separates into shreds. Scoop it out into a bowl with a spatula. Add the remaining 2 tablespoons of oil and stir-fry the bamboo shoots, mushrooms, and scallion for 2 minutes. Add the cooked chicken and toss to heat through.

Stir the sauce well, making sure the cornstarch and sugar are dissolved; then pour it into the wok and cook, stirring and tossing, until the sauce has thickened and coats the chicken.

Put the filling in a bowl and let it cool; then refrigerate. (The filling is much easier to handle when it is cold.)

FILLING AND COOKING THE NOODLE SHEETS

The noodle sheets must be soft to be filled, so it's best to use them the same day they are bought or made. Keep them stacked in a plastic bag at room temperature. If, however, you've refrigerated them, reheat them according to the instructions on page 233.

If the sheets are store-bought, cut them into squares about 4 by 5 inches. Homemade ones, prepared in a 6-inch skillet, should be about 4 to 5 inches in diameter. You should have about twenty-four squares or circles.

For commercial sheets, spread 2 tablespoons of filling all along one lengthwise edge and roll tightly into a cylinder. For homemade noodle circles, spread the filling across the middle and roll the sheet up and over the filling. Lay the cylinder on a generously oiled plate that you will later use for steaming. Continue to form the rolls and line them up on the plate, making sure there is oil between the rolls, too. An 8-inch plate can handle about eight to ten filled rolls. When you are finished, cover the plate with plastic, for up to several hours if you wish. Refrigerate if you are keeping them for more than a few hours.

Steam the chicken rolls over high heat for 10 minutes, or 12 minutes if they've been refrigerated. Transfer them to individual plates, serving two per person for a first course or four to six as lunch. Garnish with the coriander or watercress.

Variation: Pork, turkey, or beef can be used instead of chicken.

Beef with Sha He Noodles

牛
肉
炒
沙
河
粉
 NIU ROU SHAO SHA HE FEN

This dish of sliced beef and bean sprouts tossed with Sha He noodles would go very well with a cold salad such as Celery Cabbage with Dried Shrimp Salad (page 305), and Steamed Dumplings, Beijing-Style (page 145).

Yield: Serves 4 as a light meal

½ pound flank steak
2 whole scallions, split and cut in 2-inch sections
3 cups fresh mung bean sprouts
4 tablespoons peanut oil or corn oil

1½ pounds soft Sha He noodles, in ½-inch wide strips (page 233)
½ teaspoon coarse salt
½ teaspoon sugar
1 tablespoon dark soy sauce

THE MARINADE

1 teaspoon minced fresh ginger
1 tablespoon dark soy sauce
2 teaspoons cornstarch

1 tablespoon dry sherry or water
1 tablespoon peanut oil or corn oil

Slice the flank steak against the grain into pieces ⅛ inch thick and 2 inches long. Put them in a bowl, add the marinade, and toss well. Refrigerate the meat for a few minutes, or longer if you wish.

Put the sliced scallions on a plate with the bean sprouts.

Heat a wok over medium heat until hot. Add 3 tablespoons of the oil and, when it is hot, add the beef, stir-frying quickly until the meat just loses its redness and the slices separate. Scoop them out onto a plate. Wash the wok clean.

Add the last tablespoon of oil to the wok and heat briefly over medium heat. Add the Sha He noodles and stir gently to heat them through. Sprinkle the salt, sugar, and soy sauce all over the noodles and toss to mix. Add the cooked meat; then scatter the scallions and bean sprouts over the noodles and meat. Using a spatula, lift and toss gently from the bottom of the wok to make sure the noodles don't scorch. When the bean sprouts are just cooked but still crisp, transfer the contents to a large heated platter and serve immediately.

Variation: Use sliced chicken breasts or pork with the same marinade; also, for a meatless dish, substitute 1 pound fresh mushrooms for the meat: Slice them and then stir-fry them in 3 tablespoons of oil until they get dry; add soy sauce to taste.

Rice Cakes

Savory

Sweet

Plain Rice Cake

 NIAN GAO

This is the white, unseasoned rice cake, about ½ inch thick, that has a soft, somewhat chewy texture. The basic point is that it is made with flour created from soaked rice. Traditionally one ground the soaked rice into wet flour with stone wheels. Then the flour was steamed, kneaded with a stone mortar and pestle, and shaped into small rolls by hand. This project was a once-a-year event in my family's house, and we did it just before the New Year, since these cakes symbolize prosperity.

In New York's Chinatown there is a factory still making fresh old-fashioned plain rice cakes. It does use machines to speed the process, however. Electric-driven grinders grind the presoaked rice. Then the ground rice, including the water, is put in a muslin bag and the water is pressed out by machine. The result is fresh water-ground rice flour. A powerful steamer then steams the wet ground flour, which is immediately kneaded by machine into a soft dough. The cakes are formed by hand. The only cooking in this process is the steaming of the flour. No seasoning is added.

Fresh rice cakes are sold in plastic bags in the refrigerator section of Chinese markets. Also for sale are imported pre-sliced frozen and dried cakes from China. Both need soaking in cold water for at least one day or up to two weeks in the refrigerator.

Korean frozen rice cakes, already sliced, are chewier in texture than the Chinese cakes. They are made with Japanese rice and are sold in all Oriental markets. They must be soaked for at least one day before being used in Chinese dishes. The Chinese ones are better for stir-fry dishes. Soak them in water to defrost them. Keep them in the water till ready to use; then drain.

This recipe is for those who cannot purchase fresh plain rice cakes, or for those who would like to create a texture more to their own taste by using different proportions of the two kinds of flour. You could make a rice cake that is softer, harder, or chewier than this one. To make a softer one, use more glutinous rice; to make a harder one, use less; to make a chewier one, use all Japanese rice.

Since I can get dried water-ground rice flour, I have skipped the soaking and pressing steps here. But if you can't get dry flour, you will have to include them, which means soaking the two kinds of rice or one (Japanese) for at least four hours. Then, in a blender, blend the soaked rice in batches, including the water, to make a very fine liquid powder. Pour the mixture into a muslin bag, close the bag tightly, and press out the water by weighing it down with a heavy object, such as a six-pack of beer or a pot of water. It will take several hours for the water to exude. Break the resulting rice flour into small bits like the consistency of damp cornmeal, and follow the recipe for steaming and kneading.

Yield: 4 cakes, totaling 1 pound

2 cups dried long-grain rice flour, water-ground preferred
1 cup dried glutinous rice flour (sweet rice flour), water-ground preferred

¾ cup cold water, approximately

Put the two kinds of rice flour in a food processor fitted with the steel blade. Turn the machine on and pour the water through the feed tube. The flour will begin to look like granulated sugar. If the flour becomes a dough, meaning there is too much water at this point, add more flour and it will separate again.

Line a steamer with a fine-holed piece of stiff nylon mesh or mold a piece of aluminum foil into a deep pie-plate shape and place in a steamer. Loosely and evenly shake the flour into the lined steamer. Steam the flour over high heat for 20 minutes. Meanwhile, clean and rinse the food-processor bowl and keep it wet.

When the flour is cooked, put it in the food processor immediately and turn the machine on. The processing takes about 30 seconds to produce a smooth dough that hasn't yet stuck to the sides of the bowl. Dip your fingers in some oil and remove the dough. Knead the dough while it is still hot on a lightly oiled work surface until it becomes very smooth; this takes less than 1 minute.

Roll the dough into a long sausage shape about 1 inch in diameter. Divide the roll into four pieces. Flatten each piece to a ¾-inch thickness. Cover and let the pieces cool completely. These are the finished rice cakes.

You can keep the rice cakes for a week in the refrigerator if they are submerged in water and covered in plastic. To freeze them, slice them when cold on the diagonal so they are 1½ inches long and ¼ inch thick, and put them in a tightly closed plastic bag.

Stir-Fried Rice Cakes (Savory)

炒　CHAO NIAN GAO

年

糕　In the eastern provinces of Jiangsu and Zhejiang, this is a very popular dish—rice cakes that are stir-fried till soft with meat and vegetables. They make a marvelous light meal all by themselves, either as lunch or an afternoon snack. The dish is traditionally served during the New Year. The words *nian gao* are a homonym for "prosperity for the New Year," so the dish is used as a greeting for one's guests. These rice cakes would be beautifully complemented by Shanghai Spring Rolls (page 105) and Jujube Red Date Rice Cake (page 247).

Yield: 4 servings

1 pound fresh, frozen, or dried sliced rice cakes (page 241)

1 cup shredded pork, about ½ pound, semi-frozen for easy slicing

6 large dried Chinese mushrooms, soaked in warm water till soft, stems discarded, caps shredded, ¼ cup liquid saved

½ cup shredded bamboo shoots

3 cups shredded celery cabbage

¼ cup finely chopped preserved red-in-snow (Ma Ling brand preferred)

6 tablespoons peanut oil or corn oil

1 tablespoon dry sherry

1½ tablespoons dark soy sauce

1 teaspoon coarse salt

Soak the frozen or dried sliced rice cakes in water for at least one day at room temperature or for several days in the refrigerator. Drain before cooking. Fresh rice cakes can be used the day they are made or up to a few days later. Slice the rice cakes thin—about ¼ inch thick.

Set in separate piles on a platter or tray the prepared mushrooms, pork, bamboo shoots, celery cabbage, and red-in-snow.

Heat a wok until very hot. Add 2 tablespoons of the oil, heat over medium-high heat, and stir-fry the pork just until the pieces lose their pinkness. Splash in the sherry, then add 1 tablespoon of the soy sauce. Add the mushrooms and stir and toss for about 1 minute more. Transfer the entire contents of the wok to a bowl. Wash the wok clean.

Heat 2 more tablespoons of oil in the wok over medium-high heat. Stir-fry the bamboo shoots, celery cabbage, and red-in-snow for a few seconds. Add the salt and the reserved ¼ cup of mushroom water, and stir and toss for 2 minutes. Return the pork mixture to the pan, mix lightly with the vegetables, and cook, tossing, for about 1 minute. Transfer to a bowl. Up to this point the dish can be cooked ahead of time.

When you are ready to finish the dish, drain the sliced rice cakes. Heat a wok or large skillet, add the remaining 2 tablespoons of oil, and heat. Stir-fry the rice cakes gently for 2 minutes, or until the cakes are slightly soft and translucent. Add the remaining ½ tablespoon of soy sauce, then the meat and vegetables, stirring together until the cake slices are just soft and the dish is hot.

To double, prepare the dish twice.

Variation: Sliced beef or chicken with other vegetables can be used instead of pork and celery cabbage.

Cantonese Turnip Cake

 LUO-BO GAO

 White turnip cake is a Cantonese *dim sum* specialty, usually made around the time of the New Year. It combines the smooth texture of a rice cake with the tangy pungency of turnip and dried shrimp. The cake is steamed in pans, then served either hot as is or pan-fried with oil.

Yield: 8 servings

2 pounds Chinese white turnips (*luo-bo*)
2 Chinese sausages
4 dried black Chinese mushrooms, soaked in warm water for 30 minutes
¼ cup dried shrimp, soaked in ¼ cup dry sherry for 15 minutes
4 tablespoons corn oil
2 tablespoons finely chopped preserved vegetable (Zha Cai) (page 321)

1 teaspoon coarse salt or to taste
¼ teaspoon white pepper
1 tablespoon light soy sauce
1 pound fresh water-ground long-grain rice flour, broken into fine meal, or ¾ pound water-ground long-grain rice flour (page 322), about 3 cups

PREPARING THE CAKE INGREDIENTS

Peel the turnips and grate them by hand or in a food processor; you should have about 4 cups. Finely chop the sausages, mushroom caps (discard the stems), and shrimp (reserve the sherry).

Heat a wok, add 2 tablespoons of the oil, and heat; then add the sausages, mushrooms, shrimp, and preserved vegetable and stir-fry for 1 minute. Sprinkle the sherry on top and then transfer everything to a bowl.

Heat the same wok, add the remaining 2 tablespoons of oil, and stir-fry the grated turnips for 2 minutes. Add the salt, pepper, and soy sauce. There should be some liquid in the pan; if not, add ½ cup water. Cover and simmer for 10 minutes, or until the turnips are very tender.

Meanwhile, use a rubber spatula to mix the rice flour with water: Fresh rice flour takes 2½ cups; dried rice flour, 3 cups. Line two small loaf pans (7½ × 3½ × 2 inches) or one gingerbread pan (8 × 8 × 2 inches) with plastic wrap.

Add the sausage mixture to the turnips in the wok. Gradually pour the flour mixture into the wok and then stir constantly over medium-low heat until the flour is partially cooked and has become a sticky dough—about 5 minutes. Pour the turnip dough into the prepared baking pan (or pans). Smooth the top and thump the pan after it is filled to remove any air bubbles.

STEAMING THE CAKE AND SERVING IT

Prepare a steamer and bring the water to a boil. Steam the cake over medium-high heat for 30 minutes. The texture should be smooth and not sticky. Slice it into 2-inch squares ½-inch thick and serve hot with oyster sauce on the side for dipping. You can make the cake ahead of time by cooling the steamed cake and refrigerating it, unsliced, for two days or freezing it for a month. Cut into squares and steam for 5 minutes. Or pan-fry the squares in a little oil for a few minutes on both sides until lightly browned.

White Turnip Cake

SU LUO-BO GAO

This plain white turnip cake, steamed in pans, acts like the starch in a meal. It is a wonderful basic food if you need to serve a meatless dish. In addition to complementing eggs, it would be delicious in a light soup, such as Drop Noodles in Two Soups (page 90) or Best Chicken Broth (page 77).

Yield: 8 servings as a light meal

3 **pounds Chinese white turnips**
  (luo-bo)
4 **tablespoons corn oil**
2 **teaspoons coarse salt or to taste**

½ **teaspoon white pepper**
1 **pound water-ground long-grain**
  rice flour, about 4 cups

INGREDIENTS FOR FRYING THE CAKE

2 **tablespoons corn oil**
1 **teaspoon minced garlic or 1**
  tablespoon minced scallion
  soy sauce

2 **large eggs**

PREPARING AND STEAMING THE CAKE

Peel the turnips and grate them by hand or in a food processor; you should have about 6 cups. Heat a wok and add the oil; stir-fry the turnips over medium heat for 1 minute. Add the salt and pepper. Cover and simmer over medium-low heat for 10 minutes, or until the turnips are very tender.

Mix the rice flour with 3½ cups water, then gradually pour the mixture into the turnips, stirring constantly, until the flour is partially cooked—2 to 3 minutes.

Have two small loaf pans (7½ × 3½ × 3 inches) or one gingerbread pan (8 × 8 × 2 inches) ready, lined with plastic wrap. Scrape in the turnip dough. Smooth the top and thump the pan to remove any air bubbles.

Prepare a steamer and bring the water in it to a boil. Steam the cake over medium-high heat for 45 minutes, checking after 30 minutes to make sure you have enough water in the steamer. Add more boiling water if needed. Cool the cake; then put it in the refrigerator to chill.

FRYING AND SERVING THE CAKE

When it is chilled, cut the cake into slices 2 inches square and ½ inch thick. Pan-fry about eight to ten pieces until lightly browned. Cut the browned cake again into bite-size pieces and set aside.

Heat a wok with 2 tablespoons of oil. Add 1 teaspoon minced garlic or 1 tablespoon minced scallion and the cut-up turnip cake and stir-fry gently for 2 minutes. Sprinkle some soy sauce on top to taste and immediately pour two beaten eggs all over the cake cubes. Stir around lightly until the eggs are cooked. Serve hot.

Variation: Another way of serving this plain *luo-bo gao* is to make a vegetable soup or chicken soup with some green vegetables and add the cut-up steamed cake without browning it. This becomes a light meal with a soup.

Jujube Red Date Rice Cake (Sweet)

 TSAO ZI NIEN GAO

This is a classic Chinese cake, particularly in its texture, which is slightly chewy but not sticky. The color is chocolate brown. The cake is usually served as a dessert or snack offering during the New Year celebrations.

No egg is used in this cake, which is flavored with jujube red dates, a fragrant and delicious fruit with no comparable substitute. If you can't find them, however, try the recipe without them for the texture. Use 1½ cups dark brown sugar instead of the jujube red date jam and white sugar. It is an unusual treat, and it's very easy to make. It can be served at room temperature when freshly made or refrigerated for 4 to 8 hours and served cold.

After two days of refrigeration, the cake texture will become mealy. To offset this, cut it while still cold into 1-inch wedges and then reheat it in a steamer or toaster oven or pan-fry it with a little oil. I like to toast the wedges in the toaster oven until they are slightly charred—the cake is very soft this way, with a texture almost like chocolate taffy.

Yield: Two ¾-inch-thick 8-inch-round cakes; 8 servings; 16–32 wedges

1 pound water-ground glutinous rice flour (sweet rice flour), about 4 cups	½ cup granulated sugar or to taste
½ teaspoon baking soda	1¾ cups water
11-ounce can purée of jujube red dates (date jam)	½ cup corn oil
	1 or more dried jujube red dates for decoration (optional)

MAKING THE BATTER

Sift the flour with the baking soda once and set aside.

With a rubber spatula, scrape out the jujube jam from the can to a large mixing bowl. Add the sugar and water. Stir with the spatula to dissolve the jam and sugar in the water. Gradually add the flour to the mixture and stir until the batter is very smooth. Gradually add the oil to the batter and stir until the mixture is totally integrated.

Line two 8-inch round cake pans with plastic wrap. Scrape the batter into the cake pans and smooth the top with the spatula. Decorate the center of the cake with the dates, if desired.

STEAMING THE CAKES

Set up a bamboo steamer with two tiers, and bring the water to a boil. Place one cake on each tier, cover, and steam over high heat for 30 minutes. The cake on the bottom tier may have some water on top of it after being steamed; use a paper towel to blot it off immediately after steaming. If you are using an improvised steamer—a large pot with a rack or tin can with ends removed—pour boiling water to within 2 inches of the bottom of the cake pan. Cover and steam the cake for 30 minutes over high heat (or for 1 hour if you pour the batter into one 9-inch round cake pan).

Remove the cake from the steamer and let it cool in the pan. Serve at room temperature or cold. The cake, covered with plastic wrap, can be kept in the refrigerator for one week and in the freezer for one month. (Instead of being steamed, the cake may be baked without plastic wrap in a preheated 350° oven for 45 minutes.)

Red Bean Glutinous Rice Cake (Sweet)

豆　DOU SHA YAN ZI

沙

丸　These small white oval cakes filled with a dark red bean purée are quite

子　unusual; the dough is steamed before it is formed into the cakes, and that is the only cooking involved. They are a favorite snack with both the Chinese and the Japanese. Although they are usually served at room temperature, in warm weather I prefer to chill the cakes for 2 to 3 hours.

Store-bought cakes are very sweet, and the texture isn't quite to my taste. This recipe is very easy and can be adjusted to produce the sweetness and texture you like. Simply add more or less sugar in the filling for sweetness and more or less water to the dough to make a softer or chewier texture.

The Japanese Mochiko-brand sweet rice flour (glutinous rice flour) is preferred for this recipe. There is a coconut filling at the end of the recipe to use as a substitute for the red bean paste if you wish.

Yield: 12 oval cakes 2 inches in diameter

½ **pound Japanese sweet rice
  flour (glutinous rice flour),
  about 1¾ cups**
1¼ **cups cold water**

3 **tablespoons sugar**
1 **cup cold Red Bean Paste
  (page 184)**
½ **cup cornstarch for coating**

STEAMING THE DOUGH

Put the flour in a mixing bowl and gradually add the water while stirring with a wire whisk. When the mixture is like a smooth, thick batter, add the sugar and stir thoroughly.

Transfer the dough to an 8-inch round cake pan and steam it over high heat for 20 minutes.

MAKING THE CAKES

While the dough is steaming, set out a shallow dish with ¼ cup of the cornstarch in it and a large platter sprinkled with a little cornstarch. Divide the red bean paste into twelve portions and set aside near the work area.

When the dough is fully steamed, place it, in its pan, on the work surface, and with a spatula, cut the dough into twelve wedges without removing them from the pan. Lift out one wedge with the spatula and put it in the cornstarch dish. It will be sticky and hot, so use a butter knife to push the dough off the spatula into the shallow dish. Dip your

fingers in some cornstarch and push the dough into a 2½-inch circle. Put about 1 tablespoon of bean paste in the center. Press and pinch the edges of the dough together and lift the cake into your palm. Pinch and twist the edges some more so the bean paste is completely enclosed. Turn the cake to the smooth side and shape it into a 2-inch-wide oval cake. Set aside on the platter sprinkled with cornstarch.

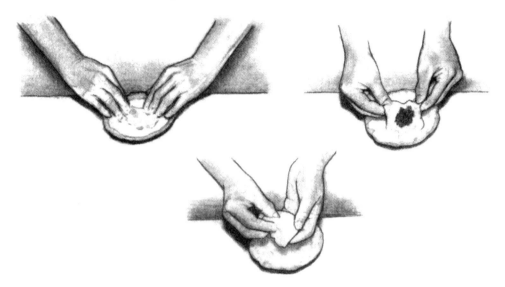

Repeat the process with the rest of the dough as rapidly as you can, so that the dough is still hot, making it easy to form smooth cakes. If the dough gets too cold, heat it up in the steamer for 5 minutes.

When the finished cakes are cool, brush off any excess cornstarch, put them on a plate, and cover with plastic wrap. They can sit for up to 8 hours at room temperature or in the refrigerator for 2 to 3 hours; longer will make them crack. They may also be frozen; to serve them, simply let them thaw completely and present them cold.

To double, prepare the recipe twice.

Variation:

COCONUT FILLING

½ cup sweetened flaked coconut, finely chopped	2 tablespoons roasted peanuts, finely chopped
2 tablespoons white sesame seeds, toasted till light brown	1 tablespoon sugar or to taste
	1 tablespoon corn oil

Mix the ingredients to use as a filling instead of red bean paste. For other types of filling, see Red Bean Paste (page 184).

Note: You may put a decorative dot of red food coloring on each cake when they are completely cool. This will give the dessert an authentic Chinese look.

Rice Dumplings

Glutinous Rice Dumplings with Pork Filling

XIAN ROU TANG TUAN

These are soft dumplings filled with savory, juicy ground pork and boiled. They are traditionally eaten with a Chinese porcelain spoon—you spoon yourself one dumpling at a time, bite off a piece with the meat and juice, and leave the rest in the spoon, to avoid losing any of the delicious juice to the cooking water the dumplings are served in. Since porcelain doesn't conduct heat, the spoon won't burn your lips. The point is, the dumplings are tastiest when hot. The plain cooking water in the soup bowl should be drunk in between eating each dumpling; it is very refreshing.

Yield: 4–6 servings as a light meal

THE FILLING

½ pound ground pork
⅛ teaspoon msg
1 teaspoon coarse salt
1 tablespoon dark soy sauce

½ tablespoon sesame oil
2 tablespoons chicken broth
Dash white pepper

THE DOUGH FOR THE DUMPLINGS

2 cups water-ground glutinous rice flour

¾ cup hot water, approximately

MAKING THE FILLING
Put the pork in a mixing bowl and add the remaining filling ingredients. With chopsticks or a wooden spoon, stir in one direction until the meat holds together. Set the filling in the refrigerator while you make the dumplings.

MAKING THE DOUGH
Put the flour in a large mixing bowl. With chopsticks or a wooden spoon, mix in the hot water a little at a time; then use your hands to knead the dough in the bowl until it is soft and smooth—about 1 minute. If the dough is a little dry, wet your hands and knead it until soft and smooth. Let the dough rest in plastic wrap while you work one portion at a time.

Take one-quarter of the dough from the plastic wrap. Roll it around a few times in your hands until it is soft and very smooth; then divide it into five pieces. Press one piece at a time with your fingers to make a cup large and thin enough to hold 2 heaping teaspoons of filling. With the thumb of one hand pressing down on the filling, use the thumb and forefinger of the other to push the edges of dough up over the filling and pinch together, making a pointed ball. Make it as smooth and neat as possible without rolling it in your palms because they are not round. Set the dumplings, not touching one another, on a tray lined with plastic wrap. Continue with the remaining dough; you should have twenty dumplings.

Cover the dumplings with more plastic wrap and refrigerate if you aren't going to cook them immediately. They can be chilled for up to a few hours, covered tightly with plastic wrap. You could also freeze them for up to one month, but defrost them completely in the refrigerator before boiling them.

COOKING AND SERVING THE DUMPLINGS
Bring 10 to 12 cups of water to a rapid boil. Drop in the dumplings one by one. With a wooden spoon, gently stir once or twice to make sure the dumplings aren't sticking; the rapidly boiling water will also help prevent this. Cook the dumplings for 7 to 8 minutes over medium heat, or until they float, look translucent, and start to puff up a little.

When the dumplings are done, ladle three or four of them into individual soup bowls, with enough cooking water to cover. Eat them as described in the introduction to the recipe.

Glutinous Rice Dumplings in Chrysanthemum Leaf Soup

米 茼 TONGHAO CAI NUO MI YAN ZI TANG

丸 蒿 Here is one of those heavenly meatless souplike meals so loved by the
子 菜 Chinese. The dumplings are faintly sweet, and the chrysanthemum leaves
    also have a sweet, fragrant flavor. You can find chrysanthemum greens in
汤 糯 Chinese or Japanese markets during the spring and summer.

Yield: 40 dumplings; 6 servings for a light meal

10 large dried black Chinese
   mushrooms
 1 bunch chrysanthemum greens,
   about 1 pound
 3 tablespoons corn oil
 2 teaspoons coarse salt

4 cups Best Chicken Broth (page
   77) (dilute with half water if
   using canned), or 4 cups water
   plus ¼ teaspoon msg for a
   vegetarian dish

THE DOUGH

2 cups water-ground glutinous
   rice flour (sweet rice flour)

¾ cup hot water

PREPARATIONS

Wash the mushrooms and then soak them in 1½ cups warm water until
soft. Remove and discard the stems. Finely shred the caps and reserve
the soaking water without the residue.

Pick over the chrysanthemum greens, selecting tender leaves and
stems; you should have about 4 cups. Wash them several times and
drain well.

MAKING THE DUMPLINGS

Put the flour in a large mixing bowl and gradually add the hot water to
form a soft dough. Knead the dough in the bowl until it is very soft and
smooth. If the dough is dry, wet your hands and knead more until the
dough is smooth. Working half of it at a time, roll it in your palms to
smooth it; then break it into twenty pieces. Roll each piece between your
palms to make a smooth ball. Put the dumplings without touching one
another on a tray lined with plastic wrap. Repeat with the other half of
the dough; you should have forty dumplings.

Cover the dumplings with another sheet of plastic wrap and refrigerate if you aren't going to cook them immediately. They can be chilled
for up to a few hours, covered with plastic wrap, or frozen for up to one
month.

COOKING THE DUMPLINGS AND THE SOUP

Heat 3 tablespoons of oil in a large saucepan. Add the mushrooms and
stir-fry for 1 minute. Add ½ teaspoon of the salt. Add the chicken broth
or the mushroom-soaking water with enough water to make 4 cups and

bring to a boil. Add the remaining salt and taste the soup to correct the seasoning. The soup may be done ahead of time up to this point.

Add all the glutinous rice balls to the boiling broth. Within 2 minutes the dumplings will float to the top; at this point add the greens and stir them into the soup. When the soup returns to the boil, the greens have cooked enough. Ladle the soup, greens, and dumplings into individual soup bowls and serve very hot.

Ningbo Glutinous Rice Dumplings Filled with Sesame Seed Paste

宁
波
猪
油
汤
粞

NINGBO ZHU YOU TANG TUAN

This is a famous dessert or snack from Ningbo, in the Zhejiang province. During the Chinese New Year it is symbolic of family happiness. It is also appreciated in other areas as well and available frozen in American Chinese markets. The frozen ones are large, but of good quality; homemade ones, however, are much better—all you need is a little patience.

Yield: 40 dumplings; 6 servings

THE SESAME SEED PASTE FILLING

1½ cups black sesame seeds
  1 cup cold pork leaf lard or
    unsalted margarine

1½ cups extra-fine sugar

THE GLUTINOUS RICE FLOUR DOUGH
FOR THE DUMPLINGS

2 cups water-ground glutinous
  rice flour (sweet rice flour)

¾ cup hot water, approximately

MAKING THE FILLING
Preheat the oven to 350 degrees. Rinse the sesame seeds with water in a very fine strainer or one lined with cheesecloth. Spread them out over a baking sheet and bake for about 30 minutes or until they are fragrant-smelling, stirring them twice during that time so they cook evenly. Let

them cool; then use a rolling pin to crush and roll the seeds into powder. If you need to, finish this step with a mortar and pestle in several batches.

Remove any skin on the surfaces or between the layers of the leaf lard. In a bowl, squeeze the lard into a purée with your fingers. Add the sesame seed powder and the sugar. Squeeze until the mixture is fully integrated. If you use unsalted margarine, simply mix it well with the sesame seed powder and sugar, using a spoon. Put the sesame paste in a plastic bag and pat it into an 8- by 6-inch oblong that is about ½ inch thick. Then refrigerate it to chill. (If made with margarine, the paste won't harden much.)

The paste may be prepared ahead of time and kept in the refrigerator for months. You should have about 2 cups.

MAKING THE DUMPLINGS AND STUFFING THEM

Put the flour in a large mixing bowl. With chopsticks or a fork, mix in the hot water a little at a time; then, use your hands to knead the dough in the bowl until it is soft and smooth—about 1 minute. If it cracks during the kneading, wet your hands with water and continue to knead until smooth. Keep the dough in plastic wrap and refrigerate it if you don't use it within several hours.

Cut the chilled sesame seed filling with lard into ¾-inch cubes and let them stand to soften a bit. If made with margarine, scrape off a little at a time with a butter knife.

Take one-quarter of the dough at a time out of the plastic wrap. Roll it a few times between your palms to make a thick rope about 10 inches long. Break this into ten pieces. Press one piece at a time with your fingers to make a cup shape that is large and thin enough to enclose a cube of filling, or 1 teaspoon if made with margarine. Put the sesame seed paste cube in the cup; then push the edges of the dough up over the filling. Pinch and twist off a small piece of dough; this will seal the edges well.

Roll the ball between your palms to make a perfect round, dabbing a little water on your palms and fingers from time to time; the water helps to seal and smooth the surface. Make the other dumplings; you should have forty.

Place the filled dumplings, not touching one another, on a tray lined with plastic wrap. Cover with another sheet of plastic wrap. The dumplings may be made ahead of time and kept in the refrigerator for up to 24 hours or in the freezer for up to one month.

COOKING AND SERVING THE DUMPLINGS

Bring 6 cups of water to a rapid boil over medium-high heat. Drop the dumplings in one by one and cook for 3 minutes, gently stirring once or twice with a wooden spoon so the dumplings don't stick. When they are ready they will float to the top and look translucent.

For an individual serving, ladle six rice dumplings into a soup or dessert bowl and cover with some of the cooking water. Eat the dumplings with a porcelain spoon, biting away half at a time—they are very hot, so they shouldn't be swallowed whole. The cooking water is a refreshing drink between bites of the rice dumplings.

Variation: Red bean paste (page 184) can be used instead of sesame seed paste.

These filled dumplings (in place of plain rice dumplings) are also wonderful in Sweet Wine Rice Soup (page 263) as a dessert after a banquet.

Cantonese Fried Glutinous Rice Dumplings

  XIAN SHUI JIAO

These deep-fried dumplings have a slightly chewy, crisp exterior, a soft, smooth inside, and, in the middle, a tasty pork-and-shrimp filling. (The proportions below are enough for two recipes. Make one and either freeze the remainder or use it to make Steamed Dumplings, Canton-Style, page 147.) They are a Cantonese treat usually made during the New Year, but nowadays they are also a popular *dim sum* offering for tea lunch or a snack. To make a full meal, serve them with Roast Pork with Tossed Noodles (Roast Pork Lo Mian) (page 63).

Yield: 16 half-moon dumplings 3 inches in diameter; serves 8 as an appetizer; 4 as a light meal

THE FILLING

- 2 tablespoons peanut oil or corn oil
- 1 teaspoon minced fresh ginger
- 2 tablespoons minced whole scallions
- ½ pound ground pork
- ½ pound raw shrimp, shelled, deveined, and chopped
- 2 large dried black Chinese mushrooms, soaked, stems discarded, and finely chopped

- 2 tablespoons chopped bamboo shoots
- 1 tablespoon light soy sauce
- 1 teaspoon coarse salt or to taste
- ⅛ teaspoon white pepper
- ¼ teaspoon sugar
- 1 tablespoon cornstarch combined with 2 tablespoons water

THE DOUGH

- 2 cups water-ground glutinous rice flour
- ¼ cup all-purpose flour
- 4 teaspoons sugar

- 1½ teaspoons baking powder
- 2 tablespoons lard or other shortening
- 1 cup hot water, approximately

3–4 cups oil for deep-frying

MAKING THE FILLING

Heat a wok until hot, add the oil and heat, then add the ginger and scallions and stir-fry for a few seconds, till fragrant. Add the pork and stir-fry until it is partially cooked—about 1 minute. Then add the shrimp, mushrooms, bamboo shoots, soy sauce, salt, pepper, and sugar. Stir-fry, tossing and turning, for 2 minutes.

Mix the cornstarch and water well; then pour into the pan and stir and toss till the sauce thickens. Transfer the filling to a bowl and let it cool. Then cover and refrigerate it while you make the dough.

MAKING THE DOUGH

Combine the flours, sugar, and baking powder in a large mixing bowl, make a well in the center, and put the lard in this well. Gradually pour about three-quarters of the hot water into the well while you stir with chopsticks or a wooden spoon until the lard is incorporated and the flour is totally damp. If there is some dry flour remaining, add the rest of the water 1 tablespoon at a time until the flour is damp. Pat and knead the dough in the bowl until it is soft and smooth—about 1 minute. Do not overwork the dough, since the gluten that develops will make the dough tough. If you are not making the dumplings immediately, refrigerate the dough wrapped in plastic.

SHAPING AND DEEP-FRYING THE DUMPLINGS
Divide the dough in half. Keep one half covered while you break the other into eight pieces. Working one piece at a time with your fingers, flatten it into a circle 2½ inches in diameter and about ¼ inch thick. Put about 2 heaping teaspoons of filling in the center and fold the circle in half. Press the edge to thin it first; then twist the edge to create a scalloped effect. (You could also press the edge with the tines of a fork to scallop it.) Place the finished dumplings, not touching one another and scalloped edge up, on a tray lined with plastic wrap.

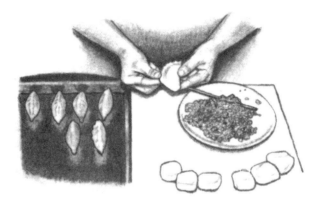

Heat the oil in a wok to 350 degrees. Drop in only five dumplings at a time, so they won't stick to one another. Turn them gently with chopsticks as they fry, so they will be evenly browned on all sides. In about 3 minutes they should be done—a light gold color and slightly puffed. Drain them on paper towels. Serve the dumplings hot or warm.

Already-fried dumplings can be kept in the refrigerator for two to three days or in the freezer for a month. Reheat refrigerated dumplings in a preheated 450-degree oven for 8 minutes, frozen ones for 10 minutes.

Glutinous Rice Dumplings in Sweet Wine Rice Soup

 JIU NIANG YAN ZI

 This is a very popular dessert in the Shanghai area—a refreshing wine-fragrant taste most welcome after a Chinese meal. This soup is traditional as a breakfast or snack for a birthday person. The apricot halves and dumplings may be replaced with poached eggs, or you may add more cooked or canned fruits such as peaches or pears and omit the rice dumplings.

Yield: 8 servings

1 can unpeeled apricot halves (17 ounces)	**1½ cups wine rice, including the juice, preferably homemade (see recipe, page 263)**
¼ cup sugar or to taste	

THE DOUGH

1 cup water-ground glutinous rice flour (sweet rice flour)	**½ cup hot water (leave out 2 tablespoons, adding as needed)**

Put the flour in a large mixing bowl and gradually add the 6 tablespoons of hot water to form a soft dough. If the dough is dry, add more as needed, ½ tablespoon at a time. Knead the dough in the bowl until very soft and smooth, about 1 minute.

Line a tray with plastic wrap. Take one-quarter of the dough at a time, roll it in your palms to make a smooth cylinder, then break it into twenty to twenty-five pieces. Roll each piece between your palms to make a smooth ball. Put these dumplings on the tray without touching.

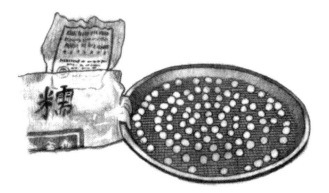

Repeat with the rest of the dough until you have eighty to one hundred. Cover the dumplings with another sheet of plastic wrap and refrigerate if you aren't going to cook them immediately. They can be chilled up to a few hours; covered with plastic wrap or frozen for up to 1 month.

Prepare eight small rice bowls. Drain the apricot halves, putting 2 pieces of apricot in each bowl, skin side up, and set aside. In a saucepan, bring 3 cups of water to a boil, then add the glutinous rice balls. The balls will float on top and fluff up slightly when they are done, about 2 minutes. Add the wine rice, stir, and break up the rice balls in the water. Add ¼ cup sugar or to taste. When the water boils again, dish out into the rice bowls. Serve hot. The soup may be served cold, but chill only briefly so that the dumpling's texture will remain soft and chewy.

Wine Rice

酒 JIU NIANG

酿
、 This wine rice can be easily made at home and stored in your refrigerator
酒 indefinitely. As with some wine, age will improve its mellowness. It makes
fragrant sweet soup or sauce for seafoods. Extract the residual and use
药 the liquid as rice wine for drinking and cooking.

The cold wine rice can be served as is, or combined with dried fruit. For example, soak and submerge ½ jar of dried prune in ½ jar of cold wine rice including the juice for one to two weeks. Keep jar in the refrigerator. This can be used as dessert including the wine rice and juice.

Yield: 5 to 6 cups

3 cups glutinous rice (sweet rice)   **2 teaspoons flour**
2 teaspoons wine yeast (Jiu-yao)

Wash the rice in cold water several times; drain. Put the rice in a 2-quart heatproof bowl. Add 3 cups of cold water and let soak for 30 minutes. Wine yeast is sold in solid form, so you must mash it before using. Measure out 2 teaspoons and mix with flour. Set aside.

Place the bowl containing the soaking rice in a large pot filled with cold water. The cold water should be 1½ inches below the bowl's rim. Cover and bring to a boil. Steam over medium-high heat for 45 minutes. You may have to add more boiling water during this time, so have boiling water ready on another burner. After cooking, the rice looks shiny with grains separated, soft but slightly chewy.

Transfer the steamed rice to a large colander and rinse thoroughly, first with cold water, then with warm water, and let drain for 5 minutes. Rinse a 2-quart earthenware casserole with warm water and dry well. Sprinkle the yeast and flour on the rice and mix thoroughly. Put the rice in the prepared casserole, gently patting the rice down to make a 1-inch well in the center down to the bottom of the casserole. Cover, place the slightly warm casserole in an insulated bag or wrap it in a heavy blanket, and leave it in a dark place for one and a half to two days. By this time a sweet liquid will have accumulated in the well and at the sides.

Transfer the wine rice to a glass container. Cover tightly and keep in the refrigerator, where it may be stored indefinitely. Be sure the juice covers the rice. Serve cold or hot.

New Year's Sesame Seed Balls

 MA TUAN

These large, hollow sesame-seed-coated balls are an eastern and southern specialty for the Chinese New Year festival, a two-week holiday time of feasting and visiting. They are deep-fried till golden brown, and because of the heat and pressing during the cooking, they inflate like balloons. They are fun to make, and their sesame fragrance and chewy texture are superb, much loved by the Chinese. They are served warm or at room temperature, as a snack or dessert.

Yield: 30 balls 3 inches in diameter

**1 pound water-ground
 glutinous rice flour**
**1¼ cups light brown or white
 sugar**
**1¼ cups boiling water,
 approximately**

**1 cup Red Bean Paste
 (page 184)**
¼ cup white sesame seeds
**6 cups peanut oil or corn oil for
 deep-frying**

FORMING THE SESAME SEED BALLS

Put the rice flour in a large mixing bowl. Dissolve the brown sugar in the boiling water; then stir the sugar water into the flour until the flour is all damp. Add more hot water if the flour appears too dry. (Since rice flour has no gluten in it, the dough's softness depends on the amount of water used.) Pat and knead the dough in the bowl until it is soft and smooth.

Break off half the dough and roll it a little between your palms; if it isn't smooth, wet your hands and roll it again. Then break it into fifteen pieces. Roll each piece between your palms into a ball about the size of a walnut. Cover with a damp towel or plastic wrap.

Take a ball of dough and press an indentation into it, making a deep cup. Place 1 teaspoon of filling inside and close the cup, making sure you completely cover the filling with the dough. Pinch and twist off

a small piece of dough and seal the edge well. Roll the filled ball between your palms to make it perfectly round. (If the ball feels dry,
dampen your palms with a little water while rolling.) Then roll the ball
in sesame seeds, pressing gently, until the entire surface is covered and
the seeds adhere to the dough. Prepare the other half of the dough and
cover the finished balls with a damp towel or plastic wrap.

FRYING THE SESAME SEED BALLS

Heat a wok over medium heat. Add the oil and heat to about 350 degrees. Lower in a few balls at a time and let them cook slightly. When
the sesame seeds have turned light brown, apply some pressure to the
balls with the back of a large ladle, pressing them against the bottom or
side of the pan. Do this continuously, pressing each ball until it blows up
to about three times its original size and the sesame seeds turn golden

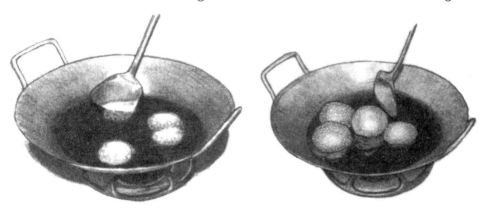

brown; this takes about 5 minutes. Each time you press down on a ball
with the back of a large ladle, it will automatically turn over and expand
a little. The trick is to work all the balls in separate turns, until they have
tripled in size, pressing each one separately and quickly going on to the
next during the 5-minute process. You'll soon develop a knack for doing
this.

Drain the sesame seed balls on paper towels and serve them warm
or at room temperature. They should be eaten with your hands, as a
dessert or a snack.

Already-cooked sesame seed balls can be reheated in a preheated
450-degree oven for about 5 minutes, or until they puff up again.

Doughs Made from

Beans

and Other
Starches

≡

Cellophane
(Mung Bean)
Noodle
Dishes

≡

Cellophane Noodles (Mung Bean Noodles)

 FEN SI

Cellophane noodles (mung bean noodles) or *fen si*, which are popular throughout China, Southeast Asia, and Japan, are made of mung beans and tapioca starch; they require heavy machinery and very high heat in their manufacture and for that reason are very difficult to make at home. I have not included a recipe here; instead, purchase them dried. They are sold in 2-, 4-, 8-, and 16-ounce packages and are readily available and inexpensive. They have a long shelf life—up to one year or more—and, like dried rice sticks, are of very good quality.

Cellophane noodles must be soaked or boiled first if they are to be used later in a soup or a stir-fried dish or deep-fried when used dry as a garnish. The Chinese don't really consider them "noodles" in the sense of a starch, because they're made of mung beans, so rice usually accompanies them in a meal. Following are several recipes for cellophane noodles that call for different methods of preparation.

Stir-Fried Cellophane Noodles with Fresh Mushrooms

 XIAN GU FEN SI

Here is a simple, satisfying dish of mushrooms and cellophane noodles flavored with a rich chicken broth. It could be served with rice or by itself. The dish can be made ahead of time and reheated over low heat, tossing, until hot. Since the noodles change texture when chilled, it is best not to refrigerate it, however.

To double, make the dish twice.

Yield: 4 servings

4 ounces cellophane noodles
1 pound fresh mushrooms
6 tablespoons peanut oil or corn oil

½ teaspoon coarse salt or to taste
2 tablespoons light soy sauce
1½ cups Best Chicken Broth (page 77)

Soak the noodles in hot water for 20 minutes; then drain them and set them aside until they are almost dry. Cut them into 4- to 6-inch lengths with scissors so they are easier to serve.

Rinse any dirt off the mushrooms and drain well. Slice them and set aside, but cook them as soon as possible so they won't change color.

Heat a nonmetallic pan (so the mushrooms will not become too dark), add 3 tablespoons of the oil, and heat until hot. Add the mushrooms and stir-fry over medium-high heat for about 5 minutes, or until almost all the juice has cooked away. Add the salt and stir and toss a little more. Scoop the mushrooms out into a bowl.

Heat the same pan, then add the remaining 3 tablespoons of the oil and heat. Stir-fry the noodles for 1 minute. Add the soy sauce and the cooked mushrooms and toss briefly. Add the chicken broth and bring to a boil. Cover and let the noodles and mushrooms cook over medium-low heat for 5 minutes, or until the broth is completely absorbed.

Taste to adjust the seasonings. Toss the noodles with chopsticks or a fork until they are fluffy and dry. The dish should be served hot. This dish will keep in a 200-degree oven, covered, for up to 1 hour.

Ants on a Tree

 MA YI SHANG SHU

The fanciful name of this spicy, hot dish applies to its appearance, since the bits of beef among the cellophane noodles look a little like ants on tree branches. The dish is a specialty of Sichuan province and is usually made with pork and served with rice. I have doubled the traditional amount of noodles so the dish can become a light meal in itself.

Yield: 4 servings

4 ounces cellophane noodles
½ pound ground beef (top round)
5½ tablespoons peanut oil or corn oil
2 tablespoons Hot Chili Bean Paste, Sichuan- or Hunan-Style (page 302) or to taste

1 teaspoon sugar
1½ cups Best Chicken Broth (page 77)
3 tablespoons minced whole scallions

THE MARINADE

1½ tablespoons light soy sauce
2 teaspoons cornstarch
1 tablespoon chicken broth

1 tablespoon peanut oil or corn oil

Soak the cellophane noodles in hot water for 20 minutes; then drain and set aside until almost dry. Cut them into 4- to 6-inch lengths with scissors so they are easier to cook and to serve.

Put the meat in a mixing bowl, add the marinade ingredients, and mix well.

Heat a wok over medium heat until very hot. Add 5 tablespoons of the oil, heat, then add the beef. Quickly stir-fry until the meat loses its pinkness and is separated into bits. Add the chili paste and sugar; stir and mix well. Add the cellophane noodles and the broth and bring to a boil. Cover and cook for 5 minutes, or until all the broth is absorbed.

Toss the noodles until they are dry and fluffy. Add the minced scallions and the remaining ½ tablespoon oil and toss. Scoop out to a platter and serve hot. The dish may be kept covered, in a warm oven (200 degrees) for up to 15 minutes.

To double, prepare the dish twice.

Variation: Ground pork can be used instead of beef. In that case, omit the oil in the marinade.

Carrots and Chinese Mushrooms with Cellophane Noodles

 CHAO FEN SI

This dish is perfect in hot weather, since it can be served at room temperature as well as hot. (Do not chill it, however, since the texture of the cellophane noodles would turn mealy and opaque in color.) I loved this dish when I was growing up, and in 1978, after thirty years' absence from China, I had it again in Shanghai—and loved it all over again. The mushroom flavor is magnificent, and the dish is visually stunning.

Yield: 4 servings

12 dried Chinese mushrooms
4 ounces cellophane noodles
4 cups carrots cut in matchstick
  strips 2 inches long (a
  mandolin makes the best cut),
  loosely packed

6 tablespoons corn oil or peanut
  oil
4 tablespoons light soy sauce
2 teaspoons coarse salt or to taste

Rinse the mushrooms briefly; then soak them in 1 cup of warm water for 30 minutes, or until soft. Drain them, but reserve ½ cup of the water. Cut off and discard the stems and shred the caps into very fine strips. Set aside on a plate.

Soak the cellophane noodles in 4 cups of cold water in a saucepan for 5 minutes. Bring to a boil, turn off the heat, cover, and let the noodles stand for 10 minutes. Drain and set aside until they are almost dry, and then cut them with scissors into 4- to 6-inch pieces. Set them aside on a plate with the mushrooms. Put the shredded carrots on the plate, too.

Heat a wok or large skillet until hot, add the oil and heat, then stir-fry the carrots over medium-high heat for about 2 minutes. Add the mushrooms, then the noodles, and stir-fry together for another 2 to 3 minutes. Add the soy sauce, salt, and reserved mushroom water.

Cover and cook over high heat for about 2 to 3 minutes, or until the sauce is absorbed. Then uncover and stir and toss the noodles until fluffy dry. Serve hot, warm, or at room temperature.

To double, prepare the dish twice.

Cellophane Noodle Soup
with Hot and Sour Shrimp

酸　SUAN LA XIA MI FEN SI TANG
辣
虾　Good cellophane noodles will not get soggy even when they are over-
米　cooked, and fortunately most of them on the market are of good quality.
粉　This light lunch dish is especially easy to prepare.
丝
汤　*Yield: 4 servings as a light meal; 8 servings as a soup*

4 ounces cellophane noodles

2 tablespoons corn oil or peanut oil

40 medium dried shrimps, ½ inch in diameter (if large ones are used, break them in half and use 20)

2 tablespoons dry sherry

2 tablespoons dark soy sauce

4 cups Best Chicken Broth (page 77), or water (add ¼ teaspoon monosodium glutamate if water is used)

¼ teaspoon white pepper

2 tablespoons cider vinegar

Coarse salt to taste

1 tablespoon sesame oil

1 tablespoon finely chopped scallion

Soak the cellophane noodles in 1 quart of just-boiled water, and let them remain in the water until it cools. Drain the water, leaving the noodles in the pan.

Heat a wok over moderate heat for 30 seconds, then add the oil and swirl. Add the shrimp and stir-fry for 2 minutes, then sprinkle the sherry over the shrimp. Add the cellophane noodles, soy sauce, and broth or water. Bring to a boil and let the liquid simmer for 5 minutes. Add the white pepper and cider vinegar. The saltiness of the dried shrimp varies, so taste the soup before adding any salt and adjust according to your taste. Then add the sesame oil and chopped scallion.

Using chopsticks, scoop the cellophane noodles into individual soup bowls first, then ladle the soup and other ingredients into each bowl. Serve with chopsticks and soup spoons.

Cellophane Noodle Soup with Pork Omelets

蛋
饺
粉
丝
汤

DAN JIAO FEN SI TANG

The shape and color of these pork-filled omelets resemble those of old gold ingots and are a symbol of wealth for the New Year. *Dan jiao* ("egg omelet") traditionally is made with pork wrapped in a thin crepe or fried beaten egg; these must be prepared individually.

I have simplified this classic holiday dish: here the ground pork and beaten eggs are mixed together and fried into tiny omelets. They can be made ahead of time and refrigerated. Adding them to the soup is their reheating. This makes a satisfying hearty soup; it would be very good accompanied by Scallion Pancakes (page 162) or Sesame Seed Bread (page 167) with filling or other dumplings and buns in the book.

Yield: 6 servings

¼ **pound ground pork**
2 **ounces cellophane noodles**
½ **pound tender celery cabbage (the inner leaves)**
4 **extra large eggs, well beaten**
4–5 **tablespoons peanut oil or corn oil**

4 **cups Best Chicken Broth (page 77) or canned broth diluted by one-half with water**
1 **teaspoon coarse salt or to taste**
¼ **teaspoon sugar**

THE MARINADE

1 **tablespoon finely chopped scallion**
½ **teaspoon coarse salt**
1 **tablespoon light soy sauce**

1 **tablespoon dry sherry**
1½ **tablespoons cornstarch**
2 **tablespoons chicken broth**

MAKING THE OMELETS

Put the ground pork in a mixing bowl, add the marinade ingredients, and mix well. Cover and refrigerate to chill slightly.

Soak the cellophane noodles in hot water for 20 minutes. Drain and set aside until almost dry, and cut them with scissors into 4- to 6-inch lengths. Set aside on a large plate. Cut the celery cabbage into 2- by 1-inch strips and set aside on the plate with the cellophane noodles.

Mix the beaten eggs with the meat just before cooking, so the egg color remains golden after cooking; if done too much in advance, the soy sauce and meat will turn the egg color brown.

Heat a 10- to 12-inch skillet (preferably nonstick) over medium heat until hot. Add about 1 tablespoon of the oil and swirl to coat the bottom of the pan. With a spoon, take 1 tablespoon of the egg-and-meat mixture and spread it in the pan to make about a 2½-inch omelet. Working quickly, spread out as many little omelets as the pan will hold. While the omelets are still soft in the center, fold them in half with a small spatula to make half-moon shapes, pressing the edge, and cook until lightly browned. Turn the omelets and brown the other side. Then transfer them from the pan to a plate.

Repeat the process, adding more oil as needed, until the omelet mixture is used up. You will have twenty-four to twenty-six tiny omelets.

They can be made in advance; cover with plastic wrap and refrigerate for up to 8 hours if you wish.

MAKING THE SOUP

Heat a casserole, pour in the remaining 2 tablespoons of the oil, and heat over medium heat; then add the celery cabbage and stir-fry for 2 minutes. Add the chicken broth, salt, and sugar and stir. Slip in the soaked cellophane noodles in a circle around the edge. Place the pork omelets on top of the cabbage in the center. Do not stir; you are trying to make a pleasing arrangement. Cover and cook over medium heat for 15 minutes, or until the cabbage is soft and tender. Serve hot.

You can make the dish ahead of time; reheat by bringing it to a boil over high heat, then lower the heat and cook till just heated through.

Variation: Ground beef, turkey, or chicken can be used instead of pork; add ½ tablespoon of oil to the marinade. Other greens, such as spinach or lettuce, may be used instead of celery cabbage. In that case lessen the cooking time a bit. If you are making the dish ahead of time, omit the greens from the first cooking and add them 2 minutes before you are going to serve the soup.

Cellophane Noodle and Meatball Soup

粉
丝
肉
丸
汤 FEN SI ROU YUAN TANG

This is a soup the Chinese often serve as a separate course in a large meal. I have doubled the amount of noodles and meatballs, so the soup can stand as a hearty meal by itself.

Yield: 4 servings

4 ounces cellophane noodles
1 pound finely ground pork,
   about 2 cups
¼ cup water
½ teaspoon coarse salt
¼ teaspoon sugar
2 tablespoons light soy sauce
1 tablespoon dry sherry

2 tablespoons cornstarch
1 large egg
4 cups Best Chicken Broth (page
   77) or 13½-ounce can chicken
   broth plus water to make 4 cups
   Salt and pepper to taste
2 cups tender spinach leaves or
   watercress leaves

Soak the cellophane noodles in 4 cups of just-boiled water for 20 minutes; then drain, cut into 4-inch-long pieces, and set aside.

Put the pork in a large bowl and gradually add the ¼ cup water while you stir in one direction with chopsticks until the mixture holds together and has some resistance. Add the salt, sugar, soy sauce, sherry, and cornstarch; mix and stir some more. Add the egg and stir until it is totally incorporated. Set the meat mixture, covered with plastic wrap, in the refrigerator.

Bring the chicken broth to a boil and then turn the heat down to a slow boil. Set a small bowl of cold water near the stove. Dip a teaspoon in the cold water and with it scoop up 1 heaping teaspoon of the meat. Shape the meat mixture into 1-inch balls in the palm of your other hand by scooping and turning the meat a few times. With the spoon, drop the meatballs one by one into the simmering soup. When they're all in the soup, let them cook for 2 minutes. Add salt and pepper to taste.

Add the greens and cook, stirring, for 1 minute. Ladle the soup into four individual soup bowls and eat with chopsticks and a soup spoon. For a very clear soup, the meatballs may be cooked in boiling water then scooped out with a slotted spoon, and added to the chicken soup to finish cooking.

Variation: If you like a peppery soup, add ¼ cup finely shredded *zha cai* (Sichuan pickled vegetable, page 321). Four very finely chopped water chestnuts can be added to the meatballs to give them some crunchiness. Ground beef can be used instead of pork.

Fish Head Chowder Casserole with Mung Bean Sheets

FEN PI SHA GUO YU TOU

Here is a recipe that goes beautifully with mung bean sheets, which are made of the same ingredients as cellophane noodles.

The Chinese adore fish heads, since they aren't squeamish at all about food and they know the meat is best near the bone. The traditional way of serving a fish head is from an earthenware pot. The pot is carried directly from the stove to the table while the liquid is still bubbling, because fish tastes best when it is piping hot. This is a one-dish meal, like a fish chowder, since the fish head has plenty of tender meat around the bone and the mung bean sheets are filling, too.

After more than 20 minutes of cooking, the fish head can easily be broken into pieces with a spoon or chopsticks. Steamed buns (page 199) or rice would be perfect accompaniments, with a cool, sweet dessert to finish the meal, such as chilled fruit or almond curd.

Yield: Serves 4 as a main course

1 two-pound fish head, from striped bass, tile, codfish, or any white fish with a collar and some flesh on the back part of the head; gills and scales removed, head split in half lengthwise for easy handling

2 ounces Tientsin mung bean sheets (about 3 round pieces 8 inches wide) (page 316)

1 tablespoon corn oil

½ teaspoon salt
Flour for dredging

4 tablespoons peanut oil or corn oil

2 half-inch slices fresh ginger, crushed

2 cloves garlic, peeled and crushed

2 whole scallions, cut into 2-inch sections

1 tablespoon cider or distilled white vinegar

2 tablespoons dry sherry

1 tablespoon brown bean sauce

3 tablespoons dark soy sauce

2 teaspoons sugar

2 cups Best Chicken Broth (page 77)

¼ teaspoon white pepper

Wash the split fish head and pat dry.

Prepare the mung bean sheets: Tear them into small pieces and put them in a pot. Cover with water and let them cook at a slow boil over low heat for 20 minutes, or less if the sheets are very thin; they should be very soft but still hold together. Then add 1 tablespoon of corn oil, turn off the heat, and let them cool in the pot.

Sprinkle the salt on the outside and inside of the cleaned fish head; then dredge with flour and shake off the excess.

Heat a wok over medium heat until very hot. Add the 4 table-spoons of oil and fry the fish head for 3 minutes on each side, or until firm and lightly brown. When you turn the fish head, add the ginger, garlic, and scallions and let them brown in the oil.

Scoop everything into a casserole (or let it remain in the wok) and set it over medium heat. Add the vinegar, sherry, brown bean sauce, soy sauce, sugar, and chicken broth. Bring the liquid to a boil; then turn the heat low. Cover and simmer for 10 minutes.

Drain the mung bean sheets and add them to the casserole or wok, gently pushing them into the sauce. Cook for another 5 minutes; the mung bean sheets should be soft and transparent by then. Add the pepper just before serving.

Variation: You could use a whole fish (about 2 pounds) instead of a fish head. And as a substitute for mung bean sheets, use cellophane noodles or fresh bean curd: Soak 2 ounces of cellophane noodles in just-boiled water for 20 minutes and then drain and cut them into 4- to 6-inch lengths. Add them to the casserole and cook for another 5 minutes. If using fresh bean curd, cut one large square (5 × 3 × 2 inches) into 1-inch cubes and add them to the casserole 5 minutes before the dish is done.

Special Dishes

**Including
Taro Fritters,
Yam Gold Coins,
Congees, and
Tofu Crackers**

Potato Buns

肉
末
山
芋
饼 ROU MO SHAN YU BING

In this unusual recipe mashed potatoes are seasoned and filled with chopped beef that has been cooked. The small round potato buns are then shallow-fried to a crisp brown. They are an excellent accompaniment to vegetable soups; try them with Best Chicken Broth with ham (page 77) or the meatless soup in Drop Noodles in Two Soups (page 90).

Yield: 16 buns

2 **pounds baking potatoes, about 5 medium-size**	2 **tablespoons light soy sauce**
1 **tablespoon corn oil or peanut oil**	¼ **cup chicken broth**
2 **tablespoons grated carrots**	½ **cup all-purpose flour**
½ **teaspoon coarse salt**	2 **tablespoons cornstarch**
2 **teaspoons sugar**	2 **tablespoons black sesame seeds (optional)**
	1 **cup corn oil**

THE FILLING

½ **pound ground round beef, about 1 cup**	1 **teaspoon sugar**
2 **teaspoons cornstarch**	2 **tablespoons dark soy sauce**
	1 **tablespoon dry sherry**

MAKING THE BUNS

Wash the potatoes. Cover with water and cook for 30 minutes, or until a knife can be inserted easily. Drain and let them cool until they are easy to handle.

Meanwhile combine the filling ingredients and mix them thoroughly. Heat a wok, add 1 tablespoon of the oil, and stir-fry the seasoned meat for 2 minutes—until it loses its pinkness. Do not overcook. With a slotted spoon, put the meat on a plate and discard the oil, if any.

Peel the potatoes, put them in a mixing bowl, and mash them with a potato masher until fairly smooth. Add the grated carrots, salt, sugar, soy sauce, and broth. Mash the potatoes thoroughly with the seasonings. Transfer them to a pot, preferably a nonstick one. Heat them over moderate heat until they are hot but not browned. Add the flour, and stir with a wooden spoon until the flour is cooked—about 2 to 3 minutes.

Let the mixture cool and then divide it into sixteen portions. Dip your fingers in some cornstarch and take up one portion of the mashed potatoes at a time. Shape into a 3-inch disk and fill with 1 tablespoon of the filling. Push the sides together to enclose the filling, then press the center down to make a flat bun 2½ inches in diameter. Sprinkle some sesame seeds on the tops of the buns and press them in gently so they stick to the dough.

FRYING THE BUNS
Heat ½ cup of oil in each of two 10-inch skillets to 350 degrees, and fry eight buns at a time in each for 2 minutes on each side, or until a brown crust forms. Transfer to a platter and serve hot.

The buns can be made ahead of time: Cover with plastic and leave at room temperature; then reheat them over low heat in an uncovered skillet with no oil, giving them about 2 minutes on each side, until they are piping hot.

Fried Taro
Fritters with Pork Filling

芋 YU TOU JIAO or WO TOU KO

头
角 One of the most unusual doughs from China comes from the taro, a plant with large green leaves sometimes called elephant ears and, to the point here, tuberous root stalks that are edible. The tubers are usually about the size of baking potatoes; the 4-inch-wide stalk is often cut into long pieces. When the taro tubers are very fresh, the sprouting ends are pink. In the Western hemisphere there is a large taro called *malanga* that is excellent for making the "pastry" necessary for this recipe; the stalks of the tubers are as big as large eggplants.

Taro is available most of the time in Chinese or Spanish markets. They should be stored as you would potatoes—in a cool, dark place.

When cooked, taro has very smooth texture and a faintly sweet taste not unlike chestnuts. In this recipe it is boiled and mashed, then combined with wheat starch (flour from which all gluten has been removed) to make a dough that is shaped into shells. The Chinese fill them with a mixture that can be either sweet or savory. The dough is then pressed into an oval, fritterlike shape. When the fritters are deep-fried, the dough takes on a flaky crust, with holes in it like a fragile bee-hive, but remains smooth inside. These fritters would make a wonderful hors d'oeuvre or appetizer as well as a main course. Steamed Dumplings, Canton-Style (page 147) or Roast Pork with Tossed Noodles (page 63) would complement them beautifully.

Yield: Thirty-two 2-inch fritters

THE FILLING

½ **pound pork shoulder**
1 **large chicken leg (about 6 ounces)**
2 **tablespoons dried shrimp**
2 **tablespoons minced bamboo shoots**
2 **tablespoons minced whole scallion**

1 **teaspoon salt**
½ **teaspoon sugar**
1 **tablespoon dry sherry**
1 **tablespoon oyster sauce**
1 **teaspoon sesame oil**
⅛ **teaspoon white pepper**
1 **tablespoon cornstarch**

THE DOUGH

1 **large or 2 small taro roots or tubers, about 2 pounds**
4 **ounces wheat starch, about 1 cup**
1 **cup boiling water, approximately**
1½ **teaspoons coarse salt**

1 **tablespoon sugar**
¼ **cup lard, at room temperature**
1 **teaspoon sesame oil**
Dash white pepper

4 **cups peanut oil or corn oil for deep-frying**

THE FILLING
Put the pork and the chicken leg in a large saucepan with water to cover. Bring to a boil, skim off any foam, cover, and simmer on low heat for about 40 minutes. Meanwhile soak the shrimp in 2 tablespoons of warm water for 20 minutes. Then chop them fine and set aside with the minced bamboo shoots and scallion.

With a slotted spoon, remove the pork and the chicken leg from the saucepan, reserving ½ cup of the broth. Bone the chicken leg and discard the bone and half of the skin. Dice the meat, plus the remaining skin, and dice the pork, either by hand or in a food processor, using the pulse action—for both chicken and pork, you want 1⁄16-inch dice.

Put the chopped chicken and pork in a mixing bowl. Add the chopped shrimp, bamboo shoots, salt, sugar, sherry, oyster sauce, sesame oil, and pepper. Mix well and set aside.

Pour the ½ cup reserved broth into a small saucepan, add 1 tablespoon of cornstarch, and mix well. Heat the mixture, stirring, until it thickens. Add the chicken-and-pork mixture and the minced scallion and cook for about 1 minute more. Scoop the filling out into a bowl and let it cool. If you are doing this hours or even a day ahead of time, cover and refrigerate.

THE DOUGH
Wash and peel the taro and cut into halves. Put them in a pot with water to cover. Bring to a boil, lower heat, and simmer for 30 minutes or until a knife can be inserted easily. Drain thoroughly and let them cool just until they are easy to handle; they must still be hot, however, so they are easy to mash, making a smooth purée.

While the taro is cooking, put the wheat starch in a mixing bowl and make a well in the center. Pour in about ¾ cup of the boiling water while you stir with a wooden spoon until the flour is just damp—if you need more water, add the remaining water 1 tablespoon at a time. Knead in the bowl with your hands for about 1 minute to make a soft but not sticky dough; wrap in plastic and set aside.

Mash the taro by hand, as you would potatoes, with a potato masher. Remove any hard pieces of taro you find during this process. Put the mashed taro on a work surface and, using the heel of your hand, push it against the surface until it is a very smooth dough—this will take 3 to 5 minutes. (At this point you should have about 2½ cups, or 1¼ pounds, of it.)

Spread the taro out flat and put the wheat starch dough, salt, sugar, lard, sesame oil, and pepper in the center. With your hands, mix

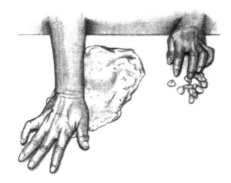

and work all the ingredients together to form a dough. Then continue pushing and kneading it into a smooth dough until the wheat starch is evenly distributed. Divide it in half and cover with plastic wrap.

MAKING AND DEEP-FRYING THE FRITTERS

Working with half of the dough at a time, roll the dough on a work surface with your hands into a long sausage shape. Cut it into sixteen pieces. With your fingers, press a well in the center of one piece. Put 2 teaspoons of filling in the well. Close the dough around the filling to seal tightly. Roll the fritter around in your palms to make a miniature football shape.

Continue to make filled taro fritters and cover them with a towel to prevent them from drying out.

Heat the 4 cups of oil in a wok until very hot—about 375 degrees. This high temperature is important, since the taro shells won't hold together if the oil isn't hot enough. Test the oil with one fritter first. When the fritter holds (does not disintegrate), lower the heat to medium-low to prevent browning and fry for 2 to 3 minutes more. Deep-fry the fritters a few at a time, raising the heat before putting in each batch and then lowering it once all the fritters are in the oil. They will take 2 to 3 minutes to cook. Lift them out with a flat strainer or slotted spoon and drain them on paper towels. Remove the flakes of dough in the oil, if any, from time to time.

The fritters are still crisp after two hours if you leave them at room temperature. If you want them very hot, keep them in a low oven (200 degrees) with the door ajar for up to an hour. In a covered container, they can be kept in the refrigerator for a week and in the freezer for a month. Reheat them on a cookie sheet in a 400-degree oven for 5 minutes, or until crisp and hot.

For serving, the small grease-proof paper eclair cups are excellent for holding the taro fritters.

Yam Gold Coins

山
芋
金
钱
饼

SHAN YU JIN QIAN BING

A sweet, dainty dessert, this is also very easy to prepare and can be done ahead of time and reheated. My favorite chef, the late T. T. Wang, often made this dessert at his restaurants in New York, Shun Lee Palace and Shun Lee West. Sometimes he skipped the filling, using minced fresh water chestnuts in the yam. He always poured hot syrup on top when serving them.

Yield: 12 servings; 48 coins

1 large yam or sweet potato, about 1 pound
1 cup glutinous rice flour (sweet rice flour), approximately

¼ cup sugar or to taste
¼ cup Red Bean or Red Date Paste (page 184)
Corn oil for shallow-frying

Boil the yam until a knife can be inserted easily—about 30 to 40 minutes. Remove and let it cool.

Peel the yam, put it in a large mixing bowl, and mash it until smooth with a potato masher. You should have about 1 cup. Add the rice flour and sugar and mix to make a soft dough. The dough should be easily manageable by hand. Add more rice flour if the dough is too soft. Divide the dough in half and roll one half on a lightly floured work surface with your hands into a cylinder about 12 inches long and then divide it into twenty-four pieces.

Put flour on your fingers and shape it into a 1½-inch-wide circle, the center thicker than the edges. Put 1 teaspoon of red bean paste in the center; then gather the edges to enclose the filling. Roll the dough in your hand to make a smooth ball and then flatten it into a coin shape. Set aside as you make the remaining coins.

Heat a 14-inch (preferably nonstick) skillet over medium-low heat until hot. Add about 2 tablespoons of oil, swirl, and heat. Pan-fry all the gold coins for 3 minutes on each side, or until they are lightly browned, very soft, and slightly puffy.

Serve the yam coins hot or warm. They can be cooked ahead of time and refrigerated for up to two days, covered with plastic wrap. Reheat in a lightly oiled pan or low oven.

Variation: For added sweetness, pour 2 to 3 tablespoons of maple syrup on top of the hot yam coins before serving them.

Miniature Split-Pea Cakes

 WAN DOU NI

This steamed purée is a brilliant green and is cut into small cubes and eaten cold. It was a favorite dish of the Empress Dowager Ci Xi in the nineteenth century, and because it was a court dish, it is still served in Beijing's best restaurant, Fangshan, which specializes in imperial food.

Yield: 32 cubes

4 ounces dried green split peas, about ⅔ cup	**¼ cup sugar or to taste**
	3 tablespoons all-purpose flour

PREPARING THE CAKE
Pick over the peas, discarding any bad ones; then wash and drain them. Put the peas in a saucepan with 3 cups of water and bring to a boil. Turn off the heat, cover, and let the peas sit for 30 minutes. Bring to a boil again and cook, covered, over low heat for 1 hour, simmering, or until the peas are very soft. After the cooking there should be about 2 cups, including the liquid; add water if there isn't that amount. Stir in the sugar until it dissolves.

Using a food processor with the steel blade, pour in the peas and liquid and process for 1 minute, or until the mixture becomes a very smooth, thin paste. Sprinkle in the flour and pulse the processor a few more turns, until the mixture is smooth.

STEAMING THE CAKE

Line a 6-inch-square cake pan or small bread pan with plastic wrap and scrape the purée into it; smooth the surface.

Set up a steamer and bring the water to a boil. Steam the cake over high heat for 20 minutes. Let it cool, cover with plastic wrap, and chill it in the refrigerator until firm—at least 4 hours.

With a sharp knife, unmold the cake bottom-side up and cut it into ¾-inch cubes. Serve cold, as a dessert or a sweet snack.

Miniature Red Bean Cakes

红
豆
糕
HONG DOU GAO

As with the split-pea cake, this one consists of very few, simple ingredients. Here the beans are cooked until very soft, but they aren't puréed, giving the cake a chewy texture.

The fragrance of red beans reminds me of eating red bean popsicles, which were abundant in China during the summer; the Chinese believe red beans are very helpful to the digestive system during hot weather. In fact, you can make popsicles with this recipe; simply insert sticks in the cooked cubed cakes and freeze them, wrapped in plastic.

This cake would be stunning served side by side with the split-pea cake (page 291), not only because of the contrasting red and green colors, but also because of the contrasting textures—this one chewy, the other smooth.

Yield: Forty ¾-inch cubes

**4 ounces dried red beans, about
    ½ cup**

**5 tablespoons sugar or to taste
¼ cup all-purpose flour**

PREPARING THE BEANS

Pick over the beans, discarding any inferior ones. Wash and drain them; then put them in a saucepan with 3 cups water. Bring the beans to a boil, cover, and let the beans sit in the water for 30 minutes. Then bring to a boil again and cook over low heat for 1 hour, or until the beans are very soft but still retain their shape.

Set up a steamer and line either a 6-inch-square cake pan or a small bread pan with plastic wrap or make an aluminum foil pan. The cake will be only ¾ inch thick.

When the beans are soft, there should be just enough liquid to cover the beans—about 2 cups; if not, add enough water to make that amount. Stir in the sugar until it dissolves. Remove from the heat and let the mixture cool.

With a rubber spatula, gently stir in the flour, making sure there are no lumps in the batter. Then pour the batter into the prepared pan.

STEAMING THE CAKE
Set up a steamer and bring the water to a boil. Steam the cake over high heat for 20 minutes. Let it cool; then refrigerate it covered with plastic wrap until it is firm—at least 4 hours. Unmold the cake, bottom side up, and cut it into ¾-inch cubes. Serve cold.

Water Chestnut Cake

 MA TI GAO

The Chinese don't favor very sweet desserts. This loaf cake, served slightly chilled, is faintly sweet and has a smooth texture broken up by the crunch of chopped water chestnuts. Its pale gray appearance can be brightened with a garnish of fresh mint leaves or cubed fruits such as watermelon or papaya.

Yield: 10 servings

> 2 cups water
> ⅔ cup sugar
> ½ cup water chestnut flour
> ½ cup water

> 10 peeled fresh or canned water chestnuts, finely chopped
>
> One 6 × 3 × 2-inch mold or small bread pan

Combine the 2 cups of water with the sugar in a saucepan and bring to a boil. Turn the heat down to keep the mixture at a slow simmer.

Meanwhile, mix the water chestnut flour with ½ cup of water, making sure the powder is in suspension. Slowly pour this into the sugar water, stirring constantly, and keep stirring until the mixture thickens and becomes translucent. Stir in the chopped water chestnuts.

Pour the mixture into the mold and let it cool to room temperature—about 3 to 4 hours. Then slice the cake into 1-inch-thick pieces, arrange them on a serving plate, and chill them in the refrigerator for 10 minutes. It is best to serve this cake just slightly chilled, because if it gets too cold it tastes starchy. Keep any leftover cake at room temperature, covered with plastic wrap.

Variation: The sliced cake is also delicious hot. Brush both sides of the slices with oil and broil them for 5 minutes; there is no need to turn them.

Chicken Congee

鸡 JI ZHOU
粥

Chicken congee reminds me of boarding school in Sichuan province during World War II. Plain congee (a thin rice cereal) was the staple dish at breakfast, accompanied by side dishes of pickled vegetables, fried beans, and, on rare occasions, scrambled eggs. The congee was always served piping hot. You tried to eat the congee in a hurry, because if you were slow, you wouldn't get seconds.

I learned the trick to it from my male classmates. First you fill the rice bowl to the brim with congee. Then, holding the bowl with the palm of your hand, you put your mouth against the rim and suck the congee while your palm turns the bowl. With one breath of sucking along the rim of the bowl, you can swallow a quarter of a bowl of congee. This is because the congee is cooler at the rim. If you needed three bowls to quell your hunger, it didn't take long to get them with this method.

Plain congee, cooked with rice and water only, is a traditional Chinese breakfast offering. An occasional plain congee breakfast in the United States is relished by those who grew up in China; for those who aren't used to it, it might appear rather tasteless at first. If the congee is made with chicken, however, it becomes a delicious light lunch.

This can be classified as a thick soup, and it is real comfort food for someone who is ill. It is light, easily digested, and nourishing. To make the chicken congee more interesting, instead of the chicken breast, pieces of fish and meat can be added before serving.

Plain congee and chicken congee go well with starchy dishes, such as *jiao zi* (boiled or fried dumplings, pages 135 and 141), Scallion Pancakes (page 162), or Deep-Fried Devils (page 172).

Yield: 6–8 servings

1 **chicken, 3½–4 pounds**	1 **cup rice (for a very smooth**
3 **quarts water**	**congee, use ½ cup glutinous**
2 **teaspoons coarse salt or to taste**	**rice and ½ cup long-grain rice)**
1 **tablespoon dry sherry**	

MAKING THE CHICKEN BROTH

Remove the breast of the chicken and set aside covered with plastic wrap, then quarter the remaining chicken. Put the chicken quarters with 12 cups of water in a large pot. Bring to a boil and skim off any foam; then add 1 teaspoon of salt and the sherry. Lower the heat so the water is very gently simmering; then cover the pot and cook for about 1 hour.

Add the chicken breast, and continue to cook for 20 minutes more. Turn off the heat and let the chicken cool in the broth; then refrigerate the breast, covered with plastic wrap, for use later in the dish; pick the rest of the meat off the bones, wrap in plastic, and refrigerate for use in other dishes. Skim off all the fat and discard, along with any residue in the broth. Strain the broth through cheesecloth; there should be about 10 cups.

MAKING THE CONGEE

Add the rice to the broth, raise the heat to high, and bring to a boil. Stir thoroughly once; then turn the heat to very low and simmer gently with the pot covered for about 2 hours. When the congee is ready, it will be a thick, smooth starch solution with cracked rice kernels in it.

(An electric casserole is a perfect pot to cook congee in. On medium heat, with the casserole covered, cook the rice in the chicken broth—or in water for plain congee—for 4 hours or longer.)

With your fingers, remove and discard the bones and skin from the reserved chicken breast and shred the white meat into small strips. Stir them into the hot congee and cook just long enough to heat the chicken through. Add the remaining salt or to taste and serve immediately, very hot. In China congee is eaten in rice bowls with spoons.

Congee made with or without chicken broth can be prepared ahead of time and kept in the refrigerator until needed. Reheat by adding a little water and mixing well, place on low heat, and slowly warm it until piping hot.

Optional Garnishes for Chicken Congee: Use 1 cup finely shredded Romaine lettuce and ¼ cup finely shredded Sichuan *zha cai*—salted celery knobs. Sprinkle the top of each bowl with 2 tablespoons of lettuce and 1 teaspoon of *zha cai*. Use the rest for seconds.

Millet Congee

 XIAO MI XI FAN

 Millet is a nonglutinous grain, one of the oldest cultivated foods on earth. It was a Chinese staple in the north long before the introduction of wheat or rice. It was usually eaten boiled, since it cannot be used as flour. For this recipe use the yellow proso variety, which has been carefully hulled; it is available at health food stores.

This soup is usually drunk plain, without seasonings, as an accompaniment to *jiao zi* dumplings (pages 135 and 141) or Cantonese or Shanghai spring rolls (pages 95 and 98) and some relish (pages 302–309) or other store-bought preserved vegetables, such as pickled lettuce, the Narcissus brand from the People's Republic of China or the Wai-Chuan brand from Taiwan.

Yield: 4–5 cups

½ cup yellow millet, without husks

5 cups cold water, for a thin millet congee
¼ teaspoon baking soda

Put the millet in a large saucepan, add the water, baking soda, and bring to a boil. Adjust the heat to a simmer, partially covered, and cook for 20 minutes, or until the millet is very soft and the consistency of the dish is that of a thick soup. Sweeten it a little with sugar or honey if you wish. Serve hot during the winter and warm during the summer.

Tofu Crackers

 JIA CHANG QIAO GUO

These crunchy fried crackers are inexpensive and easy to make—and they are a very tasty and nutritious snack. They look like corn chips and, oddly enough, taste a little like them. They would be perfect to serve with drinks.

Yield: 100 crackers 1 by 2 inches

1 three-inch square firm bean curd, ¾ inch thick	**1 tablespoon cold water, approximately**
1 cup unbleached all-purpose flour	**1 tablespoon black sesame seeds**
1 teaspoon coarse salt	**Oil for deep-frying, about 3 cups**
1 tablespoon peanut oil or corn oil	

Put the bean curd in a large mixing bowl, and with the back of a large spoon mash it into a smooth paste. Add the flour, salt, and oil and mix with your fingers to incorporate the flour. Stir in the cold water and sesame seeds; then knead the mixture in the bowl into a soft but not sticky dough. Place the dough on a lightly floured surface and knead it some more—about 2 to 3 minutes. Cover with plastic wrap and let it rest for 15 minutes.

The mixing can be done in a food processor. Leave out the black sesame seeds when processing and mix them in by hand so that the dough will not become a grayish color.

Divide the dough in half. Working with one half at a time on a lightly floured surface, roll the dough into a very thin sheet about 12 by 8 inches. Cut the sheet with a pastry cutter into strips 2 inches long and ¾ inch wide. You'll have approximately fifty strips. Stack them loosely and cover them with a dry dish towel to prevent them from drying out. Repeat with the other half of the dough.

Heat the oil in a wok until very hot—about 375 degrees. Fry the crackers in several batches until crisp and golden brown—about 3 minutes—stirring a few times during the frying so they brown evenly. Drain well on paper towels.

The fried crackers will stay fresh in a tin can for many weeks.

Note: Soft bean curd may be used, but it must be weighted first. Wrap it in a towel, put a board on top, and place a pot of water on top; let it sit for 1 hour. The water will have been released and the bean curd will be firm.

Variation: To make twisted bow ties out of the dough strips, cut a slit in the center of each strip almost to each end; then take one end and bring it through the slit from the back.

Sauces
and
Relishes

Sauces

Hot Chili Bean Paste (Sauce), Sichuan- or Hunan-Style   302

Scallion and Ginger Sauce   303

Black Bean Chili Sauce   304

Relishes

Celery Cabbage with Dried Shrimp Salad   305

Sweet-and-Sour Cucumbers or Cabbage with Hot Pepper   306

Cantonese Pickled Vegetables   307

Sichuan Pickled Cabbage   308

Shanghai Pickled Turnips   309

We Chinese often use relishes as side dishes with a meal; that is why home pickling is very important in Chinese households. We believe the concentrated flavor of the relish will stimulate one's appetite. You need only a very small amount to accompany your meal.

Almost every country has its own way of pickling vegetables in brine, vinegar, or oil, using different spices. The Chinese are no exception. In fact, there are quite interesting regional differences—hot, sour, or soy sauce plus sugar and various spices. The important item is coarse salt; the vegetable is either put in salt water or salted ahead of time to draw out the liquid, then processed with other seasonings. The result is to make the vegetable crispy and give a more intense flavor. Drawing out the liquid also eliminates any "raw taste." Even vegetables for salads, such as bean sprouts, are blanched in water. Someone who cooks authentic Chinese dishes will never serve mung bean sprouts that have not at least been blanched, because the Chinese find the raw taste very unpleasant.

Most sauces for dips mentioned in this book are very simple ones: for fried food, usually Zhejiang vinegar or wine vinegar combined with chili pepper oil; for steamed dumplings, shredded ginger and vinegar or oyster sauce. Also included are a few more complicated sauce recipes (page 139) for other dumplings.

The Hot Chili Bean Paste in this chapter is a basic hot chili sauce, made from brown bean sauce with fresh and dried hot chili peppers and other seasonings added. You can adjust it to your taste.

In China, the seasoning and spices are added to a bean sauce in different proportions in different regions. In Sichuan large amounts of hot peppers and crushed peppercorns are used; in the northern provinces, garlic and scallions; in Zhejiang and Jiangsu provinces, moderate amounts of sugar; and in Canton, large amounts of sugar, garlic, and spices. There are no set rules as to the amounts of seasonings or spices added to a bean sauce. It is a question of availability and of personal taste.

In Sichuan or Hunan cooking, in general, hot pepper dishes are not used for a main meal, especially a banquet meal, but there is always a very hot chili pepper sauce to use as a dip and pickles as side dishes to increase the appetite or to use as accompaniments for rice.

If you don't have time to pickle vegetables, they are readily available in jars or cans, most of them with soy sauce. For instance, Pickled Lettuce Stalks (page 320) are very good. Sauces (paste) are also available in jars or cans. One of them, made in New York City, is called Hunan Paste, and it is quite good.

Sauces

Hot Chili Bean Paste (Sauce), Sichuan- or Hunan-Style

辣椒豆瓣醬 LA JIAO DOU PAN CHIANG

The degree of hotness in any pepper dish depends on the number of hot peppers put into it. You can vary the proportion of hot to sweet peppers to suit your taste. This paste has an average hotness.

The ¼ cup of brown bean sauce denotes the Sichuan style; if you use 2 tablespoons of salted black beans and 2 tablespoons of brown bean sauce, the sauce becomes Hunan style. This type of paste is both made here and imported from China; it can be purchased in Chinese markets under different brands, in small jars and in cans. One of them, made in New York City, is called Hunan Paste, and it is quite good. This paste, both homemade and store-bought, will keep for months in the refrigerator.

Yield: 1 cup

20 **dried hot chili peppers, each about 1½ inches long**
1 **pound fresh sweet red peppers**
6 **tablespoons corn oil**
2 **small cloves garlic, minced**

¼ **cup brown bean sauce (for Hunan style, use 2 tablespoons salted black beans and 2 tablespoons brown bean sauce)**

Soak the dried hot peppers in ½ cup water until they are soft and the wrinkles have smoothed out. Drain, saving the soaking water. Wash the fresh red peppers and dry them thoroughly. Cut out the seeds and pith, then chop them in large chunks and set aside.

In a food processor fitted with the metal blade, chop the two kinds of peppers separately and place them in two different bowls. Or chop both peppers by hand separately till finely chopped. Be careful with the hot peppers; don't rub your eyes.

Heat the oil in a heavy saucepan with an asbestos pad on the burner. Add the hot peppers and garlic and stir and cook in the oil for 2 minutes. Add the bean sauce, sweet peppers, and the hot-pepper soaking water. Bring to a boil, then lower the heat and cook uncovered for about 30 minutes, or until the liquid has evaporated. Stir often during this time.

Let the paste cool completely. Keep it submerged under the oil that floats to the top when you transfer it to a jar with a tight lid. It will keep at room temperature for two to three weeks, or in the refrigerator indefinitely.

Scallion and Ginger Sauce

Yield: ½ cup

2 teaspoons minced fresh ginger	3 tablespoons light soy sauce
2 tablespoons chopped whole scallion	2 teaspoons red wine vinegar
	¼ cup chicken broth
2 tablespoons sesame oil	1 teaspoon sugar

Heat the sesame oil in a small saucepan over low heat. Add the ginger and scallions, and let them sizzle for 10 seconds. Add the remaining ingredients and heat together for another 10 seconds, stirring. Divide the sauce into individual dip dishes.

Black Bean Chili Sauce

Yield: ½ cup

1 tablespoon light soy sauce
1 tablespoon dry sherry
2 teaspoons sugar
¼ teaspoon coarse salt or to taste
2 tablespoons chicken broth or water
2 tablespoons chopped whole scallions

2 tablespoons corn oil or peanut oil
2 tablespoons salted black beans, rinsed and drained
1 teaspoon chili pepper flakes
1 clove garlic, finely chopped

Put into a small bowl the soy sauce, sherry, sugar, salt, chicken broth, and scallions and mix well. Set aside.

Heat the oil in a small saucepan. Add the black beans and chili pepper and cook for 1 minute. Stir in the garlic and cook 30 seconds. Remove from heat, add the bowl ingredients, and stir to mix well. Adjust seasonings with salt if you wish. Divide the sauce into individual dishes.

Relishes

Celery Cabbage
with Dried Shrimp Salad

 XIANG CAI BAN XIA MI

This salad is served at Auntie Yuan's Restaurant in New York, which is famous for its home-cooked Chinese food. It has a refreshing taste and goes beautifully with any pasta dish.

A small amount of dried shrimp in a salad acts a little like cheese in a Western salad: It gives the vegetables a spark of flavor.

Yield: 2 cups

4 cups packed shredded celery
  cabbage, the white, tender
  inner leaves
4 small scallions, white part
  only, finely shredded
½ cup chopped fresh coriander
  leaves and tender stems
1½ teaspoons coarse salt or to
  taste
1 teaspoon sugar

2 tablespoons lemon juice
2 tablespoons finely minced
  dried shrimp or to taste
  (preferably the pink ones, a
  sign they've been freshly
  stocked; the more expensive
  kind)
1 clove garlic, finely minced
1 teaspoon sesame oil

Combine the celery cabbage, scallions, and coriander in a large mixing bowl. Add the salt, toss, and let it sit for 20 minutes.

Drain and discard the water, but do not squeeze the cabbage dry. Add the sugar, lemon juice, shrimp, garlic, and sesame oil. Mix, tossing, then cover and refrigerate until ready to serve.

Sweet-and-Sour Cucumbers or Cabbage with Hot Pepper

SUAN LA HUANG GUA, BAI CAI

These sweet-and-sour relishes with hot chili peppers are an excellent side dish for any pasta meal, and the concentrated flavor of the relish will stimulate one's appetite. They are very easy to make and can be prepared ahead of time—in fact, they taste even better after a day or two. The charred dried whole chili peppers are very hot, so do not eat them unless you are accustomed to the spiciness.

Yield: 1½ cups

2 large or 4 small cucumbers, or 4 cups finely shredded celery cabbage, the tender stems only	2 tablespoons corn oil or peanut oil
2 teaspoons coarse salt	4 dried red chili peppers, each about 1 inch long

THE SAUCE

1½ tablespoons sugar	1 tablespoon distilled white vinegar

MACERATING THE VEGETABLE

Wash the cucumbers and cut off and discard both ends. If the skin is very hard, scrape it off. Cut each cucumber lengthwise in half. Using a teaspoon, scrape out the seeds and pulp (if you are using seedless cucumber, there's no need to scrape). Lay each cucumber half cut side down and slice it very thin crosswise, so the slices are about 1/16 inch thick. If you are using the cabbage stems, cut them into very fine shreds about 2 inches long. You should have about 4 cups.

Put the cucumber or cabbage in a large mixing bowl, add the salt, and toss to mix well; then lightly press the mass down and let it macerate for at least 4 hours or up to 8 hours at room temperature. The vegetable should be limp. Drain off the water without squeezing the vegetable.

MAKING THE SAUCE AND ADDING THE VEGETABLE

Combine the sauce ingredients in a heatproof dish, stirring to dissolve the sugar, and set aside.

Heat the oil in a small saucepan over medium heat for 30 seconds, add the dried chili peppers, and fry them for about 2 minutes, or until they are almost black. Remove the pan from the stove, then stand back and pour the hot oil and peppers into the sauce—it will sizzle strongly. Pour this sauce-and-oil mixture over the cucumbers or cabbage and toss to mix well.

The relish can be eaten right away or kept in a container in the refrigerator overnight or longer—up to two weeks.

Cantonese Pickled Vegetables

广
东   QUANGDONG PAO CAI
泡
菜   Cantonese pickled vegetables are sweet-and-sour rather than spicy, rely-
      ing on the natural spiciness of the vegetables used. For instance, the
      hearts of mustard greens (the tender inner part) have a strong mustard
      flavor after pickling. Young fresh ginger root, available in early summer,
      has a light but fragrant hotness. Because the vegetables are pickled in a
      solution of vinegar, sugar, salt, and water, they are very crisp. Other firm
      vegetables, such as sliced cucumbers or carrots, would also be delicious
      pickled this way.

Yield: 1½ cups

4 cups hearts of Chinese mustard   1 teaspoon coarse salt
greens (the inner part), cut into
pieces 1 × 1 × 2 inches, or
combined with ¼ cup scraped
and thinly sliced ginger root
(optional)

THE PICKLING SOLUTION

6 tablespoons distilled white   6 tablespoons sugar
vinegar   ¼ teaspoon coarse salt

Put the vegetables in a large mixing bowl, sprinkle on the salt, and toss to distribute the salt. Set aside for 2 hours to macerate.

Drain off the water and, using your hands, squeeze most of the water from the vegetables. Put them in a glass jar.

Combine the pickling solution ingredients in a saucepan and stir to dissolve the sugar. Bring the solution to a boil and let it cool completely. Pour the cool solution into the jar; it should completely cover the vegetables. Let the jar sit in the refrigerator overnight.

Serve the pickled vegetables cold. They can be kept for three months, refrigerated.

Sichuan Pickled Cabbage

四
川   SICHUAN PAO CAI
泡
菜   The Chinese often use relishes as side dishes with noodle and dumpling meals—they increase your appetite. Sichuan pickled cabbage is a delicious homemade relish, and it can be made all year round. It can be served as a side dish or used as a seasoning ingredient, cooked with meats or vegetables for noodle toppings. If you keep it in an aged brine for a long time, it will develop a very tasty sauerkrautlike flavor.

I always have a jar of aged brine in my refrigerator. The trick is to keep the brine free from bacteria by adding salt to the liquid from time to time. Always use absolutely clean utensils to pick out the cabbage or stir the liquid. In one Sichuan restaurant in New York they even brought aged brine with them from China.

Other vegetables, such as cut-up cauliflower; peeled broccoli stems; Chinese white turnips (luo-bo), the skins only scraped lightly; young green beans; peeled carrots; or young fresh peeled ginger (available in Chinese markets in early summer) may be used instead of cabbage or combined with it in the same jar. Two to four fresh chili peppers may be used instead of dried ones.

Yield: Serves 4 as a side dish

1 pound green cabbage (use the inner white leaves only)
3 tablespoons coarse salt
4 cups cold water

½ teaspoon Sichuan peppercorns (optional)
4 dried hot chili peppers, or ½ teaspoon chili pepper flakes or to your taste

Cut or tear the cabbage into 1½- by 1-inch pieces; you should have about 6 cups.

In a 2-quart wide-mouth jar, dissolve the salt in the water. Add the peppercorns and chili peppers. Mix well, then add the cabbage and press it down to the bottom within the liquid. Cover and keep the jar at room temperature for one day, then in the refrigerator for about three days. Remove the cabbage with clean, dry chopsticks or a fork and serve it cold. The brine will improve the flavor after two or three times of pickling Store the relish jar in the refrigerator.

You may continue to use the brine. Add more fresh cabbage as a batch of it is used up. Stir in about 3 teaspoons of salt each time you add fresh cabbage. Cabbage soaked in aged brine will be pickled in one to two days. After you've added cabbage twice to the brine, replace the peppers if you like. When the liquid isn't enough to cover the cabbage, it is time to make a half recipe of brine and add that to the original.

Shanghai Pickled Turnips

  JIANG LUOBO

This soy sauce pickle is neither sour nor hot. It is a popular relish dish in east-central China. The skin of the large white turnip gives this pickle an extra crispness. The young kohlrabi, when it is in season, can also be used.

Yield: 2 cups

1 medium white turnip (white radish, which the Japanese call "daikon"), about 1 pound	2 tablespoons soy sauce, or to your taste, preferably Kimlan brand (page 325)
1 teaspoon coarse salt	1 tablespoon sesame oil
2 teaspoons sugar	

With a small knife, lightly scrape the turnip's skin, so that only the thin outer layer is scraped off (the skin of the white turnip is very firm; it is best for pickling). Wash the turnip and dry well with paper towels. Cut the turnip into ½-inch cubes; you should have about 3 cups. Place the turnips, salt, and sugar in a 1-quart glass jar. Cover the jar and shake well so that the turnips are coated with the seasonings. Leave for 1 hour at room temperature or refrigerate overnight.

Pour off the accumulated liquid from the jar and discard. Add the soy sauce and let marinate for at least 2 to 3 hours. Add sesame oil and serve cold, or leave the turnip in the jar and keep it in the refrigerator up to a month (these pickles taste better after a day or two). Remove as much as you need, add few drops of sesame oil, and serve as side dish for noodles or dumplings.

Glossary

BAMBOO SHOOTS, WINTER

冬笋 *Dong Sun*

In the winter, when bamboo shoots first begin to grow, they are collected by digging them up from underground. That is why these shoots are called winter bamboo shoots. They are relatively small in size and are the best tasting of all bamboo shoots. They have a smooth beige-colored shell and, when peeled, are about the size of medium pinecones.

Shoots are best eaten fresh. In recent years, during the Chinese New Year, they have become available at the Kam Kuo market in New York City. They are very expensive, but they can be kept in the refrigerator for up to one month unpeeled if the shell has no black spots and the whole piece is firm.

When bamboo shoots are preserved, they lose much of their flavor. The crisp texture remains, however, which is much admired by the Chinese.

Winter bamboo shoots are canned unseasoned, packed in water; the best brand is Narcissus from China. Once the can is opened, submerge the shoots in their own liquid or in cold water and refrigerate them in a covered jar. If you change the water in the jar every four to five days, you can keep the bamboo shoots fresh for several weeks.

BEAN CURD, PRESSED, PLAIN AND SEASONED

白豆腐干 豆腐干 *Dou Fu Gan (Pai Dou Fu Gan and Wu Xiang Dou Fu Gan)*

When more water is pressed out of firm bean curd, it becomes pressed bean curd. Its texture becomes much firmer than that of regular bean curd, almost like a firm cheese. Pressed bean curd may be bought either plain or seasoned.

The plain curd is white and the seasoned is cooked in soy sauce and star anise, giving it a brown color. The size of the seasoned pressed bean curd varies depending on the manufacturer, ranging from 2 × 2 inches to 2 × 4 inches and ½ to ¾ inch thick. The two types are available in most Chinese markets and in some local Oriental food shops.

Pressed bean curd can best be stored submerged in salted water—1 tablespoon salt to 2 cups water—in a covered container. If kept in the coldest part of the refrigerator, it will stay fresh for several weeks.

BEAN CURD, TENDER AND FIRM

豆
腐

嫩
豆
腐

老
豆
腐

Dou Fu (Nen Dou Fu and *Lao Dou Fu)*
When a coagulant is added to boiled soybean milk, the milk curdles. After removing some of the water from the curdled bean milk, the result is tender bean curd. It is cut into 4-by-4-inch squares about 1½ inches thick.

When a coagulant is added to soybean milk of a different concentration and some of the water is removed, the milk becomes firm bean curd. This is cut into 3-by-3-inch squares about ¾ inch thick.

Bean curd spoils easily, so it should be submerged in water in a covered container and placed in the coldest part of the refrigerator. If the water is changed every other day, it can be kept unspoiled for at least a week if it was fresh when purchased. Also available in supermarkets are sealed boxes containing bean curd and water, with preservative added. They last up to two weeks.

BLACK BEANS, SALTED

豆
豉

Dou Chi
Small dried black beans, preserved through soaking, steaming, fermenting, and adding salt and spices, are used to flavor bland foods, such as steamed fish or chicken. They come in small plastic bags, in jars, or in cans. The beans are sold in Chinese markets. They can be refrigerated in a jar and kept indefinitely.

BROWN BEAN SAUCE, GROUND OR WHOLE BEANS

原 磨
晒 原
豉 豉

Yuan Shai Chi (whole) and *Mo Yuan Chi* (ground)
Brown bean sauce, which is more like a paste, is made from fermented soybeans and wheat flour mixed with salt and water. The beans in the sauce may be either ground or left whole. (I use the whole brown bean sauce, which has a better flavor for my variations on the sauce, which has fresh and dried red peppers and other seasonings; see page 302.)

To this basic bean sauce spices and other seasonings are added, forming many varieties from different parts of China. In Sichuan, large amounts of hot chili pepper and crushed Sichuan peppercorns are added; in the northern provinces, garlic and scallions; in Zhejiang and Jiangsu provinces, moderate amounts of sugar; in Canton, large amounts of sugar, garlic, and spices. These brown bean sauces are sold in cans or jars.

If the bean sauce is from a can, it should be transferred to a jar and kept in the refrigerator. It will not spoil for a long time. Bean sauce can be found in many Oriental food stores.

CHILI PEPPER OIL

La Yu

Hot pepper oil is often added to the toppings for noodles or used as a dip for meat-filled dumplings to give the food an extra spicy taste. This hot pepper oil is made simply by frying hot pepper flakes and paprika. The oil turns red and its taste becomes pungent. The pepper flakes are removed and can be used in other dishes. Store the oil in a bottle, where it will keep for months. You can also purchase the oil already made.

CHILI PEPPERS

La Jiao

There are many kinds of chili peppers, and the degree of hotness varies. The thin red or green ones, about 3 to 5 inches long, are widely available fresh at vegetable stands; dried, the red ones are sold in plastic packages in Oriental or Spanish markets. They are about 1 inch long. However, you can use any hot chili pepper you desire. If you cannot get whole peppers, either fresh or dried, use chili pepper flakes.

CHINESE CABBAGE (BOK CHOY OR BAI CAI)

Bok Choy or *Bai Cai*

Bok choy is eaten at different stages of growth. The *bok choy* sold in Chinese or American markets is fully grown, with white stems, dark green leaves, and sometimes yellow blossoms in the center. Doubly wrapped in a paper bag and then a plastic bag, it will keep in the refrigerator for up to three weeks if the vegetable is fresh and free from excess moisture. Soak the vegetables in cold water before you use them.

CHINESE CELERY CABBAGE (LONG HEAD AND SHORT HEAD)

Tianjin Bai Cai (long head); *Shandong Bai Cai* (short head)

Long-head Chinese celery cabbage originally came from Tianjin in the north of China. It has a pale yellow color and a tightly wrapped elongated head. Two-thirds of the plant is stem, while the leaves are comparatively small. The tender stem is excellent for making relish.

Short-head Chinese celery cabbage, also called Napa cabbage, is very similar to the long-headed variety, except that its leaves are curlier and it has a shorter and fatter head. It is named after the province of Shandong in the north.

Both varieties will keep well for up to three weeks in the refrigerator if they are doubly wrapped in a paper bag and then a plastic bag.

CHINESE CHIVES
韭菜 *Jiu Cai*

Chinese chives are a perennial plant of the onion family. Their dark-green grasslike leaves are used for flavoring and sometimes as a vegetable. The chives start growing in the early summer; later on, tiny bulbous heads grow on top; they are sweeter than the leaves.

Chinese chives are sold only fresh, by the bunch, in Chinese and Oriental vegetable stores. They have a strong aroma and spoil easily. They should be stored in the refrigerator double bagged (placed first in a paper bag or wrapped in paper towels, then in a plastic bag). Depending on the freshness of the chives, they can be kept for up to a week.

CHRYSANTHEMUM GREENS
茼蒿菜 *Tonghao Cai*

Edible chrysanthemums, though cultivated, grow like weeds. They should be eaten before they begin to bloom. The vegetable is harvested by picking off the top several inches of stem where the stems are still tender and fragrant. They are sold by the bunch in Chinese and Japanese vegetable stores. If doubly wrapped in a paper bag and then a plastic bag, they will keep for a few days. Soak them in cold water to revive them.

CORIANDER
香菜 *Xiang Cai*
芫荽

Coriander is an herb of the parsley family and looks like delicate Italian parsley. Its taste is very unusual–sharp, cool, almost medicinal. A Chinese cook would use coriander leaves and tender stems as a Western cook would use parsley. It is sold by the bunch.

It keeps fresh in the refrigerator for a few days if the roots aren't removed and it is put in a paper bag and then a plastic bag.

FIVE-SPICE POWDER
Wu Xiang Fen

Five-spice powder is a combination of many seasonings, much as curry powder is made of a combination of spices. It is used for seasoning poultry, meat, and fish. The powder can be a combination of star anise, fennel seeds, cloves, cinnamon bark, Sichuan peppercorns, licorice, ginger, and nutmeg. Different brands use different combinations of spices, so the aroma and taste vary.

FLAT FISH FILLET, DRIED
扁 *Bian Yu*
鱼 This is a dried unsalted fillet made from a small flat fish similar to butterfish. The dried fish can be refrigerated in a sealed plastic bag and kept indefinitely.

HOISIN SAUCE AND SWEET BEAN SAUCE
海 *Hai Xian Jiang* and *Tian Mian Jiang*
鲜 Hoisin sauce and sweet bean sauce are both made from basic brown
酱 bean sauce. Hoisin sauce, from Canton, has large amounts of sugar,
、 garlic, and spices added. It is very popular in the United States, because
甜 it was established abroad so long ago. The Cantonese use hoisin sauce to
面 spread on Peking duck.
酱 The sweet bean sauce, from Beijing, has less sugar added than hoisin sauce, so it is saltier. The duck restaurants in that city use this sauce on the duck. Both regions use their sauce in many other dishes as well. If the sauce has been canned, transfer it to a jar and put it in the refrigerator, where it will keep indefinitely.

JUJUBES (RED DATES) AND JUJUBE DATE JAM
枣 *Hong Zao* and *Zao Ni*
子 Jujubes are a fruit that comes from the northern part of China. When
、 fresh, they are green, crisp, and sweet. They are generally available
枣 dried and have a crinkled skin and dark-red color. Their size varies
泥 from that of seedless grapes to that of large olives. They are best stored in the refrigerator or freezer and are sold in Chinese markets in plastic bags.

Jujube date jam comes in 11-ounce cans. The Evergreen brand product from China is excellent.

LOTUS SEED PASTE

蓮
蓉
Lian Rong

Lotus seed paste is cooked lotus seeds mashed into a paste, with a little added sugar. The 7-ounce canned Szechuan brand from Taiwan is good.

MUNG BEAN SHEETS

粉
皮
Fen Pi

Mung bean sheets, like cellophane noodles, are made from mung bean flour and tapioca flour. The sheets must be soaked before using them. They are transparent when warm and opaque when cool. They are sold dried, in stacks of 8-inch-round sheets, eight to ten sheets in a stack. Kept in plastic bags, they will stay fresh indefinitely at room temperature.

MUNG BEAN SPROUTS

绿
豆
芽
Lu Dou Ya

Mung bean sprouts are one of the most popular Chinese vegetables in the United States. They can be found in almost every large city supermarket. If they are very fresh and stored in a plastic bag, they will keep in the refrigerator for two to three days.

MUSHROOMS (CHINESE BLACK MUSHROOMS AND WINTER MUSHROOMS)

香
菌
冬
菇
Xiang Jun and *Dong Gu*

Dried black Chinese mushrooms are the most popular type of mushrooms used in Chinese dishes, as a complementary vegetable for its flavor. Soaking them in warm water for 30 minutes will bring the mushrooms back to their original shape. Winter mushrooms are a thicker variety of black mushrooms; they are grayish black and after soaking become even tenderer than black mushrooms. They are also more expensive and have a better flavor and aroma. The better grade of these mushrooms needs at least 1 hour to redevelop.

MUSTARD GREENS

芥
菜
Gai Cai

Both the stems and leaves of mustard greens have the color of a greening apple. The mature plant has a very loosely wrapped head, and each individual stem is wide and has a full, ruffled leaf. Doubly wrapped in a paper bag and then a plastic bag, it will keep for up to three weeks in the refrigerator.

NOODLES, CELLOPHANE (TRANSPARENT NOODLES OR MUNG BEAN NOODLES)

粉
丝 *Fen Si*

Cellophane noodles are made from dried mung beans that are soaked and then water-ground into flour; then tapioca flour is added. The noodles are opaque when cool and transparent when hot. This transparent quality is the reason the noodles are called cellophane noodles. They are sold dried, in bundles weighing 2, 4, 8 ounces, or 1 pound; they are inexpensive and keep indefinitely at room temperature.

NOODLES, FRESH EGG

蛋
面 *Dan Mian*

Fresh Chinese egg noodles usually come in two to three widths, between 1/16 inch and 1/8 inch. Packaged in 1-pound plastic bags, they are kept in the refrigerated section of Chinese grocery stores. See page 28 for storage and other information.

NOODLES, FRESH EGGLESS

白
面 *Bai Mian*

Fresh Chinese eggless noodles usually come in two widths, 1/8 inch and a little less than 1/4 inch. Packaged in 1-pound plastic bags, they are kept in the refrigerated section of Chinese grocery stores. See page 28 for storage and other information.

NOODLES, RICE (RICE STICKS)

米
粉 *Mi Fen*

Rice noodles are a southern specialty made from ground long-grain rice. They are thin, white, and uneven. They come in two thicknesses—one slightly thicker than cellophane noodles and the other very fine, thinner than angel's hair pasta. These noodles require only a brief boiling in water for the thick kind or a few minutes soaking in cold water for the very fine before they are cooked with other food. Rice noodles can be stir-fried or dropped into soup, and they can also be deep-fried into crisp sticks.

Rice noodles are available dried, in wads wrapped in paper in 1-pound packages. Each package is divided into four wads for easily accessible serving portions. They are sold in Chinese food markets. Most of the brands are equally good. No refrigeration is needed.

NOODLES, SPINACH

菠
菜
面

Po Cai Mian

Spinach noodles come in dried form in Chinese markets. The noodles have been steamed and are therefore slightly shiny, slightly darker in color, and a little heavier. The Long Life brand is very good. Neatly wrapped in cellophane, the 250g (8.8 oz) package is a product of the People's Republic of China.

NOODLES, SHRIMP ROE AND VELVET CHICKEN

虾 蚝
子 味
面 酱

Xia Zi Mian and *Ji Rong Mian*

Most shrimp roe and velvet chicken noodles come in small patties or nests. They have been steamed, so the noodle patties are golden and shiny. Their texture is firmer than that of fresh noodles, so they take longer to cook. After cooking, the noodles are much bouncier and fluffier than fresh noodles.

NOODLES, YI FU

伊
府
面

Yi Fu Mian

Yi Fu noodles come in plastic bags or boxes. They are sold already fried, then dried, so they are puffy. They will keep at room temperature for up to two months.

OIL

油

The liquid oil that the Chinese prefer to use in cooking is flavorless oil, such as corn oil or peanut oil or a vegetable oil from cotton seeds or soybeans. An oil with a strong flavor is easily detectable in a delicate dish such as stir-fried Chinese cabbage (bok choy).

Frying in oil can be done with high heat (375 degrees and up), moderate heat (around 350 degrees), or low heat (250 degrees to 300 degrees). If you don't have a thermometer, you can test the temperature of the oil with a piece of scallion or a green vegetable leaf. The scallion does not sizzle when placed in oil at low heat. If it sizzles but remains green for a little while, the heat is moderate; if it browns immediately, the heat is high.

Deep-frying as a method of cooking tends to scare people because they immediately think of greasy food. However, if the food is cooked properly, it is often not any more greasy than food that has been stir-fried.

One method of deep-frying uses the oil to generate very high heat. The extremely hot oil puffs up the item you are cooking. For instance, heat the oil to 385 degrees and fry some rice noodles or cellophane noodles. They will puff up in seconds, and the noodles have hardly had the chance to soak up any oil. The result is a puffy crispy noodle.

Deep-frying can also be done with the oil at a mere 300 degrees. This temperature is hot enough to seal the delicate coating but will not overcook the food; the result is a velvety texture. This is a precooking technique used before stir-frying. Many cooks call it "velveting in the oil"; the literal translation is "hot wok and warm oil." For this method of cooking, the wok must be well seasoned, which means you heat a clean wok until hot, pour in about ½ cup oil, swirl it around until it is very hot, about 1 minute, then pour off the oil and reserve it. Now your wok is well seasoned, and your coated food will not stick, especially those foods coated with egg white and cornstarch.

The oil can be reused up to three times without adding clean oil. For instance, when frying spring rolls (egg rolls), you will have to add more oil after thirty to forty pieces. That means, half used oil and half clean oil. You can use the oil continuously without any danger of the oil's burning.

I like to store leftover oil in an earthenware pot or a glass jar at room temperature and this will keep up to a month. Remove floating bits with a strainer. The remaining residue will settle in the bottom of the jar in about one day, so when you reuse the oil, just pour it off the top and add some clean oil for stir-frying or deep-frying. Remember: The oil used to deep-fry fish should be saved exclusively for this purpose. It will be too strongly flavored for general use.

The oil used for the "velveting in the oil" method may return some liquid from the food. I usually keep this oil in the refrigerator because it will spoil in a day or two at room temperature.

OYSTER-FLAVORED SAUCE

蚝
味
酱
Hao Wei Jiang

For the last fifteen years I have been unable to buy real oyster sauce. It is probably too expensive to produce. What is offered now instead is oyster-flavored sauce, which is made with oyster extract and salt, cornstarch, and monosodium glutamate. I usually buy the Hop Sing Lung or Lee Kum Kee brands, both from Hong Kong. Store the bottle in the refrigerator, where it will keep indefinitely.

PEPPERCORNS, SICHUAN

花
椒
Hua Jiao

This peppercorn has a different flavor from the ordinary black peppercorn in that it is not peppery but gives a numbing sensation to the tongue. It also has a distinct aroma after roasting in a dry skillet. The peppercorn has dark red husks that are open. The seeds are not enclosed in the hulls and are a darker red, almost black. After roasting the peppercorns for several minutes, crush them with a rolling pin and keep them in a tightly capped jar.

PICKLED VEGETABLES

Salting, drying, and drying after salting are the ancient methods the Chinese used to preserve food. In all regions of China the vegetables of the cabbage and turnip family are preserved, each region producing different flavors. Some vegetables are named after the places in which they're produced. These specially preserved vegetables are shipped all over China for use in cooking.

Most pickled vegetables contain a large amount of salt, and only small amounts are used to complement a dish. An entire can or jar cannot be used at one time. Store the remaining vegetable in a jar with a rustproof cover. It will keep for a long time in the refrigerator.

PICKLED LETTUCE STALKS

香菜心 *Xiang Cai Xin*

Pickled lettuce stalks are sold canned. They are overgrown stalks that have been peeled, thinly sliced, and then pickled in soy sauce. The color is reddish brown. They are a tasty accompaniment for soup noodles and congee. They come in a 7-ounce can and keep indefinitely in a covered jar. The Narcissus brand from China and the Wei Chuan brand from Taiwan are both excellent.

PICKLED RED-IN-SNOW CABBAGE

雪菜、雪里蕻 *Xue Cai*

The people of Zhejiang and Jiangsu provinces pickle a delicious crisp green that is literally translated as "red-in-snow." This vegetable is like turnip tops, and both the leaves and stems are preserved. It is grown in the United States and can be bought fresh in Chinese markets.

To preserve it yourself, figure on 5 pounds fresh tender red-in-snow and ¾ cup coarse salt. Wash, drain, and dry the vegetable. Place layer upon layer of the leaves in a large pot, sprinkling salt on top of each layer. Set a heavy object on top to press down the leaves, and let them sit for two days. Pack the salted vegetable firmly into a wide-mouth jar and pour in the saltwater to cover the vegetable. Cover tightly. The salted leaves will be ready to eat after one week. Cut them to the desired size. If you store the jar in the refrigerator, the vegetable will keep indefinitely.

Red-in-snow also comes in a 7-ounce can labeled pickled cabbage; it is cut into 2- to 3-inch sections. The best brand is Ma-ling, produced in China.

PICKLED SICHUAN STEMS

四　*Sichuan Zha Cai*
川　*Zha cai* is a preserved vegetable, a specialty of Sichuan province. It con-
乍　sists of a special variety of mustard greens found only in China; the many
菜　knobs on the stem are pickled with salt and minced hot chili pepper.

Zha cai is greenish-brown in color, hot and salty in taste. It comes either chopped or in chunks and is packed in jars or cans. If it tastes too peppery, rinse it under cold water to eliminate some of the hot chili flavor before cooking.

Zha cai is a piquant seasoning for noodle dishes, especially vegetarian ones. It will keep indefinitely, if refrigerated in a covered jar. *Zha cai* is available in Oriental food shops and Chinese markets.

PICKLED TIANJIN CABBAGE

天　*Tianjin Dong Cai*
津　This vegetable is a famous product of the city of Tianjin. It is the leaves
冬　and stems of Chinese celery cabbage, cut into small bits and preserved
菜　with salt, garlic, and other spices. Its color is light brown, and it is
packed very tightly in earthenware or glass jars. These jars are labeled Tientsin, the old transliteration from the Chinese. Transferred to a covered jar and refrigerated, Tianjin *dong cai* keeps indefinitely. It is available in Oriental food stores and Chinese markets.

RED BEANS AND RED BEAN PASTE

红　*Hong Dou* and *Hong Dou Sha*
豆　In Chinese cooking red beans are used often in sweet pastries in the
、　form of paste. The paste can be homemade or bought in cans; the 18-
红　ounce canned Companion brand from Taiwan is very good. Dried red
豆　beans are sold by weight in plastic bags and can be found in many Ori-
沙　ental food stores.

RICE CAKES

宁　*Ningbo Nian Gao*
波　Rice cakes are a specialty of the seaport city of Ningbo in Zhejiang
年　province. They are commonly called Ningbo rice cakes and are made
糕　from a mixture of water-ground flours from long-grain and glutinous

rice. Fresh rice cakes can be bought in Chinese markets in plastic bags containing stacks of eight to ten rectangles 5 by 1½ by ½ inch.

They can be kept in the refrigerator for up to two months by slicing and submerging them in cold water and then changing the water weekly. (You could also slice and freeze them.) They are also sold already frozen, in slices. However, for stir-fried rice cake dishes, I prefer soaking frozen rice cakes in water, as is done with the fresh ones before using them, since the texture will be softer and smoother after soaking.

Never leave rice cakes uncovered for more than 10 minutes, because the dry air will crack them. Rice cakes also come dried; these must be soaked for at least a few days or for up to two months. As with the fresh ones, you should change the water weekly.

RICE FLOUR

粘
米
粉

Zhan Mi Fen

Rice flour is ground from long-grain rice. It is used for making cakes and shells to wrap either sweet or salty fillings.

RICE FLOUR, GLUTINOUS (SWEET RICE FLOUR)

糯
米
粉

Nuo Mi Fen

Sweet rice flour is ground from glutinous rice. It is used in the same way as plain rice flour, although they aren't interchangeable. Sweet rice flour has a softer texture than plain rice flour. Japanese sweet rice flour is less glutinous than that of the Chinese.

RICE FLOUR, WATER-GROUND

水
磨
粉

Shui Mo Fen

Grinding rice with water is another method of making rice flour. Long-grain or glutinous rice kernels are soaked in water and ground while wet. Afterward the excess water is squeezed out. This method produces a finer texture than that of dry-ground flours. Since 1984 this flour, in a dry powder form, has been widely available in Chinese markets. A product of Thailand, both the Erawan and KTK brands are excellent. The flour keeps indefinitely if tightly sealed and stored at room temperature.

Fresh water-ground rice flour is sold by Chinese bean curd factories in large cities. Because of easy spoilage, it is sold only during cooler weather in lumps by weight. It is used the same way dry rice flour is, although less water is added when mixing the dough. This flour must be kept in the coldest part of the refrigerator and stays fresh only for two to three days; however, you could freeze it, tightly wrapped, for several weeks.

RICE VINEGAR, ZHEJIANG VINEGAR, AND CHINKIANG VINEGAR

浙 镇
醋 江
香
醋

Zhe Cu and *ChinKiang Xiang Cu*

Zhejiang and Jiangsu provinces produce a very good rice vinegar, with a mild and mellow flavor and a rich brown color. It is most often used as a dip.

The most popular Zhejiang vinegar is the Zhe Cu, or Great Wall, brand; the most popular ChinKiang vinegar is the Golden Plum brand. The latter has the stronger flavor. Both are sold in bottles and may be stored at room temperature.

SEAWEED, GREEN (GREEN MOSS)

苔
条

Tai Tiao

This mosslike seaweed is green in color. It comes dried, in wads or in matted chips. When it is fried in oil, it has a special vegetable fragrance and a slight iodine taste. It is used as a flavoring.

SESAME OIL

麻
油

Ma Yu

Chinese sesame oil has a strong nutlike fragrance and taste. In northern China it is used as a cooking oil, but generally it is used as a final flavoring. The pale sesame oil that comes from the Middle East is made from raw sesame seeds; it has a completely different flavor and is unsuitable for Chinese cooking. Sesame oil is available in most Oriental food shops. It should be covered tightly to retain its fragrance.

SESAME SEED PASTE

芝
麻
酱

Zhi Ma Jiang

In northern China sesame seed paste is used to make dressings for salads or sauces for noodles. It comes in a jar covered with oil. I find most of the brands to be quite bitter, so I substitute creamy peanut butter and add sesame oil to make the sauce for cold noodles (page 72).

SESAME SEEDS (WHITE AND BLACK)

白 黑
芝 芝
麻 麻

Bai Zhi Ma and *Hei Zhi Ma*

Sesame seeds are round, almost flat black or white seeds, slightly larger than poppy seeds. They are often used for their flavor. When toasted, they have a wonderful fragrance. These seeds can be ground to make a paste or to obtain oil. Like the Italians, the Chinese often top their pastries with these seeds. Raw sesame seeds can be bought in Italian and Chinese food markets and many supermarkets.

SHRIMP, DRIED
Xia Mi

Dried shrimp are a variety of small shrimp that are prepared by salting, shelling, and finally drying them, so that their flavor intensifies during the process. Their size varies; the best are those that are about 1 inch in diameter curled up. They should be pink in color (the more expensive kind).

To redevelop dried shrimp, soak them in dry sherry or water for about 10 minutes.

They come in ½- or 1-pound plastic packages; store them at room temperature in a covered glass jar for a few months or in a covered jar in the refrigerator, where they will keep indefinitely.

SHRIMP ROE
Xia Zi

Sold in Chinese markets by the ounce, they are a dark reddish brown and look like fine sand. Refrigerated in a jar, they will keep indefinitely.

SMITHFIELD HAM
Hui Tui

The American Smithfield ham has the nearest taste and texture to the Chinese Jinhua and Yunnan ham, which are important seasoning ingredients in Chinese cooking.

Smithfield ham can be bought either cooked or uncooked. Gourmet food shops sell the cooked variety, but Chinese meat markets usually sell it uncooked in thick slices or whole. Since the ham is quite salty, it should be soaked, cleaned, and then cooked.

For a 3-inch-thick slice of untrimmed and uncooked ham, first soak it in cold water for 1 hour. Then rinse and scrape it under hot water, cut off any black or yellow parts, and remove the bone marrow. Rinse the ham slice again and put in a pot just large enough to hold it. Cover the ham with water 1 inch above, bring the water to a boil, and let it simmer, covered, for two hours. With tongs, remove the ham, let it cool, then wrap it in plastic, and put it in the refrigerator; it will be easier to slice thin when it is completely cold. The ham can be kept in the refrigerator for up to three weeks or in the freezer for two months.

If you're pressed for time, you may parboil the whole piece of ham in water for five minutes instead of soaking it in cold water for one hour, then proceed to clean. The cooking time (at a slow simmer) for a three-inch piece of ham should be about two hours or until a knife inserted in the center portion goes in easily.

The water the ham cooked in is delicious combined with chicken soup. Remove all the fat, bottle the broth, and freeze it to use later. It's wonderful when added (about ½ cup) to noodle broth. Even better is cooking a thick piece of ham with a chicken (Best Chicken Broth, page 77), so that you have chicken, soup, and ham all at once. The salt in the ham will be reduced by cooking the meat in the chicken broth, but its flavor will be retained.

If you cannot obtain Smithfield ham, try smoked pig's knuckles, which are widely sold in supermarkets. They are not as tasty as Smithfield ham, but they are a good substitute.

Smithfield ham is wonderful with noodles, whether hot or cold. You need only a little bit, because the ham's salty flavor is strong and it should just add zest to the dish.

SOYBEAN MILK
豆 *Dou Jiang*
浆 Soybean milk is extracted from soaked soybeans that have been ground with water; it is then strained through cloth. The straining removes the husk and most of the solid residue from the beans. The white liquid obtained is the bean milk, which contains most of the protein of the beans. Bean milk must be brought to a boil to get rid of the strong bean flavor. It is usually served hot as a beverage with Deep-Fried Devils (page 172) and Sesame Seed Bread (page 167) as part of breakfast. It should be stored in the same manner as regular milk.

SOY SAUCE, LIGHT AND DARK (THIN AND THICK)
酱 *Jiang Yu*
油 Soy sauce is the most important seasoning liquid in Chinese cooking. It comes in various sizes of containers and in many brands. Most manufacturers produce two kinds of soy sauce—dark and light. The light is used for delicate dishes and for dipping. Dark soy sauce usually contains molasses, making it thicker. It is used whenever a deep-brown color is wanted, as in red-cooked dishes.

The brand I used most for this book is Amoy, from Hong Kong. It is saltier than many other brands, but I use less. I also use the Kimlan brand from Taiwan for dipping, since it is less salty than many brands and very flavorful—good for this purpose. Soy sauce does not need refrigeration.

STAR ANISE

八 *Bai Jiao*

角 This anise comes in the shape of an eight-pointed star and differs slightly in flavor from aniseed. Often it is used to flavor beef or pork as one would use bay leaf.

TAPIOCA FLOUR

西 *Xi Mi Fen*

米 Tapioca flour or starch comes from the root of the tapioca plant. The
粉 root starch is ground into flour and also made into two sizes of granules: The large granules are called fish eyes and the smaller ones pearls. Tapioca flour is used for making shells to wrap shrimp or meat fillings. The shells made from this starch have a crisp texture and transparent appearance.

TIGER LILY BUDS (GOLDEN NEEDLES)

金 *Jin Zhen*

针 Tiger lily buds come from a special type of lily. They are dried and used as a complementary vegetable, often in combination with tree ears. Soak them in boiling water for about 15 minutes and then remove the hard ends. The water used for soaking is generally discarded.

　　Tiger lily buds are sold dried in packages; look for very light brown ones, which are more flavorful since they are fresher than darker ones. They keep for a month if sealed in a tightly covered jar or can.

TREE EARS (CLOUD EARS OR BLACK FUNGI)

木 *Mu Er* or *Yun Er*

耳 Tree ears, a small tree fungus, are also called cloud ears. When dried,
， they have the nondescript appearance of dark chips. They vary in color
云 from dark brown to gray to black. After soaking, if they are of good
耳 quality, they have the shape of the petals of double petunias. To redevelop them, simply soak them in cold water for 1 hour (if you are in a hurry, use boiling water to have them ready in 30 minutes). Remove and discard the hard woody substance at the stem, if any, and rinse them several times.

　　The flavor and taste, though mild, can be compared to nothing in American cooking, so it is best to taste them for yourself.

TURNIPS, WHITE (WHITE RADISH OR ICICLE RADISH)

白 *Bai Luobo*
萝
卜 Many varieties of turnips are suitable for Chinese cooking. The best flavor comes from large white ones, about 8 inches long and 2 to 3 inches wide. This type of turnip can be cooked until tender without becoming mealy. They can keep for about two weeks wrapped and refrigerated.

WATER CHESTNUT FLOUR

马 *Ma Ti Fen*
蹄
粉 Water chestnut flour is used to make batters and to thicken sauces. It gives a shiny glaze or light crust to cooked food. This flour is also used for making cakes. Since only a small amount is used to thicken a sauce, the flour is sold in half- or quarter-pound packages as well as in larger packages. Many Chinese grocery stores carry this special flour.

WATER CHESTNUTS

马 *Ma Ti*
蹄 Water chestnuts are actually not part of the chestnut family. They are the starchy stalks of a water plant whose leaves grow above the water. They are available fresh, canned, and powdered. Fresh water chestnuts, available all year round and imported from Hong Kong, are so superior in texture and flavor that they cannot be compared with the canned.

Fresh water chestnuts are difficult to peel (a time-consuming process) but are well worth the effort. Canned water chestnuts retain only the texture of the fresh ones, not the flavor. They are available in most supermarkets; fresh ones can be obtained only in Chinese grocery stores and in specialty shops. The fresh ones do not spoil readily, so they can be kept in the refrigerator, covered, for about three weeks. Once peeled, they keep well in the freezer. Powdered water chestnuts are discussed above.

WHEAT STARCH

澄 *Cheng Fen*
粉 When the protein part of wheat flour is removed to make gluten, the remaining part is called wheat starch. This is sold in 1-pound packages; store it tightly closed at room temperature.

WINE RICE AND WINE YEAST

酒酒 *Jiu Niang and Jiu Yao*
酿药 Wine rice is fermented rice. It can be made at home using wine yeast,

which is available in Chinese markets. Wine yeast comes in large grape-sized balls and is a fermenting agent. Ready-made wine rice comes in glass jars, soaked in its own sweet liquid. It can often be found in large Chinese markets. Wine rice must be stored in the refrigerator.

WOOD EARS

木 *Mu Er*

耳 Dried wood ears are a very large tree fungus, black on top and white on the underside. After being soaked in warm water, some of them expand to 6 inches in diameter and they become dark brown on both sides.

Wood ears don't have much real flavor or fragrance, but their texture, prized by the Chinese, is wonderful though hard to describe—it is, say, a resilient crispness. Wood ears are greatly enhanced when combined with fresh or dried mushrooms.

WRAPPERS, CANTONESE SPRING ROLL

广 *Guangdong Chun Juan Pi*

东 Cantonese spring roll wrappers are sold in 7-inch squares, by the
春 pound; they are wrapped in wax paper. Each pound contains fourteen
卷 to twenty-five wrappers, depending on their thickness. They will keep
皮 fresh for up to one week in the refrigerator and for one month in the freezer. They must be thoroughly defrosted before you use them.

WRAPPERS, WONTON

馄 *Huntun Pi*

饨 In general, wonton wrappers are sold in 1-pound packages and in two
皮 thicknesses. Thick ones, usually made from eggless noodle dough, number about 80 per package; thin ones, numbering about 120 per package, are made from egg noodle dough; sometimes pasta flour or cornstarch is used.

Wonton wrappers keep fresh for about one week in the refrigerator and one month in the freezer. After you thoroughly defrost them, wrap them in a damp dish towel for an hour or longer before using them.

WRAPPERS, SHANGHAI SPRING ROLL (EGG ROLL)

上 卷 *Shanghai Chun Juan Pi*

海 皮 Shanghai spring roll wrappers are either square or round and resemble
春 doilies about 7 inches in diameter. They are packed in stacks of ten to twenty-five pieces in plastic bags. After you bring them home, put them

in tightly sealed plastic bags and store them in the refrigerator for one week or in the freezer for one month.

After you defrost frozen wrappers, wrap them in a damp dish towel for a few hours before using them. See directions for reheating the wrappers on page 101.

WRAPPERS, SHAO MAI

烧
卖
皮
Shao Mai Pi

Most shao mai wrappers are made from egg noodle dough; they are round and very thin and about 3½ inches in diameter. Shao mai wrappers are sold in 1-pound packages. They keep fresh for about one week in the refrigerator and one month in the freezer. The Japanese 3-inch-round shao mai wrappers are very good; they are made of an eggless flour-and-cornstarch dough, which is very smooth after cooking. They are usually sold frozen, labeled *jiao zi skin.*

WRAPPERS

燕
皮
Yen Pi

A specialty of Fukien province, this is a wrapper made from ground pork rind that is pounded into a paste and combined with wheat flour and liquid to make a dough. The dough is rolled into a thin sheet, which is then air-dried.

Uncooked *yen pi* is grayish white. The Narcissus brand from China comes in an 8½-ounce box that is kept in the refrigerated section of Chinese food stores. They will keep for up to three months in the refrigerator if tightly wrapped in plastic wrap.

Index

About the Author

Florence Lin was born and raised in Zhejiang and Wuhan provinces, the daughter of a silk merchant. She became interested in the regional cuisine of China while still a child, a "favored" daughter accompanying her father on business trips around the country. The love of Chinese culture and cuisine these trips instilled remained with Mrs. Lin long after she had emigrated to the United States and married; however, at first the demands of a growing family made cooking simply a necessity. In 1960, at the persuasion of a close friend, she began teaching classes at the China Institute in America located in New York City. Twenty-five years, thousands of students, and five books later, Florence Lin still marvels at the diversity and rich heritage of Chinese cuisine. She is the former principal food consultant for Time-Life's *Cooking of China* (Food of the World series). Previous publications by the author include *Florence Lin's Chinese Regional Cookbook* 1975, *Florence Lin's Chinese One-Dish Meal Cookbook* 1977, *Florence Lin's Cooking with Fire Pot* 1978, *Florence Lin's Chinese Vegetarian Cookbook* 1976 (all from Hawthorne/Dutton), and *Florence Lin's Chinese Vegetarian Cookbook* (Shambhala, 1983). The recipes included in her *Complete Book of Chinese Noodles, Dumplings, and Breads* are the result of her years of teaching and her frequent travels throughout China. She lives in New York City.